Meows from the Manse

Meows from the Manse
―――― Purrs from the Parsonage ――――

Barry Blackstone

RESOURCE *Publications* • Eugene, Oregon

MEOWS FROM THE MANSE
Purrs from the Parsonage

Copyright © 2022 Barry Blackstone. All rights reserved. Except for brief quotations in critical publications or reviews, no part of this book may be reproduced in any manner without prior written permission from the publisher. Write: Permissions, Wipf and Stock Publishers, 199 W. 8th Ave., Suite 3, Eugene, OR 97401.

Resource Publications
An Imprint of Wipf and Stock Publishers
199 W. 8th Ave., Suite 3
Eugene, OR 97401

www.wipfandstock.com

PAPERBACK ISBN: 978-1-6667-4358-6
HARDCOVER ISBN: 978-1-6667-4359-3
EBOOK ISBN: 978-1-6667-4360-9

08/11/22

I KNOW HE WILL NEVER READ OR UNDERSTAND THIS DEDICATION, BUT IT IS ONLY PROPER THAT I ACKNOWLEDGE AND RECOGNIZE MY INSPIRING CAT IN THIS DEDICATION. EDDIE WAS A ONCE IN A LIFETIME PET AND COMPANION. HE TAUGHT ME ABOUT GOD AND HIS WORD FOR MORE REASONS THAN THE LESSONS I HAVE RECORDED IN THIS BOOK. I AM GRATEFUL TO THE GOOD LORD FOR SENDING AN *"ANGEL UNAWARES"* (Hebrews 13:2) FOR THE YEARS (2005–2021) THAT WE WERE TOGETHER.

**TO GOD BE THE GLORY,
GREAT THINGS HE HAS DONE IN EDDIE!**

Other Books of Barry Blackstone

Though None Go With Me
Rendezvous in Paris
Though One Go With Me
Scotland Journey
The Region Beyond
Enlarge My Coast
From Dan to Beersheba and Beyond
The Uttermost Part
Homestead Homilies
Rover: A Boy's Best Friend
North to Alaska and Back
Another Day in Nazareth
Sermonettes from the Seashore
Earth's Farthest Bounds
Angling Admonitions
Beyond the Bend
Expendable

Contents

Acknowledgement | xi

Introduction: Eddie's Exhortations (Job 12:7, 9, 10) | xiii

CHAPTER ONE: Using Trust Against Fear (Psalms 9:5, 11) | 1

CHAPTER TWO: Love Pure Love (I Corinthians 13:13) | 4

CHAPTER THREE: Stepping Outside Your Comfort Zone (Philippians 4:13) | 7

CHAPTER FOUR: That Besetting Sin (Hebrews 12:1) | 10

CHAPTER FIVE: Callings and Choices (Matthew 22:14) | 13

CHAPTER SIX: The Pursuit of God (Hosea 6:3) | 16

CHAPTER SEVEN: Fellowship with God (I John 1:3) | 19

CHAPTER EIGHT: Why We Are Drawn to God (John 6:44) | 22

CHAPTER NINE: An Arranged Marriage (Genesis 24:4) | 25

CHAPTER TEN: Holiness Unto the Lord (Exodus 28:36) | 28

CHAPTER ELEVEN: Sober and Vigilant (I Peter 5:8) | 31

CHAPTER TWELVE: Following Hard After God (Psalms 63:8) | 34

CHAPTER THIRTEEN: Legalism Versus Liberty (Galatians 5:1) | 37

CHAPTER FOURTEEN: The Need for Simplicity (II Corinthians 1:12) | 40

CHAPTER FIFTEEN: Traveling Light (Luke 12:15) | 43

CHAPTER SIXTEEN: A Single Solitary Life (Philippians 2:6-8) | 46

CHAPTER SEVENTEEN: Letting Go (Philippians 3:13) | 49

CHAPTER EIGHTEEN: Confronting the Contentious (Romans 2:8) | 52

CHAPTER NINETEEN: The Tyranny of Things (Mark 10:22) | 55

CHAPTER TWENTY: Do the Work of an Evangelist (II Timothy 4:5) | 58

CHAPTER TWENTY-ONE: The Need to Escape (Psalms 71:2) | 61

Chapter Twenty-Two: Training Up a Child (Proverbs 22:6) | 64
Chapter Twenty-Three: Constant Companionship (Hebrews 13:5) | 67
Chapter Twenty-Four: Apprehending God (Psalms 34:8) | 70
Chapter Twenty-Five: A Lesson from a Gadabout (Psalms 56:8) | 73
Chapter Twenty-Six: The Victory That Overcomes the World (I John 5:4) | 76
Chapter Twenty-Seven: An Appointment with the Almighty (Genesis 3:8) | 79
Chapter Twenty-Eight: Listening to a Quarrel (Colossians 3:13) | 82
Chapter Twenty-Nine: Learning to Listen (I Samuel 3:10) | 85
Chapter Thirty: Appeasing the Lion (II Timothy 4:17) | 88
Chapter Thirty-One: Hospitality (Romans 12:13) | 91
Chapter Thirty-Two: The Doctrines of Devils (I Timothy 4:1) | 94
Chapter Thirty-Three: The Creator-Creature Relationship (Psalms 57:5) | 97
Chapter Thirty-Four: Adopted (Romans 8:15) | 100
Chapter Thirty-Five: Best Friends (Proverbs 18:24) | 103
Chapter Thirty-Six: It's a Male Thing (Acts 8:16) | 106
Chapter Thirty-Seven: Lyra Sojourner Newswanger (James 1:27) | 109
Chapter Thirty-Eight: Harvey Wallhanger (Psalms 59:11) | 112
Chapter Thirty-Nine: A Daybreak Meditation (Psalms 1:2) | 115
Chapter Forty: Wonderfully Made (Psalms 139:14) | 118
Chapter Forty-One: Protecting a Pearl (Matthew 13:45, 46) | 121
Chapter Forty-Two: If animals could talk? Maybe they can! (Numbers 22:28) | 124
Chapter Forty-Three: Give Attention to Reading (I Timothy 4:13) | 127
Chapter Forty-Four: And Eddie Makes Ten (Leviticus 27:32) | 130
Chapter Forty-Five: Go Tell that Old Fox (Luke 13:32) | 133
Chapter Forty-Six: Home Alone (Jeremiah 15:17) | 137
Chapter Forty-Seven: Behold the Fowls of the Air (Matthew 6:26) | 141
Chapter Forty-Eight: Chicken Concepts from a Cat (Matthew 23:37) | 144
Chapter Forty-Nine: The Life of an Animal (Proverbs 12:10) | 148

CONTENTS

CHAPTER FIFTY: Sun on Your Face (Numbers 6:25) | 152
CHAPTER FIFTY-ONE: Max the Disabled Dog (Exodus 4:11) | 156
CHAPTER FIFTY-TWO: An Angel Unawares (Hebrews 13:2) | 160
CHAPTER FIFTY-THREE: A Christmas Miracle (Genesis 31:49) | 164
CHAPTER FIFTY-FOUR: Scarface (Galatians 6:17) | 167
CHAPTER FIFTY-FIVE: An American Shorthair Companion (Exodus 32:27) | 170
CHAPTER FIFTY-SIX: Trusting by Senses (Hebrews 5:14) | 174
CHAPTER FIFTY-SEVEN: Following the Master's Commands (John 15:14) | 178
CHAPTER FIFTY-EIGHT: Faithful to a Fault (I Corinthians 4:2) | 181
CHAPTER FIFTY-NINE: Available for Anything (II Corinthians 8:19) | 185
CHAPTER SIXTY: Eddie and the Mailman (Matthew 7:7) | 189
CHAPTER SIXTY-ONE: The Nature of Eddie (Hebrews 4:13) | 193
CHAPTER SIXTY-TWO: Paw Prints in the Snow (II Corinthians 2:11) | 198
CHAPTER SIXTY-THREE: Seeing Christ Everywhere (Luke 24:44) | 202
CHAPTER SIXTY-FOUR: Red Spot (Revelation 12:3) | 208
CHAPTER SIXTY-FIVE: Beatitudes According to Eddie (Matthew 5:2, 3) | 212
CHAPTER SIXTY-SIX: Wonderful Graces (I Peter 4:10) | 216
CHAPTER SIXTY-SEVEN: Purring and Praying (Philippians 4:6) | 220
CHAPTER SIXTY-EIGHT: The Comforting Cat (II Corinthians 1:3) | 223
CHAPTER SIXTY-NINE: Does a Cat have a Soul? (Job 12:10) | 226
CHAPTER SEVENTY: Eddie and Judah (Genesis 29:35) | 229
CHAPTER SEVENTY-ONE: The Sentinel of the Brush Pile (Jeremiah 51:12) | 233
CHAPTER SEVENTY-TWO: The Death of a Pearl (Revelation 17:4) | 236
CHAPTER SEVENTY-THREE: Sadie Mae, the Frightful Feline (II Corinthians 7:5) | 239
CHAPTER SEVENTY-FOUR: Scaredy Cat (Job 18:11) | 242

Postlude: An Ode to Eddie (Psalms 148:7, 10, 13) | 246

Acknowledgement

I WOULD NOT HAVE gotten this book project finished if not for the editing and compiling by my friend and sister-in-Christ, Rosemary Campbell. I would like to thank her for the numerous hours and many days she spent in Florida in the winter of 2021/2022 reading and correcting the errors in the original script. Thanks again Rosemary for all your work; may you share in the eternal rewards of this book.

Introduction

Eddie's Exhortations

"But ask now the beasts, and they shall teach thee . . .
Who knoweth not in all these that the hand of the Lord hath wrought this?
In whose hand is the soul of every living thing . . ."

—JOB 12:7, 9 10

November 1, 2005

The day Eddie first came into my life.

I AM WRITING THIS preface to a very unique book from a Christian horse camp in Canada. I am on my 21st trip to minister with the gracious folks of the CSSM (Canadian Sunday School Mission) at Hampton Bible Camp. I started this ministry in 1986 and have only missed three camps in 24 years. An event took place at the first chapel service that aged me more than you know. I asked if any in the room of 80 campers and counselors were over 24 years of age. No hands went up. It struck me that every soul in the room wasn't even born that first summer I traveled from my home in Maine to Hampton, New Brunswick. I was certainly ministering to an entirely new generation, and it reminded me that the Lord was still working on me and working through me.

So what a better time or place to start recording the spiritual effects of one of God's creatures then at a Christian summer camp that uses animals as a draw for the bringing of young people into an environment where the Good Lord can be introduced and where His Dear Son Jesus can be exalted. Away from the distractions of the modern world and the devices that keep kid's minds deluded with ungodly things versus the godly virtues of the Christian life. While waiting my next chapel, I thought it time I started on a writing project that I have had on my heart for nearly four years now. A spiritual look into the practical teaching of a simple tomcat I call "Eddie, Eddie, Eddie" and what he has taught me about his Creator and mine.

When you spend your time surrounded by kids and animals, you have a tendency to turn a little childish yourself. This same affect comes each and every time I drive onto the campus of Hampton Bible Camp. I have written of my exploits at this summer mission in a book I call *Fishing at Hampton*. The barnyard that is Hampton also takes me back to the days of my youth when I was raised on a working potato and dairy farm, another place and time in my life when I was surrounded by animals. Hampton Bible Camp has 24 horses and a newly born colt. Chickens, dogs, and two cats make up the rest of the herd, but because we are in the woods we have an assortment of birds in the trees, ducks on the pond, and fish in a stream that cuts directly through the middle of the property. After five days in this environment, it is not strange that I would be thinking of the greatest cat in the world, especially since Hampton now has cats. (Note: Ed and Kim Dickinson are the directors of Hampton Bible Camp and though they live just down the road from the camp their two cats often travel up to see them as they did this morning. These two active felines even joined us for staff devotions this morning.) Besides, I have just gotten off the phone with my dear wife Coleen who called for prayer requests for the weekly prayer meeting of the Emmanuel Baptist Church where I have pastored for the last 18 years. In our conversation she told me how Eddie had been searching for me since I left on Sunday. To say we are close and Eddie has dependence issues would be an understatement.

Eddie is a stray cat that came into my life after he was abandoned by his owners when they left our neighborhood in Ellsworth, Maine. Eddie sees me as his saviour and deliverer and best friend. He acts more like a dog around me than a cat. He comes when I call, he follows me wherever I go, and wonders and wanders when I am gone. We have a very unique relationship which verges on the unbelievable, yet I now have a church full of people that know of it and support it. Eddie has even become the church cat, and everybody makes exceptions for "Eddie, Eddie, Eddie." He spends the bulk of his days at the church rather than at the parsonage, and he sees the sanctuary of the church as his. In this arrangement some very important spiritual lessons have come to me while watching and observing this multi-colored feline. Often while watching him or listening to him (yes, he can talk; more later) I have been inspired with a Biblical precept that I thought I ought to record, so here I am. I have come to a place where inspiration from God's animal world is everywhere. Job said it best when he told us in the verses printed above that we ought to go to the cats (beasts) and ask them to teach us something. If God can cause a donkey to talk, why not a cat! If God can use a raven to feed a prophet, why not a cat to feed a preacher! If God can use the colt of a donkey to take Him to the people, why not a cat to lift Him up to a pastor that was in need to know God better?

I believe that it was not by accident that Eddie came into my life just a few short months before I embarked on the greatest spiritual mission and most important adventure of my life—a trip to southern India to teach at a small native Bible college. Granted, I didn't observe much at first because I wasn't looking or listening, but after four years into our relationship I know different. What is so strange is that I am by my very nature not a cat lover; that would be my wife. We have always had a cat or two in our home for our 36 years now, but I wasn't friendly with any, including our current cat Precious Patience Pearl, who is neither precious, patience, or a pearl. But my wife loves her, and I have tolerated her for over nine years now. Eddie, however, was different from day one, and, as you will see throughout this book an amazing teller of godly truth, especially in the area of the attributes of God. That is why I have given this series of short stories and sermons the title of *Meows from the Manse* or *Purrs from the Parsonage*. I know some will call me crazy and the stories I tell beyond belief and maybe a bit sacrilegious because I dare to use a cat to tell you of the things of God. I hope before you pass judgment that you will read this accounting and will check the Scriptures against what I write.

I told you at the beginning that this will be a unique book indeed, but my fervent prayer is that you will discover with me the wonderful virtues of God through my faithful friend Eddie. If the heavens and the earth can declare the glories of God (Psalms 19:1, 2) then why not a short-hair American tomcat called "Eddie, Eddie, Eddie."

Chapter One

Using Trust against Fear

"When I cry unto Thee, then shall mine enemies turn back: this I know; for God is for me . . . ?

In God have I put my trust: I will not be afraid what man can do unto me?"

—Psalms 5:9, 11

Eventually, we all must learn the lesson of what to do with fear.

I was leaving my comfort zone when I left my beloved Maine for the unknown shores of India. It had been nearly 33 years since I last ventured across the seas to do a work for God. I had been asked by the President of Kerala Baptist Bible College to come and teach for 40 days as an end of the school year special professor. I had known of the work for over twenty years, and I had desired to teach at a college level, but I never imagined that the Eternal God would choose an isolated place nine thousand miles away and by cultural standards another world. Natural fear and spiritual fear took turns challenging my heart with just why I ought to stay at home and let somebody else do it. Added to the fear and agony was the news that my dear wife of thirty-two years had developed breast cancer. Surely, I couldn't leave her. My fears abounded. So from January to October, 2005, I battled the demon of fear within and waited without to know what my God would do about my sickly wife.

It was after three operations and seven cancer treatments that covered nearly half of 2005 that I began to notice a small cat periodically stocking around the building that is the sanctuary for the people of the Emmanuel Baptist Church. At first I didn't take notice because I never had a very good relationship with any cat. I had been around cats all my life starting with the two dozen or more cats that often called the Blackstone homestead home at any one given period of time. Shortly after Coleen and I got married I realized that she had been waiting her entire childhood and early adulthood to have one cat. Because of family medical issues cats were not allowed in the Meister household so it wasn't very long into our marriage that we got our first cat. Over the years nearly another dozen cats have lived various lengths of times in the parsonages we have called home. It was then, unexpectedly, a stray that seemed to be in trouble came into my life. He was thin and wild and frail despite appearing very young. It was then my dear wife reminded me of some cat food that had been rejected by Precious Patience Pearl, and what harm would it be to share with the stray?

While planning for India, I started setting out food for "the stray." For days on end I wouldn't see the shy creature, but sure enough the food always disappeared. Often I would shout out over an empty parking lot that there was nothing to fear, but fear had full control over the abandoned kitten. I was telling myself that being afraid of India wasn't a sin in itself. I have always admired the doctor who was afraid of disease, the friend who feared debt, and, of course, I had preached for years of the importance of the Christian to fear sin. Surely, you know that nowhere in the Bible does it say, "Thou shalt not fear." And I knew that the little cat that was hiding each and every time I came near was only protecting itself from maybe another rejection, abandonment, disappointment, or, worse still, trust that had failed him already.

What we learn from the Bible is that fear can't be ignored or denied, but it must be conquered. Fear must be confronted and engaged or it will haunt, hound, and harass until it conquers us. As my new neighbor was learning each and every time he came a bit closer and showed himself a bit more, the middle age man who was feeding him could be trusted. As I watched this cat first expose himself to me, then allow me to touch him, and finally trust me enough to come into the church for his food, I realized I was doing the same with my God. As the days drew closer to my departure, the closer I was coming to complete abandonment to the will of my Master. Is this not what Jesus experienced in the Garden of Gethsemane when he yielded completely into the will of His Father? The three trips back and forth between his disciples and His praying place were a sure sign that fear was being engaged. Turmoil was experienced because like Eddie and his environment and like Barry with his new ministry Jesus was also going into a realm never entered by God before—the country of death. Near the end of that struggle, Jesus yielded His will and promptly put His trust in the Father. I watched this little stray do the same thing one morning when I called and he came as if I was a long lost friend that had finally come home after a very long trip away. Trust had conquered fear in the end, and it was then I realized, if a simple creature could learn that lesson, so should I. And I did, and I can say that my India experience was the most trusting thing I have ever done or experienced in my life, only trumped by the time at the age of seven I put my complete trust in the Lord Jesus Christ as my personal Saviour.

The exhortation I learned from Eddie is that there is only one remedy for fear, any fear, and that is best stated by the Psalmist when he wrote:

> WHAT TIME I AM AFRAID, I WILL TRUST IN THEE.
> (Psalms 56:3)

The second we feel some kind of fear coming over us, it is then we must trust. It is what Eddie does each and every time I come upon him suddenly. Eddie is still a very vigilant cat. He is still very careful around strangers, but what blesses me is that when I call his name or whistle to him, he changes quickly and comes willingly to my side. What has changed? He has come to trust me. I, too, have come to a new understanding on how to trust my God. When He calls my name, I no longer fear what He has in store for me. I tell people that from now on my life will be seen in two parts: before India and after India. My experience in trusting God was that dramatic, and, in part, I have a cat to thank because he showed me how to use "trust against fear" in a very practical way.

Postscript: I have just returned from my sixth trip to India in 16 years and again this time I went to an entirely different region full of fear, but I experienced none! And I believe I have to give some thanks to a simple stray that taught me how to trust again!

Chapter Two

Love Pure Love

*"And now abideth faith, hope, charity, these three;
but the greatest of these is charity."*

—I Corinthians 13:13

I HAVE HAD MANY loves in my life with the two greatest being my Lord (Jesus Christ) and my lady (Coleen Meister-Co passed in 2020). I could also write of the two special children the Good Lord gave me, Scott Alexander (Scott died of cancer in 2017), a soldier in the United States Army, and Marnie Lee (Marnie is married with two children), a student at Dallas Theological Seminary, but by now you know that this book is not about people. I am writing of a pet, a very special and unique cat that God sent my way to teach me some truths about Him that I had missed or forgotten in my first half century knowing of Him and about Him. I stand amazed that I am such a slow learner, but am grateful that my loving Saviour hasn't given up on me. It was for many reasons I now see that He brought an abandoned tomcat into my life to refocus my attention back on Him, and one of the attributes I have relearned about is unconditional love.

One of the best-known truths in the Bible is the fact that *"the Lord is my portion"* (Lamentations 3:24), but an even more important truth is that *"the Lord's portion is His people"* (Deuteronomy 32:9). We talk and testify that the Lord is our joy, our love, our happiness, but when was the last time you realized that you are God's joy, God's love, God's happiness? One can't read the entire Bible without coming to the conclusion that God loves to be with His people. Whether God's daily trips to Eden to visit in the cool of the evening with Adam and Eve or His command to Moses to build Him a tabernacle that He might dwell with the children of Israel on their trip from Egypt to Canaan, God simply loves to be with His people. The greatest demonstration of this love is when God sent His only beloved Son to earth to actually live among us and eventually die for us. God loves to share our presence in good times and in bad times. It doesn't make any difference because the Almighty, the Eternal God, loves to be with us unconditionally.

The first surprise to me about "Eddie, Eddie, Eddie" was the attachment between us when I finally arrived back from India. Our relationship had only just begun when I left for seven weeks to fulfill my promise to Shibu Simon that I would come and teach at Kerala Baptist Bible College. My wife will tell you that despite the fact she had to care for Eddie throughout that time (including a couple of trips to the vet because of problems he developed while living on his own), they never bonded. What is strange about that is that Coleen can make friends with about any cat. Remember, she is the cat person not me, yet she and Eddie have never bonded. Despite the absent days, immediately upon my return Eddie began to do something I have never witnessed any other cat doing, either in my house or any other. Eddie enjoys being near me, going with me, being where I am.

If I go to bed, Eddie goes to bed and stays with me until Coleen comes to bed. Though Eddie might go out early in the morning, he is always waiting for me on the porch ready to walk with me across the street to my office at the church. We have become quite the couple in the morning as we make our way through the neighborhood. People actually stop and stare as this cat follows me like a dog. He stays with me at church until late in the afternoon when he follows me back home for supper. Despite the fact he likes to spend his evening in the backyard guarding against any other cats (except for Willy, more later), when it nears dark he comes in, often just to sit in my chair with me while I watch television. Most days, the days I am around the church or parsonage, Eddie is at my side in some way or manner. Why? I believe Eddie loves to be where I am because in his own way he has affection for me. We still don't know what happened to Eddie in his first year (our vet told us that Eddie was only about a year old when he came to us), but someone failed to love him.

One of the greatest verses in the Bible on love in my opinion is I John 4:19:

WE LOVE HIM, BECAUSE HE FIRST LOVED US!

I know now that I love God because God first loved me. I know now that Eddie loves me and wants to be with me because I first fell in love with him. I didn't want to, but I did, and now I know that love cannot stand to be isolated, alienated, or neglected. I am convinced that few of Jesus early disciples understood this. There were exceptions like Mary who was always found at the feet of Jesus, in his presence, by his side, out of love. Eddie is reminding me again just how it was when I first started my relationship with Jesus Christ. I will confess in all the years (64 at this editing), despite spending most of them in the Lord's work, I had committed the sin of the Ephesians:

> *Nevertheless I have somewhat against thee, because thou hast left thy first love. (Revelation 2:4)*

Eddie has taught me that God and God's love hates rivals. Ask anyone that knows Eddie and they will tell you that he is a one-pastor cat. Eddie has taught me that I, too, need to love my Lord without limitations, without hesitations, and without any conditions. He does love me, and, if a simple feline can show such affection, I ought to be able to show such charity to my Master.

Is not this how *"God so loved the world that He gave . . . ?"* God gives pure love, and He wants pure love in return. No second fiddle with Him; no divided loyalty with Him; no lukewarm love with Him. I have watched a cat for the last four years love me that way, and I have often been rebuked in heart when I realized that I haven't been showing my Lord and Saviour anywhere near the same affection. I like Peter have often said, "You know I love you!" (John 21:17) But have I showed it, demonstrated it, by desiring to be in His constant presence to the same degree as Eddie wants to be with me? It is a humbling experience when an 11-pound cat rebukes and reproves you by his actions. My love life for God was growing thin until He send a stray cat to teach me again the basic attributes of unconditional love. Eddie has never used the word love yet, but his actions speak of the greatest of these is love. (I Corinthians 13:13)

Chapter Three

Stepping Outside Your Comfort Zone

*"I can do all things through Christ
which strengtheneth me."*

—PHILIPPIANS 4:13

WHEN I BEGAN THIS writing project with my cat Eddie being the inspiration, I told you that I had grown to love sameness, routine, and surprise-less days. It was as I watched Eddie expand his comfort zone that I expanded my own. One of the least mentioned attributes of God in my opinion is "daring." We serve a very daring God, one who left the perfection and order of heaven for the imperfection and disorder of earth. Eddie seemed to be content living under our neighbor's barn, finding a meal when he could, only venturing a few houses up or down School Street, but one day he decided to test the faithfulness of the local preacher as he tempted him with a couple of square meals every day. In time Eddie's daring paid off because he was adopted into the Blackstone family with all the privileges of Precious Patience Pearl and actually more (Eddie gets to go outside unattended, the Pearl never). Eddie wasn't the first animal to step outside his comfort zone and be rewarded by being used of God to do wonderful things.

Recently, I finished a study in the Bible of animals God used to make a spiritual lesson unforgettable. This is what I found:

1. BALAAM'S DONKEY SPOKE AUDIBLY (Numbers 22:28). I think you know that donkey's don't talk. Talk about stepping out of your comfort zone, yet Balaam's ass did just that because God asked her to, then gave her (note she was a her not a him) the ability to speak. One of the greatest promises in the Bible in my opinion is I Thessalonians 5:24: *"Faithful is He that calleth you, who also will do it."* Moses and Nicodemus had troubles in this area, but they eventually trusted God, stepped outside their comfort zone, and spoke for Him. I, too, at

first used this excuse before God gave me the courage to speak up and speak out for Him, and He can do the same for you.

2. ELIJAH'S RAVENS SHARED THEIR FOOD (I Kings 17:6). If you know anything about ravens, you know they don't share anything, yet when God asked them to daily bring His prophet food, they did it. I know lots of people who have trouble with sharing, but we are so instructed through the teaching of Christ (Matthew 25:35-40). We live in a society that is uncomfortable with meeting the basic needs of those without. It is out of their comfort zone even to associate with the hungry, homeless, and helpless, but this is exactly what we are called to do. If a bird can do it, then every believer can do it.

3. DANIEL'S LIONS SHUT THEIR MOUTHS (Daniel 6:22). Lions just don't do this if they are hungry, and these lions were hungry (note Daniel 6:24)! Yet at the command of the Lord these savage creatures closed their mouths and curbed their appetite and left Daniel alone. We live in a world filled with chronic complainers, and the Church is no exception. Somebody is always looking for that speck (Matthew 7:1-5) in your life and telling you about it. If lions can obey God and shut their mouths, we ought to be able as well. James 3:3-5 tells us just how powerful the tongue can be, and James 1:19 tells us we ought to be slow in opening our mouth.

4. JESUS' COLT GAVE A SMOOTH RIDE (Matthew 21:5). I read once this bit of advice: "If you find a donkey on which no man has ever ridden, don't you be the first." Colts have a wild nature, but this colt gave Jesus a smooth ride into Jerusalem. Why? Because Jesus can change the basic nature of any of His creatures including you and me and shy cats like Eddie. Jesus wants us in control and controllable at all times. Temperance is the word given in God's Word, and we discover that it is one of the pieces of the "fruit of the Spirit" (Galatians 5:22-23). How smooth of a ride are you giving the people that are traveling with you?

5. JONAH'S WHALE SPIT HIM OUT (Jonah 2:10). Just so you know, it was a whale (read Matthew 12:40). Now you know fish don't give up easily anything they eat or attack. I remember a time when my brother-in-law, Larry Fox, was reeling in a small northern pike and a larger northern pike attacked it. We netted both fish, got them into the boat, and we literally had to beat the larger fish before it would let the smaller fish go. Yet, at the command of God the whale spit Jonah back onto the shore. Is there something in your life you have gotten hold of

that God wants you to let go of? Can't we be as obedient as a fish, a colt, a lion, a raven, or a donkey?[/NL 1-5]

If God can use a donkey to rebuke a prophet, God can use a cat to reprove a preacher. If God can use a raven to feed a man of God, God can use a cat to feed a starving pastor. If God can use a lion to keep safe a righteous man, cannot God use a cat (same family) to teach His man when he ought to shut his mouth? If God can use a colt to carry Him to the people, cannot God use a cat to carry a man by the name of Barry into His presence? And if God can command a fish to deposit His preacher back to his calling, cannot God use a cat to bring a drifting pastor back to his mission? I say, yes, He can, and He has. The key to any out-of-our-comfort zone experience is simply "letting go and letting God." Eddie didn't teach me this chorus, but he reminded me one day as I was pondering the proof I needed that God was using my feline friend to teach me this precept:

> Let the Lord have His way, in your life every day,
> There is no rest there is no peace, until the Lord has His way.
> Place your life in His hand, rest secure in His plans.
> Let the Lord, let the Lord have His way.

Chapter Four

That Besetting Sin

"Wherefore, seeing we also are compassed about with so great a cloud of witnesses,

let us lay aside every weight, and the sin which doth so easily beset us,

and let us run with patience the race that is set before us."

—Hebrews 12:1

WHO OF US DOESN'T have a besetting sin? In our struggle against Satan, society, and self there always seems to be a certain sin that affects us much more than any other. We might call it our haunting sin, our thorn in the flesh, that transgression that nearly always gets the best of us no matter how hard we fight it or try to flee from it. It's our "Big Grey."

Eddie came to our home in the winter of 2005-2006. Long before he arrived a dark grey tomcat periodically passed through our backyard and often found shelter under our garage. Because Precious Patience Pearl is an indoor cat, we never had any reason to give Big Grey any more than a passing glance that is until Eddie staked out his new territory. Cats are very territorial by nature, and Eddie is no exception to that rule. On any given day you will find him walking the perimeter of the parsonage and the church property across the road. When he finally realized that this would be his new home, the land on which his new residence rested was his domain, and he guards it with a passion. He is constantly marking the bushes around the two pieces of land to my wife's horror. Remember, she had no cats as a child and most of our parsonage cats have been indoor cats and female, so the ways of a male cat are still a bit strange to her. However, it is in Eddie's new arena that I at least have seen a Biblical precept being played out between my Eddie, Eddie, Eddie and Big Grey, Eddie's besetting sin.

Yesterday morning I was surprised when I left for work that Eddie wasn't at his normal place on the parsonage porch to walk with me across School Street to my office at the Emmanuel Baptist Church. It has happened before, but not often so I didn't give it a second though. After about an hour, as I always do when this happens, I went to the back door and called, "Eddie, Eddie, Eddie." Sure enough, from behind the hedge in front of the porch came that familiar face. As the lad made his way across the street I could tell instantly that something was wrong. Eddie didn't have that usual snap in his step. He was limping and moving very slowly as he approached me. My boy was hurting, but why? After a quick examination I found that his right front leg was bleeding in three places. He was covered, and I mean covered, with dirty grey hair. There was blood coming from one of his ears, and I eventually found another wound under his chin. Eddie had been in a fight, and by the looks of it had gotten the worst of the exchange!

This was not the first time Eddie had come home wounded. Unbeknown to us, he came to our home with a number of wounds that had gotten infected. Because of his shyness at first we couldn't check him over. While I was in India my wife finally was able to get him examined. Some of his old wounds had to be medically repaired so we knew quite early that Eddie was a fighter. I prefer defender (I know, a justification). I had watched on a couple of occasions when Big Grey would invade the back yard, Eddie's nature changed from a mild-mannered feline to a wild animal. It wasn't hard to figure out what had happened to Eddie on that morning he came to the church battered and bruised. Sometime during his few hours out roaming he had come face to face with his archenemy, and again they had faced off in a struggle over space. What is so interesting about this battle between Big Grey and Eddie is that Eddie allows Willy, another neighborhood cat, to come into his yard without any fighting. There seems to be something about the nature of Big Grey that turns Eddie into a brawler. Eddie's besetting sin?

I have learned that I can never really be like Christ until I come face to face with my besetting sin. I for years have made excuse after excuse about the weakness I have to a certain sin. We love to explain it away, justify it, or simply learn to live with it. I tell Eddie each and every time he fights that he really doesn't need to. He has a home, people that love him and will take care of him; yet, each and every time Big Grey crosses his path he can't walk away. How are you at walking away from your besetting sin? As you read the Bible you will discover that God speaks of "**sin in terms of beastliness**" as Glyn Evans puts it. What of the mud-loving pig and the vomit-loving dog of II Peter 2:22? There are also references to stubborn horses and wily snakes. I know that Eddie is doing what comes natural to him. His behavior is instinctive, and I will probably never change him. I am writing this the day after the big fight. After some medical care on behalf of my wife, Eddie is recovering nicely. I wish I could convince him that his besetting sin might someday kill him, but I can't. What I can do is tell you that your besetting sin is not only redeemable, but beatable.

George Whitefield once called Paul's besetting sin "The Darling Sin." Do you have one? If you do, then you must take the advice Eddie won't accept. The Bible is very clear that all sin, including "that besetting sin," must be retreated from, not resisted. We are to resist Satan (James 4:7) and flee sin (II Timothy 2:22). When we see "Big Grey" coming, we are to run, something Eddie hasn't learned as yet and to his harm. (Big Grey is about twice the size of Eddie and though Eddie has a big heart he is no match for the older, more powerful tom.) He is no coward that flees his besetting sin, but Eddie seems to think so. It is the wisest action one can take. God already knows your weakness to this sin (Psalms 139:23-24), and by now in your life you, too, know it well. It is well defined in your life, and you need to deal with it using God's tactics. I believe that a practice of strategic withdrawal is necessary each and every time that "darling sin" comes into your backyard. It is tempting to confront it, but you know you can't defeat it. I don't know if Eddie knows he can never defeat Big Grey, but I suspect he will keep trying. Unlike Eddie you have God's grace, God's Spirit, and God's Word on your side. Use them against "the sin which doth so easily beset [you]." (Hebrews 12:1)

Chapter Five

Callings and Choices

"For many are called, but few are chosen."
—Matthew 22:14

If I wrote a book about my boyhood dog "Rover" (a published book by Wipf and Stock under the title *Rover: A Boy's Best Friend*) and our youthful exploits together in the country, then I must write a book about my adulthood cat named Eddie and our spiritual adventures in the city.

It has been over forty years between personal pets. When I lost my childhood friend in the 1960s, I thought that I would never have another pet like Rover. Since that tragic day I have had at least two other dogs as pets and dozens of cats have come in and out in my life, but there never seemed to be one that could or would measure up to the standard set by Rover, that is, until a weak, skinny neighborhood stray caught my attention. I have seen in those four decades many an animal, but none has pulled at my heart quite like Eddie. It took me nearly three months to gain his trust, but once I did it developed into a wonderful friendship and fellowship—a "Rover" kind of relationship.

For the first time since Rover, I feel that I have a pet that is my kind of animal. I know that not everybody looks for the same thing in a pet. My wife Coleen loves cats and is not very fond of dogs though she loved our dog Cherry and her one pup Survivor. Because of serious issues we had to give up Cherry when our son was born. (I believe there was jealousy between baby and pet.) Over the years she looked for her ideal cat and, after nearly a dozen experiments, she finally found Precious Patience Pearl, a long-hair Maine coon cat. This nine-year old independent feline with a very unique personality came along as we faced the "empty nest" of seeing our last child leave home. I fought Pearl's coming, but nestled in the arms of my daughter, Marnie, how could I say no?

As I have mentioned already, I never looked for Eddie. He chose me, but why? My wife and I have come to believe, true or false, that Eddie was left behind when our across-the-street neighbors left town. Over the months leading up to our connection I had seen the young cat, but never really paid much attention to it. One cat in the house was enough for me or so I thought, but as winter approached I began to notice this neighborhood stray having a hard time. One day my wife saw Eddie eating the dried bread she had thrown out to the raven. Eddie was starving, and bleak were his prospects of making it through the winter. It was then I began feeding him. As I watched him devour the food I placed out for him, my heart was moved with compassion, but Eddie (if the story be told I actually started calling Eddie Ellie because I didn't know at first what gender he was) kept his distance. Weeks passed and with each feeding Eddie stayed longer and lingered closer to the hand that was feeding him. It was during those fellowship times I discovered that Eddie was more like a dog than a cat, perhaps one of the reasons I was drawn to him, Rover-like, but why was he drawn to me?

Now that our relationship has had over four years to mature, there is still one lingering question. Why me? Why in the realm of eternity did this neighborhood stray choose me for his friend? I have thought a lot about this question, but it wasn't until I came across this story out of a book (*Awake My Heart*-1960-Zondervan Publishing House) by Sidlow Baxter that an answer began to formulate in my mind. This is the tale that got me to thinking:

> The late Dr. A. C. Dixon tells how one day when he was in his garden; he heard the yelping of hunting hounds nearby, and went to look over the hedge to see what might be happening. Rushing wildly toward him was a beautiful young fawn, with panting sides, and terror in its eyes, as the hounds raced after it. For a split second it hesitated, gave one despairing look to the right and the left, then, taking its one and only chance, it leapt into the preacher's arms. All in a flash, he saw hunting in a new light, and grabbed a knobbed stick to defend the poor creature. On came the dogs, and for nearly twenty minutes Dr. Dixon fought them off, until the last one skulked away whining from his blows. Afterward the fawn would never leave him. It became the best-loved pet of the household.

Don't think Eddie's and my first encounter was that dramatic, but as I thought of Dixon's story I thought of how Eddie must have been feeling those last days in the wild. I saw no dogs chasing him, but just behind my dear cat were the hounds of hunger and cold and loneliness. They were nipping at his heels just as the hunting hounds of Dixon's tale were chasing down that baby deer. With the cold increasing and food becoming harder and harder to find, I saw my Eddie pause just like that deer many a time as he crossed the road to the Emmanuel Baptist Church. Oh, he feared me and my open arms, but there came a day when he feared the demon dogs that were chasing him more. He looked back and saw only death; he looked to the right and saw only further misery; and he looked to the left to see only a future of starvation. In that split second he realized his only hope was in the arms of a preacher who might help him escape his past neglect and future emptiness.

As with the fawn, Eddie is now a valuable member of our household. We would have a hard time imagining our life without him. As I put these thoughts into my computer, Eddie is asleep in my desk chair here in my study at the church. Now I rarely cross the road from the parsonage to the sanctuary without Eddie. Does he see me now as his protector or provider? I can't read the mind of Eddie, but this I am convinced off. There came a moment in this young feline's life when he concluded that he needed a friend, and that he found one in a middle-age pastor who was also looking for a special companion. It wasn't long after this conclusion that I realized Eddie's story was my story in relationship to the Lord Jesus Christ. I was a young seven when I realized the hounds of sin were chasing me. It was then that I saw before me the open arms of Jesus, ready and willing to shelter me through His forgiveness and grace. I like the fawn and Eddie only pondered for a quick second before I in child-like faith leaped into the outstretched arms, those everlasting arms. For the last fifty plus years (64 now) what fellowship we have had!

Chapter Six

The Pursuit of God

"Then shall we know, if we follow on to know the Lord:
His going forth is prepared as the morning; and
He shall come unto us as the rain, as the latter
and former rain unto the earth."

—Hosea 6:3

I can honestly say I first got to know God at the age of seven when in a children's church at the First Baptist Church of Perham, Maine, I gave my heart to the Lord (Acts 16:31). It was over twelve years later in a prayer room on the second floor of a dormitory at Bob Jones University in Greenville, South Carolina, that I got to know Him a bit better when I gave Him my body for His service (Romans 12:1). For over 35 years (now 53 years) I faithfully followed the Lord through four pastorates (one in New Hampshire and three in Maine) thinking I knew all there was about knowing the Lord. Just because you serve Him doesn't mean you really know Him or that He knows you. I have always been challenged by these verses in Jesus' Sermon on the Mount:

> "Not every one that saith unto me, Lord, Lord, shall enter into the kingdom of heaven; but he that doeth the will of my Father which is in heaven. Many will say to me in that day, Lord, Lord, have we not prophesied in thy name? And in Thy name have cast out devils? And in Thy name done many wonderful works? And then will I profess unto them, I never knew you: depart from me, ye that work iniquity." (Matthew 7:21-23)

What a rebuke to most of us and especially to me. Sometimes while doing the Lord's work I have failed to do the Lord's will by taking time to get to know Him better, an iniquity if you read Matthew 7:23 clearly.

Certainly, He is *"the same yesterday, and today, and forever"* (Hebrews 13:8), but what we know of Him should grow as we grow and mature in Him (II Peter 3:18). Enter stage right a cat named Eddie and the opportunity to travel to India.

During Eddie's steps to know me better and to trust me more I realized that I was venturing into the unknown with India. I knew about pastoring, but being a Bible college professor was not in my resume. I knew English, or at least most feel I have command of the English language, but Malayalam was foreign to me. I knew about the culture of New England, but the culture of Kerala? Well, I might as well have been going to another planet. It was then I realized that my only hope was to get to know God better, a new relationship for a distant, strange, and difficult calling. I would only be taking Him with me (I have written of this in a book published by Wipf and Stock Publishers (2009) out of Eugene, Oregon, entitled *Though None Go With Me*.) so I had better learn of what my God could do for me, or more importantly what I needed to do to know Him better. Besides Eddie's example, I was helped on this quest by a classic book written by A. W. Tozer called *The Pursuit of God*. It was there I found the verse printed at the introduction of this article. I found it to be true because each morning my day was planned by God and completed by God's amazing grace and supply.

I was surprised to find that Tozer's book was written from the standpoint of a busy Chicago pastor who, too, had been so wrapped up in the Lord's service that he also had stopped learning and growing in God. It was the testimony of how he refocused his priority and in turn was blessed. Just as Eddie changed his direction from going it alone to relying on me so, too, did I learn to rely more on my God? I had known the phrase "let go and let God" most of my life, but I can honestly write that it wasn't before Eddie and India that I really practiced it completely. Oh, there were times I would for an event, a situation, a circumstance be forced to rely, but more often than not I tried to figure out how I would get myself out of that situation or circumstance. With Eddie's silent exhortation and the Spirit's continual urging I learned just what it meant to "pursue God." My forty days in southern India were the most intimate times with God in our very long history, and I believe I have a cat to thank for this or at least my God for using a cat to bring me into a new knowledge of Him. Like the early and the latter rains India was both a time of refreshment spiritually and a time of renewal in my ministry. (If you will ask my flock at Emmanuel, they will tell you the man that left for India was not the man who returned.) I found a freedom there just to walk with Him and talk with Him because I found time with Him and for Him. I had watched as a young tomcat did the same for me. Over our months together we have almost become inseparable.

Where I am he is! It isn't that as his master I demand it or force it. Eddie just desires it. I am not yet as faithful to my Master as Eddie, but I am with the Psalmist growing into:

> *"As the hart [another animal] panted after the water brooks, so panteth my soul after Thee, O God. My soul thirsteth for God, for the living God: when shall I come and appear before God?"* (Psalms 42:1-2)

David was another man that got great exhortation from the animal kingdom (what of the 23rd Psalm?). For David in this psalm it was a deer, for me it was a cat, but in both cases they showed us the way to pursue God and find Him and know Him in a very unique, satisfying and fulfilling way.

Chapter Seven

Fellowship with God

*"That which we have seen and heard declare we unto you,
that ye also may have fellowship with us:*

*and truly our fellowship is with the Father,
and with His Son Jesus Christ."*

—I John 1:3

IN THIS AGE OF mass loneliness there is a glimpse of hope; within the bounds of Christian fellowship is the potential of fellowship with God. Is not this what John is teaching in the verse printed above?

If I have learned anything from my friend Eddie, Eddie, Eddie, it is the importance of developing a proper fellowship with our Creator. Oh, I have been in "the fellowship" with saints most of my life. I have felt that I knew of fellowship with God for most of that time. Only when I was left alone with God in India did I come to a deeper understanding of the true nature of the fellowship with God. The more Eddie and I have been left alone have we come to a realization of what it means to have fellowship between a preacher and a pussycat. To experience the sweetness of fellowship takes time and place, a quiet place away from the distraction of this world. Fellowship is more than just relationship (even the devil and God have a relationship), but not fellowship. For fellowship to materialize there needs to be a genuine love and desire to be in the presence of the one seeking and wanting fellowship. True spiritual fellowship in my opinion is at an all-time low. To large sections of the Christian church the art of fellowship has been entirely lost, and in its place has come that unbiblical and spiritually foreign replacement called "program." I still remember as my wife and I started our first work in Pembroke, New Hampshire, we were determined to call it the Pembroke Bible Fellowship. I was ignorant to the current changes taking place in the church and within five years the fellowship ceased to exist.

For my next three pastorates covering nearly 30 years (49 years now) I forsook fellowship, ceased to teach fellowship, and ignored this primary instruction of John. I realize now I had come at this doctrine from the wrong perspective. It is not fellowship that nourishes the soul, but God's fellowship that feeds the spirit because until the believer finds God in a personal fellowship all saintly fellowship will eventually end. Fellowship is not an end to itself, but a means to bring believers into an intimate and satisfying relationship with God that we might enter into His presence with thanksgiving and delight in the simple joy of just being with Him. Over these last four years I have watched a simple feline daily gravitate into my presence. Whether at home or work, Eddie's day begins with a desire to sit in my lap and simply be rubbed by me. He has gotten quite insistent that I take time with him, as he did this morning. I came to my study to write this article. I had been thinking about it since yesterday, and I was determined to get it into my computer. When I have something like this to get done, I am focused and don't like distractions. Meeting me on the walkway leading to the street, Eddie strolled with me step by step until we made the back steps of the church. Into the church we came and I immediately turned on my computer. Normally, I would go to the back room where I would read and pray for a half an hour or more. Unusually, Eddie sets in my lap during this quiet time. This morning I just had to get my thoughts down so no back-room time. Instantly, Eddie was in my face, on my computer, wondering why no "Eddie Time."

I wish I could say that my passion for being in the presence of God was as passionate as Eddie's desire to be with me. I have been rebuked many a morning by this little tomcat as I thought of how I had gotten my day started without a second thought of the importance of some time spent in fellowship with God. Some devotionals written by F. B. Meyer were compiled in 1972 by Baker Books under the title of *Fellowship with God*. The first article in that series was entitled *Arise, Go Up to Bethel*, a reference to God telling Jacob to return to where they had first met (Genesis 35:1). We all have a Bethel in our lives, a place where we first met and had fellowship with the Almighty, but most of us like Jacob over time have gotten so involved with life and living that we have forgotten the need to be still and know that God is still God (Psalm 46:10) and that He desires our fellowship. Was that not the reason He left Heaven every evening to walk with Adam and Eve in the cool of dusk? Unlike Eddie, our God is not pushy. Until I stopped typing and took some time to pat and feed him (Yes, feed. Eddie would rather be fed by my hand than eat out of his bowl. Spoiled, I know.), Eddie wouldn't leave me alone. God won't bug us, or He hasn't me, but now I know He is waiting patiently for us to stop what we are doing and just spend some quality time in fellowship with Him. Is that why He led Paul to Arabia after his conversion (Galatians 1:17)? Have you ever noticed how many of God's great workers were first led to a desert place, a quiet, alone place before their great missions began? (Consider, Moses in Exodus 2; Jesus in Matthew 4; David in I Samuel 22, to name a few.)

I can honestly say that Eddie is still better than me when it comes to fellowship—his fellowship with me versus my fellowship with God. I am still a work in progress, and I am so thankful that my Lord still wants to fellowship with me. Eddie is a daily reminder that what he desires of me I need to desire of God. I feel that this is another reason the Good Lord put Eddie on my path four years ago. I am discovering that the older I get in the Lord the more I need His fellowship. You would think the reverse would be true, the younger the more fellowship, but the opposite is the way it is. The older we get our desire to fellowship with Him ought to grow more. Are we not heading towards a time when complete fellowship will be our daily norm? Heaven will be an unending fellowship with the One that redeemed us and brought us into His family. Paul, perhaps, summarized it best when he wrote:

> *"God is faithful, by whom ye were called unto the fellowship of His Son Jesus Christ our Lord."* (I Corinthians 1:9)

There is no doubt we have been called, but have we chosen to join ourselves with God on a daily basis? Eddie makes that decision with me without fail, and Eddie's exhortation reminds me that I need to make that same decision with God.

Chapter Eight
Why We Are Drawn to God.

*"No man can come to me, except the Father
which hath sent me draw him . . . "*

—John 6:44

Do you know of the doctrine of "prevenient grace?" I believe A. W. Tozer defined it best when he wrote, "**That before a man can seek God, God must first have sought the man.**" You have probably figured out by now that Eddie, Eddie, Eddie has dramatically changed my opinion of cats. I must give my God all the credit for what I am about to write.

To my knowledge, I have never had a cat of my own. As I have written before, I was raised with many barn cats, and there has always been a cat or two in our home since I married my wife of 36 years (we would get 48 before her passing). Cats here and cats there, but they have always belonged to someone else. That is until a black and white cat with a brown goatee drew my wife's attention, and now I know my God's attention. This young male had been in our School and Park Street neighborhood for a while having come with our across-the-street neighbors. Soon we began to see him more often, especially after our neighbors moved out of town. The whole matter would have stayed the same if not for my wife's interest in the welfare of cats and the lessons my God had for me to learn.

At first, Ellie, my wife's name for this stray, only came around when nobody was around. For weeks we played a cat and mouse game of who would find the other first. I was trying to feed the starving kitten and, as well for my wife's sake, get to know the shy feline. Each morning I would leave the parsonage and as I walked the hundred yards to the church I would call "Ellie, Ellie, Ellie." Each morning I would set a dish of food in the stairwell of the church for this elusive stray. The draw of food became too great for Eddie so eventually I would see him waiting across Park

Street until I left the food and went into the church. Eddie was determined not to let me get too close, but I was by my very acts of kindness being drawn into a relationship I had not sought.

With each close encounter Eddie got more familiar with me and me with him, and, sure enough, one morning when I called for him he called back. Soon our morning rendezvous turned into a time of touching and rubbing his back and lap time, if just to determine that Eddie was not Ellie. What started out with food has now developed into a draw because of friendship. How do I know? As I write this devotional I am drawn outside by a small squeal from under my study window. I have heard it before, and I know by the tone that Eddie has caught a mouse. Eddie no longer hunts for food, but as at other times he simply wanted me to see what he has caught. No longer drawn by hunger, our times together have another purpose, and it is in that purpose my Lord showed me another Eddie exhortation I needed to understand.

There are some who teach that man first seeks God because there is some drive or desire in each of us. The Bible seems to suggest just the opposite. Paul, quoting the Psalmist in Romans 3:11, says:

> *"There is none that understandeth, there is none that seeketh after God."*

Before any man can even have a thought of God in a genuine way there must be a divine enlightenment present. Remember what Jesus said to Peter after His disciple had answered His question of "Who say ye that I am?" (Matthew 16:15) correctly:

> *" . . . for flesh and blood hath not revealed it unto thee, but my Father which is in heaven."* (Matthew 16:17)

We are only drawn to God when God puts that urge in us. The verse that I have printed at the beginning of this article is proof enough of this precept. God's "prevenient drawing" is what motivates us to seek God, and that impulse comes from God not us!

A man by the name of Hugel once put it this way: "God is always previous!" For me, God is always first. Not only "in the beginning God," but in the beginning of every relationship God. He starts it, continues it, and will finish it (Philippians 1:6). There can be nothing of man in the process or it will be flawed, but with God there will be no flaws. Why after half a century was I finally drawn to a cat? Why after being abandoned and neglected was Eddie drawn to me? There will be those that say it was simply the survival of nature taking over, my desire to see a stray live, or Eddie's instinct simply to live. I have learned over time to see even seemingly insignificant things as something of God. Paul wrote: "*And we know that ALL THINGS work together for good to them that love God, to them who are the called according to His purpose*" (Romans 8:28). Does this not include "cat" relationships? Do you remember Job's exhorting question that began this entire project: "*Who knoweth not in all these that the hand of the Lord hath wrought this?*" (Job 12:9) It was not by chance or circumstance, that Eddie and I met, just like it was not by luck or lottery that God and I met. I know this flies in the face of modern theology and man-made religions that want it all about man and very little about God. If only we would see that in all things, even the simple and simplistic, God is at work drawing us to Him. As this trying pastor neared the end of four decades of service, it was determined by the Almighty that he needed a fresh drawing, a new relationship. Not that the old one was wrong, but it had gotten stale, in a rout, and sadly, familiar. So God used a simple creature of God to draw that same pastor into a better understanding of his Lord and Saviour Jesus Christ.

Chapter Nine

An Arranged Marriage

"But thou shalt go unto my country, and to my kindred, and take a wife unto my son Isaac."

—Genesis 24:4

Shortly after I adopted a neighborhood stray we call Eddie, I left for a six-week missionary assignment in southern India. Winter had come to the coast of Maine, and Eddie was still an outdoor cat. It was left to my wife to try and tempt Eddie into the warmth of the parsonage and introduce him to Precious Patience Pearl, Coleen's cat.

Throughout my time in Kerala, India, I stayed in contact with my wife through the internet and phone calls. With each conversation or e-mail I asked how Eddie and Pearl were making out. The invitation for a dry and warm place to stay the winter was quickly accepted by the stray, but not all members of our family were happy about this new arrangement.

It was soon discovered that Eddie had fought a few battles in his wandering days and, once my wife found an open wound in his underbelly, a trip to the vet was in order. The wound was stitched up, and new shots were given. It was discovered that Eddie had been fixed and my wife thought that perhaps instead of a brother and sister relationship, maybe husband and wife was in order for the two cats of the parsonage. You must understand that my wife has always been a matchmaker.

As we talked about our new cat situation and the stigma of Pearl and Eddie living together, marriage seemed the only option. I told my wife of the ancient tradition of arranged marriages still practiced in India, and how I thought in time that Eddie and Pearl would be able to co-exist in our house as husband and wife, that the custom seemed to be working well in India, so why not try it with our cats. It was left to my wife, until my return, to join the two cats together. As with Eliezer going to a far country to get a bride for Isaac, I had gone to a distant land and discovered the Biblical practice of arranging marriages was still alive and doing quite well. While I was there my host Shibu Simon was in the process of finding a wife for his brother-in-law. (Two years later when my daughter went to India to teach at the same Bible College, she had the experience of actually going on a number of appointments with the Simon family as they sought a bride.) Coleen and I had determined that Eddie, despite his background, was a good match for our Pearl.

Eddie had proven with each passing day to be a very gentle and loving cat. He was easy going, playful, and very respectful of Precious. Almost from the very first encounter it was love at first sight for Eddie. Our Patience is a Maine coon cat with beautiful long, flowing hair. With her hair she looks twice Eddie's size, but in weight Eddie is much heavier. Coleen would tell me that Eddie took instantly to the Pearl. The Pearl on the other hand had other ideas about this stranger that had invaded her perfect, one-cat world of six years. Pearl was an indoor cat, the complete opposite to Eddie. Isn't the old saying "opposites attract" true? Pearl had never had to share her home, her bed, her master, or her "Fish and Shrimp," her favorite cat food. Within minutes of Eddie coming into Pearl's domain, she began to express her opinion about this new arrangement. She would have nothing to do with Eddie and would hiss and bat him each and every time he came near. Coleen even asked the vet about it. Our cat doctor simple told my wife that in a few months they would be like old friends!

The veterinarian was wrong. It has been over four years now since we tried to unite Eddie and Pearl, and to this day Pearl treats Eddie as she did on that first day. Eddie has been nothing but a gentleman about it, but Pearl still only tolerates his presence. Arranged marriages might work in India and in the Bible, but it didn't work with our cats, which brings me to this latest Eddie exhortation. You can't read the Bible without seeing the bride and the bridegroom analogy in relationship to Christ and His Church (Ephesians 5:22-33). To me there is a beautiful type in Abraham's desire to get a wife for Isaac. Abraham is God the Father, Isaac is God the Son, and Eliezer is God the Spirit. Why did the Spirit come (Acts 2), to find a "bride" for Jesus? Is not this what the Spirit is doing to this day, putting the Church together, forming the future bride of Christ? Let us not forget that the wedding is still a future event (Revelation 19) so the bride is still being sought. One of the lessons I have learned from watching Eddie and Pearl is that Pearl acts more like the bride as Eddie acts more and more like Christ each day.

No matter what Pearl has done Eddie never strikes her or treats her like she treats him. If I have learned anything about this doctrinal lesson it is found in these words by Paul:

> "*That He MIGHT present it to Himself a glorious church, not having spot, or wrinkle, or any such thing; but that it should be holy and without blemish.*" (Ephesians 5:27)

"Might" told me that this description is of a future event. Any observer of the church today certainly has a hard time seeing Paul's description. We have our share of heretical "spots," worldly "wrinkles," and believer "blemishes." We are far from holy, but we are still a work in progress, like Pearl and Eddie's relationship. That childhood chorus comes to mind:

> He's still working on me, to make me what I ought to be.
> It took Him just a week to make the moon and the stars,
> The sun and the earth and Jupiter and Mars!
> How loving and faithful He must be,
> For He's still working on me!

He's still working on us, His bride, His love at first sight, and though we often treat Him horribly He still loves us above all. Despite the mention of husband and wife in the context of Ephesians 5, Paul leaves us without a doubt of his actual topic.

> "*This is a great mystery: but I speak concerning Christ and the church.*" (Ephesians 5:32)

Daily as I watch the uneasy relationship between the Pearl and Eddie, I am reminded of the disgraceful actions of my fellow believers, and, yes, sometimes my own, and, yet, our Isaac waits patiently for Eliezer to bring Him His bride (Genesis 24:66-67). Oh, that when our day of departure comes we will be as eager as Rebekah (Genesis 24:58) to mount up to meet our Bridegroom in the clouds (I Thessalonians 4:16-17).

Chapter Ten

Holiness unto the Lord

"And thou shalt make a plate of pure gold, and grave upon it, like the engravings of a signet, HOLINESS TO THE LORD."

—Exodus 28:36

WHEN WE BROUGHT EDDIE, the neighborhood stray, into our home he was very, very thin. According to our veterinarian, Edwardo, our nickname for Eddie, Eddie, Eddie, was about a year old. How long Eddie had been on his own, we didn't know, but this I learned early—he was starving. I still remember watching him as he devoured a big can of cat food and sometimes a bowl of dry cat food as well. At first he would eat as much as I put out for him. Even when we got him into the parsonage, and to this day, he ate anything and everything put in front of him. My wife says that he stress eats, thinking each meal is his last. He seems to have a hollow leg, but he is no longer thin or light.

While in India (a trip I took shortly after Eddie came to stay in our home), I got a chance to see many a Hindu temple, a few Moslem mosques, and a number of Buddhist shrines. Without an exception at each of these shines was a Buddha idol. The classic shape is one of the most recognized images in the world. It was also the first time in which I came face to face with the idolatry that still exists on this planet. We are so sheltered in America, but in places like India the worship of other "gods" is always in your face. One night after I got back from India, I was sitting in my living room chair and Eddie came by to say hello. Sitting next to me, I noticed that his form had changed from thin and lean to Buddha-like. That night I began to call him "Buddha-belly," and the name and shape have stuck!

It was not long after I returned from India that we discovered that Eddie had either been in another fight or had cut himself crawling over some sharp object. Another trip to the vet was necessary, but this time I took him.

It was then I discovered just how far the young lad had come from our first days together. I also found out just how quiet a spirit my new friend had. Despite the numerous cats and dogs and other creatures in the clinic, Eddie remained calm throughout the ordeal. Eddie stayed calm during the long wait, and when I got him into the examination room and removed him from his cage, he still was a perfect gentleman. To my surprise the nurse weighed him, and he tipped the scale at 13 pounds, all mass and muscle despite his hour-glass shape. To this day Eddie is always ready to eat. Despite his weight he is still fit and trim because he is in constant motion. He is a wanderer and a roamer, and, despite his "Buddha-belly," he is hard as a rock. If you lift the Pearl you get air, but with Eddie you get stone. Eddie spends his days guarding his backyard and church property while the Pearl rests. We laugh at his "Buddha-belly," and for him it is a sign of better times, but for the rest of the world it is a sign of a false-faith in an object made by man.

One of the first instructions given by God to His people was to never create an image to worship. Paul writes of this in Romans:

> *"Professing themselves to be wise, they became fools, and changed the glory of the incorruptible God into an image made like to corruptible man, and to birds, and four-footed beasts [cats], and creeping things."* (Romans 1:22-23)

You know that one of the creatures worshiped in Egypt where the Israelites had left was the cat. God had brought His children out of Egypt (often a symbol of the world) to separate them from sin, and His desire was that they would become Godlike in their character and conscience. It was F. B. Meyer that said, **"Never forget that holiness is not an attainment, but an attitude!"** We are commanded to *"be ye holy; for I am holy"* (I Peter 1:16). The high priest met everyone with this phrase on the frontlet of his forehead, "Holiness to the Lord!" There is an abolition today that would remove this dividing line between holiness as God see it and the standard of holiness as man sees it.

If you think that Buddhism is only found in far off and distant lands like India, think again. Just a short walk around two corners and setting quietly is a house of meditation where Buddhism is practiced. Ellsworth is an All-American town, yet this eastern religion has crept into our community. Buddhism is a creed, a formula, and a ritual practiced resulting in a holy life, but what kind of holiness? Our land has compromised in its original faith and now allows an equality of all religions thinking that this will somehow justify us in the eyes of the world, but what about the eyes of God? Could we write the phrase "holiness to the Lord" on that house on State Street? Can you write "holiness to the Lord" over the lifestyles of most Americans? Inclusion is now a more important word than doctrine, even if that means the destruction of centuries of tradition and truth that connects us with "the faith of our fathers."

I have lived most of my life in an America that believes in a leveling-down policy rather than a leveling up philosophy. We have dropped our standards for letting young men into the armed forces because we must let the young women in also. Colleges have been forced to lower their entrance standards so all races are equal in numbers in enrollment. Society has lowered it standards for high school graduation so that more will graduate. Even in Christian circles we are following suit thinking that quantity is better than quality. One reading of the Bible will reveal that God sees things differently. He would have Gideon go into battle with 300 who wanted to be there and were brave than 30,000 reluctant cowards that really would rather be elsewhere. God's standards have always been set high, and He challenges His followers to press upward to a higher holiness. Buddhism and the other "isms" of the world live on a lower plain of expectation, while true Christianity only elevates those it calls.

The only difference between the "Buddha-bellies" in India and other places around the world and Eddie's belly is that one is worshipped and the other is washed every day with a well-fed tongue. I still smile each and every time I see Eddie sitting on a porch or in the driveway in his "Buddha" pose, and I think of how deceived the world is when they think all there is to have faith in a god is the shape of a Buddha! I love my cat, but to worship him would be wrong. Eddie is a constant exhortation that we are to worship the Creator, not the creature.

Chapter Eleven

Sober and Vigilant

*"Be sober, be vigilant; because your adversary
the devil, as a roaring lion, walketh about,
seeking whom he may devour."*

—I Peter 5:8

SHORTLY AFTER EDDIE CAME into my life I began to write down some observations about him never realizing that one day they would result in a book. One of the first recordings came under the title of "The Little Sentinel":

> Ever since Eddie came into our home to stay he has taken over guard duty responsibilities for the parsonage and sanctuary of the Emmanuel Baptist Church and for all who live within the borders of that property, including the "Pearl!"
>
> At any given hour of the day or night you can find Eddie somewhere on sentry duty or on patrol. By his very nature Eddie is a roamer, a wanderer. His restless, alert spirit makes him perfectly suited for the role he has accepted as the newest member of our family. We don't have a guard dog; we now have a guard cat. We never asked Eddie to assume this role, but maybe in his mind he is paying us back for taking him off the streets and giving him a home.
>
> Whether in the backyard guarding against an invasion of black birds or in our case on the coast of Maine seagulls or on the front walkway protecting the front porch from Big Grey, Eddie is vigilant against all who might invade "his" space during the day. You might find him on the ramp guarding the hole that leads under the garage or walking the property line at the church, but more often than not you will find him watching some part of his new domain. Early on his number one concern seemed to be the Pearl. He has become a big brother

to our female cat, and on those occasions when Pearl gets out of the house, all we need to do is send Eddie to find her and corral her back home. The protection of the Pearl seems to be Eddie's chief responsibility in his mind, and though Pearl still has nothing to do with Eddie, Eddie keeps watch against all that would molest his "Pearl."

When Eddie first came into my life, I saw this habit of making the rounds throughout the yard as just a way to stretch his legs. But after a few months watching his routine, I began to realize he was not only marking out his territory, but was willing to defend that territory against all comers. It might be the "squirrel brothers" gathering nuts for winter, or the "boys," a group of ravens that haunt our neighborhood looking for food. It matters not who they are; if they are near, Eddie is watchful.

The most dramatic action of Eddie in this area of sentinel duty is where he chooses to sleep at night. Despite his attempts to stay outdoors at times, we have set a curfew for the "fellow." Because of two trips to the vet after night fights with who knows who (probably Big Grey), we now make sure that Eddie is in before dark. Once this became a pattern we noticed that after he eats his supper he would begin to circle the downstairs. Our downstairs is laid out so you can circle from the kitchen to the living room to the dining room and back to the kitchen again. It was as if he was checking the windows and doors to see that everything was shut up and safe for the night. Once everything seems to be secure he settles down on the stairs leading upstairs. We have come to believe that it is his way of protecting his new family. I don't know what he would do against an intruder, but he thinks he is our first defense!

As I thought of what I wrote years ago about my cat Eddie, I was reminded of the challenge of Peter in the verse printed above. We, too, have been instructed in the need to be "*sober and vigilant.*" One of the instincts of a Christian ought to be the realization that we will be attacked, and that we like Eddie need to be constantly on alert. One of our duties is to guard against sins from without and self from within that would seek to devour our new found faith. Peter wrote of the devil as a cat that would devour. So what are we to do? Many years ago I was given my grandfather's brother's Bible. Uncle Ben had died in the early days of 1923. He was on his way home from Peru where he had been a pioneer missionary to an unreached people group, but had within a short time contracted a fatal disease. At his funeral on January 9, 1923, a poem was read in testimony to his service and his character. It was called "The Faithful Sentinel":

We wept not for him that his warfare is done,
That the battle is finished, and the victory is won.
But for those whom his heart loved the most,
He never gave up, he died at his post.
Almost gone is his family, and the friends of his youth,
Yet there remains a legacy of love and of truth.
His faith put to flight the alien host,
But he fell like a soldier, he died at his post.
He asked not for statue, or sculpture, or verse,
He asked not his life, or merits rehearse.
He asked but when he gave up the ghost,
That his family might know that he died at his post.
Victorious in death, for he rose as he fell,
With Him, though unseen, in Heaven to dwell!
He has crossed the great sea he has stepped on golden coast,
To take up station there to claim his new post.
And shall we the words of our loved one forget,
Oh, no, they are fresh in our memory as yet.
An example like his shall always be our boast,
We shall return to our work, we shall return to our post!

We all are sentinels in one fashion or the other. We all have a post, a territory, and a life to watch over. I ask you whether or not you will be found faithful at your duty station. I ask myself the question, do I take as seriously as Eddie my responsibility to watch over the souls of those left to my charge? I still remember the first time I read Hebrews 13:17 and understood the seriousness of its instruction:

> "Obey them that have the rule over you, and submit yourselves: for they WATCH FOR YOUR SOULS, as they that must give account, that they may do it with joy, and not with grief: for that is unprofitable for you."

Once again I have been rebuked by the faithfulness of my cat as he guards empty holes and empty fields, while I take lightly at times the serious matter of "souls."

Chapter Twelve

Following Hard After God

"My soul followeth hard after Thee:
Thy right hand upholdeth me."

—Psalms 63:8

In my old King James Bible the 63rd Psalms has this heading: "A Psalm of David, when he was in the wilderness of Judah."

In my study of David's life I have determined that this psalm was probably written during a period in David's wilderness wandering described in I Samuel 23:14. David's songs reveal a man at times who was tormented with a desire to understand why he was left by God to drift from wilderness to wilderness. I like the way A. W. Tozer put it: "**His psalms ring with the cry of the seeker and the glad shout of the finder!**" I have learned through my relationship with Eddie that there is nothing wrong with "the cry of the seeker," nor "the shout of the finder."

I mentioned in an earlier article that Eddie could talk. When I discovered that my new cat could talk like our other cat Pearl, I started reading up on the characteristics of cats. I discovered that one of the traits of some cats is that they are very talkative. Almost from day one I noticed just how vocal Eddie was. I had never heard a cat talk as much except for the exception of the Pearl, a very talkative feline, but I didn't draw the connection between the two until one day I was watching a public broadcast documentary on a group of barnyard cats in Britain.

The story was of a man who was doing research on farm cats and the social makeup of a group of cats located on a particular farm in central England. The story caught my attention, and before long I was engrossed in the concept that cats could talk, communicate. It was then I heard for the first time the word "felinese." According to this British researcher, he had determined that at least in this group of barn cats a language had developed.

After that program I began listening closer to the mews and purrs and meows and hisses coming from the mouth of Eddie. It wasn't long into my own research that I became a believer in "felinese."

When I say our cats are talkative, that is almost an understatement. I had known cats that never made a sound unless you were hurting them. Our cats talk whenever they want something or when you talk to them. I believe that is one of the reasons why I have fallen in love with Eddie. With his talking comes another window into his personality, and he has personality to burn. One would think he was a person by some of the things he tells me to do. His vocabulary amazes my wife and me because when we have heard what we think was the last variation of his meow, he comes up with another sound or tone. Over the years I have been able to identify certain sounds with certain events in Eddie's life.

For example, like most cats, Eddie loves to watch other animals. He will chase a bird, but he would rather spend hours "bird watching" out the upstairs bedroom window. If you are around when he is watching, you will hear his bird purr. Eddie would also prefer watching squirrels than chasing them up a tree. From our front porch you will see him hiding behind the hedge as the squirrel brothers play in the big maple tree in our front yard. Get close enough and you will hear a hollow meow coming from his throat. In our neighborhood is a group of ravens we call "the boys." My wife feeds the big birds with old bread, and they come around regularly. When they come to the backyard for a meal, you will find Eddie making sure they don't come too close to the house, and without fail he will be heard uttering a mellow meow. As I write this article I have been called outside by Eddie so that he can show me a baby rat that he had caught. I knew the sound as if it was felinese for "come see."

Another favorite sport for my cat after dark is to be put up to the window to see that it is dark and that it is time for him to stay in. Eddie isn't allowed outdoors after dusk because of his love of fighting Big Grey. Many months ago I was lifting him up as our custom has become when a shadow from across the street caught his attention. Again I was surprised by the tone in his meow that I had never heard before. The shadow proved to be just a man walking by the church, but Eddie was voicing his opinion about what he was doing there. If a cat could bark like a dog to warn an intruder to stay away, then I know now felinese for a "beware!"

I have pondered and wondered about Eddie before he found safety with the Blackstones. How often did he cry, whether in hunger or harm, and nobody came? I have come to believe he sought until he found. Like David of old he never stopped shouting, and, if you will, one day His Creator answered his prayer and now like David he has a right hand to hold him up; whether to a window to check the front yard at dusk or to give him treats for a job well done. Through my experience with Eddie I have a new understanding to what Paul was saying when he wrote:

> *"Yea doubtless, and I count all things but loss for the Excellency of the knowledge of Christ Jesus my Lord: for whom I have suffered the loss of all things, and do count them but dung, that I may win Christ."* (Philippians 3:8)

Paul's one desire was to follow hard after God. David's one desire was to follow hard after God. Should that not be our one desire to cry and call until we are heeded and heard? If cats can call and cry to the point that their masters can understand what they want, do we not think that the Almighty God will not hear and help us?

Whether you believe in felinese or not, I hope you will put your faith in the God that David came to trust. The context or the verse that comes before our key verse printed at the beginning of this devotional is:

> *"Because Thou hast been my help, therefore in the shadow of Thy wings will I rejoice."* (Psalms 63:7)

If my Eddie can learn that in following hard after me I will provide for him with my right hand, why can't I trust the Lord for the same reason? Why can't you?

Chapter Thirteen

Legalism versus Liberty

"Stand fast therefore in the liberty wherewith Christ hath made us free, and be not entangled again with the yoke of bondage."

—GALATIANS 5:1

I AM FINALLY READING Chuck Swindoll's well-known book *The Grace Awakening*. As I neared the halfway mark in this wonderful exhortation against the "grace killers" of our age and modern Christianity, I realized that living in the parsonage of the Emmanuel Baptist Church of Ellsworth, Maine, were two examples of this current debate in Christian circles. For the last nine years my wife and I have kept one of our cats in a legalistic state, while for the last four years our other cat has been living in perfect liberty. Precious Patience Pearl knows only law, but Eddie, Eddie, Eddie knows only grace. How did we come to this theological contrast?

Like our two felines, I, too, have lived in both camps. I started my walk with Christ squarely in the grip of legalism. For the first half of my spiritual life I knew nothing different, like our Pearl. We got our female cat as a kitten and, after a short time, decided that she would be an indoor cat. We took her to the vet and had her fixed and her front claws removed. Since that day, other than a few times she has managed to escape Precious Pearl has been living a life of bondage within the four walls of the parsonage. She is restricted in all aspects of her life. Oh, she loves to sit in a window and gaze upon a forbidden world, but never is allowed the freedom to romp and roam at will. She is bound to a set of rules that are seriously enforced; her list of do's and don'ts has become well established in her life. We have discovered that even when she gets free at times she is intimidated by her surrounding world which causes her to stop and become immobile, thereby easy to recapture. Over the years I have come to observe that those caught in the web of legalism face the same dilemma. Just like Coleen and I have with our Precious Patience Pearl.

On the other hand our approach with Eddie has been the extreme opposite. Unlike the Pearl Eddie was born free or so we think. When he came to us he was on his own with the rights and privileges of a free "tom." Both Coleen and I thought it would be cruel to restrict him to the same demands we have with the Pearl so we decided to allow Eddie the grace to come and go at his good pleasure. Just like those of us who for part of our lives have lived under some form of law, we, too, have come to an understanding of the joys of freedom under grace. Instead of being "satisfied with slavery" as the Pearl has, we have become joyful in the freedom of grace as with Eddie. With any kind of legalism, i.e., Mosaic Law comes various kinds of requirements, regulations, restrictions, rules, rites, and rituals. Long before I knew Eddie he had been liberated. If his owners had determined that he would be an outdoor cat, then he was always free. I feel, however, that he was one day just abandoned and that his liberty came from neglect, not love. It is in this very act that I see more of this marvelous teaching that is at the heart of Pauline theology.

Eddie was a lost cat in a neighborhood that had become a difficult place. Until he found me and the provisions I provided, Eddie was nearing death. Starving and sickly because of wounds he had received simply defending himself, he had liberty but no grace. Once our relationship began I determined that his independent spirit would be best served with allowing him to remain a free spirit. He was free, but now he had the grace of a loving caregiver to meet his needs. Is this not what happened when Christ found us? We were free to do as we would in the sinful life that is normal to all of us (Romans 3:23). However, as with all sin there are results that bring us under bondage. Adam and Eve had the freedom of Eden with only one area off-limits and out- of-bounds—the Tree of the Knowledge of Good and Evil. When they crossed that line, the Law caught them, and they lost their freedom. So it was with our lives when a certain sin drew us in and enslaved us within its grip. But Christ has set us free from every sin that so easily besets. Remember, it is "the truth" that sets us free (John 8:32) and "*If the Son therefore shall make you free, you shall be free indeed.*" (John 8:36) So, what happens when liberty turns into legalism? All you have to do is remember Pearl and Eddie.

Paul writes to the Galatians:

> "*O foolish Galatians, who hath bewitched you that ye should not obey the truth, before whose eyes Jesus Christ hath been evidently set forth crucified among you? This only would I learn of you,*

received ye the Spirit by the works of the law, or by the hearing of faith? Are ye so foolish? Having begun in the Spirit, are ye now made perfect by the flesh?" (Galatians 3:1-3)

Add to these words what I wrote at the beginning of this article and you will see the folly of leaving the bondage of sin for the freedom of grace only to return to another kind of bondage like legalism. Pearl has never known grace and Eddie only grace. I know how penned in Eddie feels when we leave for a few hours or a few days, and he has to spend that time inside with the Pearl. Eddie wanders and paws at the door to be let out. Pearl might whine at the door, but soon forgets why she wants to get out. Eddie knows why he wants to get out. He loves the open spaces and places, the fresh air and soft grass under his feet. Eddie has come to enjoy the freedom that comes from being able to roam at will or nap where he wants and to explore the world of the free and liberated soul. Why anyone once freed would ever love slavery again, yet that is exactly what has happened too many a Christian caught up in this heresy called "legalism."

Paul also wrote, *"For the law of the Spirit of life in Christ Jesus has made you free. . ."* (Romans 8:2). It is too late for the Pearl, but it is never too late for you. If you are caught up in some rigid, graceless religion that has taken away your freedom, then consider this—my cat Eddie has more freedom than you; if I can give such grace to a cat, then who am I to restrict my fellow believer with a set of manmade rules.

Chapter Fourteen

The Need for Simplicity

"For our rejoicing is this, the testimony of our conscience, that in simplicity and godly sincerity, not with fleshly wisdom, but by the grace of God, we have had our conversation in the world, and more abundantly to you-ward."

—II Corinthians 1:12

ONE OF THE BLESSINGS of being in the ministry for nearly four decades is the saints of God one gets to meet. A case in point was a lady by the name of Virginia Coburn. She and her husband came to my church on the coast of Maine early in that ministry. They had moved up from Georgia to build a home near his aging mother. As the years passed, both the mother and son passed leaving Virginia alone. She was the perfect example of the saintly widow in my opinion and, as age and time began to take its toll, it was decided that she ought to move closer to family. Before she left she gave me many of her husband's books as well as a few of her own. One book she encouraged me to read was A. W. Tozer's *The Pursuit of God*, one of my top ten spiritual books, and in particular a chapter on 'the need of simplicity'!

When I think about simplicity, I think about Eddie. Talk about a simple life, an uncomplicated existence. As Jesus challenged us to observe the birds, how they toil not, fret not, worry not (Matthew 6:25-34), such is the life of Eddie. Every Monday morning when I get out my checkbook and the weekly bills, Eddie goes to sleep unconcerned in the corner of my study. Each time my wife and I sit at our dining room table discussing the financial needs of the family Eddie is usually outdoor playing with Willy (another neighborhood cat) unaffected. Eddie seems to spend no time in anxiety, worry, or frustration over the current economic downturn. Why? Eddie is a classic example of a creature of God who lives in the simplicity of the thought, "If God takes care of other creatures God will take care of cats!" God's care is that simple to Eddie, but is His care that simple to us? He promised to meet our needs, period; simple, right? Remember how simple it was to talk to God when you were a child? Remember how easy it was to trust God when you were a child? Remember childlike faith? Was that not a simple time, an uncomplicated age when you just went about your business of being a child while all the time you allowed your parents to take care of all your needs? Is not that what the Bible is saying about our need to trust Him in our adulthood?

I don't ever once remember Eddie telling me as I left the house to go with my wife to get groceries, "Don't forget my treats!" Not once in the four years I have known this cat has he ever asked me to take him to the vet, lock the door at the end of the day, or give him his anti-flea medicine at the beginning of every month. Eddie lives a simple life because he has someone to take care of all the details of his life. If he has, I have, and you have, too. Paul writes of a "simplicity and godly sincerity" (II Corinthians 1:12) that affected his conscience. I would debate that a cat doesn't have a conscience, but we do. Is not the creation according to Genesis much simpler than the theory of evolution? I have been taught the doctrine of evolution for over fifty years now, and I still don't fully understand it, yet creation is straightforward and understandable to the very young. It is mankind that has made life complicated, not God. The Almighty was looking only for a simple relationship with Adam and Eve when the devil stepped in to complicate things. Life was forever changed, that is, until the Godhead decided to un-complicate things again. Was there anything simpler than the coming of Christ and the simple life He led and the simple death He died?

Despite our slow start, Eddie and I have developed a straightforward and simplistic partnership. Eddie looks to me for his food, shelter, and protection. In return I get the privilege of his companionship. Some might think that this is a one-sided relationship with one party giving a lot more than the other, and they would be right. I do give far more. I still remember the first time I spent $100 on Eddie. I was in India when my wife called with the news that Eddie needed an operation that would cost a hundred of dollars and a bit more. I had never in all the time we had cats ever spent that kind of money on an animal. At first it bothered me, but I paid the bill. I have paid other bills over the last four years equal to that first hundred, but now I don't even think about it. Why? Because it is Eddie and I am responsible. I believe Jesus did the same at Calvary. The cost was high, but it mattered not because it was for me. It is the same in your case, it was for you. I still remember the first time I heard the song "He could have called ten thousand angels to destroy the world . . . but He died alone for you and me!" Redemption made simple. Salvation made simple. Forgiveness made simple. Love made simple. *"For God so loved the world!"* (John 3:16) No exceptions, everyone is loved by God. It doesn't get any simpler than that!

Chapter Fifteen

Traveling Light

*"... for a man's life consisteth not in the abundance
of the things which he possesseth."*

—LUKE 12:15

ANOTHER LESSON I LEARNED in India that was reinforced when I returned to America was Jesus' precept that was illustrated by his classic parable of the "certain rich man." (Luke 12:16-21) Eddie is a constant reminder to me of the importance of traveling light.

Paul exhorts us to " ... *lay aside every weight* ... " (Hebrews 12:1) in our earthly race called life! One of those weights is possessions. I often think Lot's wife probably looked back to Sodom because of the fine house and treasured possessions that she had to leave behind, and we are exhorted to "Remember Lot's wife." (Luke 17:32) It is so easy to get attached to "things." I have come to believe it is one of the most dangerous deceptions in the devil's arsenal. What has happened to those caught up in the hoarding business? For me it is as simple as this basic philosophy: "**Life is not a reservoir but a channel.**"

That precept was penned by E. Stanley Jones, a famous missionary to India in the twentieth century. I have been reading his daily devotional book *Abundant Living* just before I go to bed each night. I will admit I have some very serious doubts about some of his basic Christian philosophies, but as for me on this topic he is right on. I am not as bad as some, but most of us struggle with accumulation. I have tried for most of my life to be a "channel of blessing" as the old church hymn says. I was taught and have come to believe that if God has given you more than you need, then the extra is to meet the need of someone else. I have tried to live on the bare essentials, but in the environment that is America it is so easy to stockpile and store away stuff that only takes up space and place. One of the modern movements that highlights and illustrates this concept is the "self-storage" explosion. You see these buildings everywhere now because we Americans have filled our homes (many of us two homes), our garages (many of them two or three doors), basements, and attics. Now we have so much stuff we need to rent others places to store our mountain of things.

In contrast take for example my cat Eddie. When I was in India I witnessed the greatest example of poverty I have experienced in my life. I have gone to the slums of some of our great cities, and I have been to the poor homes of many a Christian in rural America, but the poorest I have seen in America was a rich man compared to some Indians I meet in Kerala, people who literally have nothing but the cloths on their backs, who work each day just to make enough to eat and who live in huts that we wouldn't put our dog or Eddie in. While in India I did see one cat. It reminded me of Eddie because of its coloring and its thin body. When I came back home, I made the comparison that Eddie had just as many possessions as that Indian cat—none. Eddie came to me with nothing, and he still has nothing. The tragedy of this is that Eddie does now have stuff, but it is stuff I have accumulated for him. He has no self-storage place because he travels light. Some would say he needs nothing but food, clothes, and shelter. (Sound familiar?) Jesus taught:

> "Therefore take no thought, saying, what shall we eat? Or, what shall we drink? Or, Wherewithal shall we be clothed? (For after all these things do Gentiles seek :) for your heavenly Father knoweth that ye have need of all these things? But seek ye first the kingdom of God, and His righteousness; and all these things shall be added unto you" (Matthew 6:31-33).

For me the Lord has laid out the boundaries of what we need to seek and what we need to store. I do not believe the Good Lord is against you having nice things, a warm home, a good car, and a few treasures that will make your life nice. What He is against, I believe, is when "we lay up in store" so much that we forget to trust him and rely on Him. Was not that the sin of the "certain rich man?" The farmer had become so successful that he had been able to provide for himself for many years into the future. God wants us to be dependent on Him. Eddie is dependent on me, and he daily trusts me to provide for him the necessities and essentials of life. Unlike the squirrel brothers in the neighborhood, Eddie is not laying up in store for the coming Maine winter. He believes that I will do that, and he lives each day trusting in my "adding" unto him what he needs. Most would say nobody can live like that, and I would say that there are a multitude of Christians in India living like that every day. Granted, they seemingly have no option but to live like that, but I ask who is really the poorer? I still remember the time when I discovered this verse in the Revelation: "*I know thy works, and tribulation, and poverty, (But thou art rich)...*" (Revelation 2:9). I now know some of these people, and God was right. I have come to believe that we Americans are the poor Christians on this planet, and that men like Ranjan and Noah of Orissa are the truly rich!

I believe Jesus knew the human heart and its tendency to love accumulation, to forget the importance of reliance on God and the failure of making God our perpetual sustainer. As I watch Eddie day in and day out trust me for his basic needs, I am rebuked by my lack of trust, not because I have so little, but because God has blessed me with so much. But what am I doing with my much? Am I saying with the rich farmer I don't have to worry about the future? I don't have to go to God for help? I don't need but what I already have? We are rebuked and reproved over and over again in God's word because He knows our habit of hoarding both material wealth and spiritual possessions. I am now dealing with a generation of Christians that have retired too early. They are in Florida conserving their resources and reserves so they can live a few more years on this earth rather than working for God with their last ounce of energy and giving to God their last mite. They have forgotten that God has promised strength for each day and supplies what is necessary for each need. They have forgotten that **"life is not a reservoir but a channel."** Mary Maxwell says it best in her hymn "Channels Only."

> Channels only, blessed Master,
> But with all Thy wondrous power, flowing through us,
> Thou canst use us every day and every hour!

It is time we get back to traveling light, working hard, keeping little, and sharing much.

Chapter Sixteen

A Single Solitary Life

"Who, being in the form of God, thought it not robbery to be equal with God: but made Himself of no reputation, and took upon Him the form of a servant, and was made in the likeness of men: and being found in fashion as a man, He humbled Himself, and became obedient unto death, even the death of the cross."

—Philippians 2:6-8

It is a Saturday afternoon on the coast of Maine and tropical storm Danny is dumping several inches of rain on the area. I have just gotten back from a committal where I sprinkled the ashes of Ethel and Emerson Rice over a pair of rocks in a forest behind their home. Ethel died nearly 4 years ago and Emerson nearly a year. It was their final desire that their ashes be placed together over a set of stones where Emerson had proposed to Ethel nearly seventy years ago. It was a first for me, especially when you add the wind and water to what was once Hurricane Danny. The family fulfilled the couple's wishes, and I also kept a promise I had made to Emerson a few years back. What I didn't expect was the special blessing that came because of the weather.

I knew that I was traveling into a very wet no-man's land so I decided not to take my new preaching Bible with me. I went to my book shelf and took an old Bible, my original preaching Bible, instead. I figured that if I got that Bible wet it wouldn't be as bad as my new Oxford wide-margin Bible that my dear wife had spent over one hundred dollars for. I got to the appointed place a bit early, and as I waited the arrival of the Rice family (two children and their children and their children and even one fourth generation lad of 18-months by the name of Sam) I flipped through the well-worn pages of my 1972-1988 Bible. Pasted on the front page was an article that I had long forgotten, but when I reread its message it inspired this "exhortation from Eddie."

I have mentioned before that Eddie is the only cat I have ever claimed as "mine" in my nearly sixty years. Plenty of cats have passed me by, but Eddie has become very special to me. This single solitary feline has changed forever my opinion of cats and the impact animals can have on the lives of people. I know many people with a special pet, but I never thought I would one day be one of those people. Oh, I have always liked animals. I love to watch wildlife, whether birds or beasts. I was a hunter in my foolish youth, but now I prefer watching versus killing. Raised on a dairy farm I was surrounded with plenty of creatures, but only one dog by the name of Rover ever impacted my life. After his death I never again imagined that I would feel the way I do now about Eddie. The effect of this single solitary creature has changed many of my opinions and convictions. (We will have to debate in a future article as to whether animals like Eddie will be in Heaven.) As I read again these lines, I realized that Eddie was again reminding me of an old reason why I came to believe in the "single solitary life" that was Jesus Christ. These are the anonymous thoughts that inspired me then, and today on this rainy weekend afternoon have touched me again.

> He was born in an obscure village,
> The child of a peasant woman.
> He grew up in still another village where
> He worked in a carpenter shop
> Until He was thirty.
> Then for three years He was an
> Itinerate preacher.
> He never wrote a book.
> He never held an office.
> He never had a family or owned a house.
> He didn't go to college.
> He never visited a big city.
> He never traveled two hundred miles from
> The place where He was born.
> He did none of the things one usually
> Associates with greatness.
> He had no credentials but Himself.
> He was only thirty-three when the tide of
> Public opinion turned against Him.

His friends ran away.
He was turned over to His enemies and went
Through the mockery of a trial.
He was nailed to a cross between two thieves.
While He was dying, His executioners
Gambled for His clothing, the only
Property He had on earth.
When he was dead, He was laid in a borrowed
Grave through the pity of a friend.
Twenty centuries have come and gone, and
Today He is the central figure of the human
Race and the leader of mankind's progress.
All the armies that ever marched,
All the navies that ever sailed,
All the parliaments that ever sat,
All the kings that ever reigned,
Put together have not affected the life
Of man on earth as much as that
ONE SOLITARY LIFE.

Whoever wrote those lines came to the same conclusion I came to over fifty years ago. Since I gave my heart to Jesus, I have never found another that could satisfy and save like Him. His "one solitary life" has been my inspiration and my soul's satisfaction all these years. As this one cat named Eddie has changed forever how I view the animal kingdom, Jesus Christ changed how I see everything. Paul's statement printed above says it all. That single solitary life that was made of "no reputation" and "became obedient unto death" changes everything both in this life and the life to come. I must ask if you, too, have come to the same conclusion as the unknown prose writer. If you haven't met Jesus yet, let me introduce you to Him today. If a cat, a simple creature of God's making, can change the way a preacher sees The Almighty, then how much more can His Son do?

Chapter Seventeen

Letting Go

"Brethren, I count not myself to have apprehended:
but this one thing I do, forgetting those things which are behind,
and reaching forth unto those things which are before."

—Philippians 3:13

I AM INSPIRED AGAIN by an unknown author and the message he or she penned. This example of spiritual prose has caused me to re-examine another illustration from the life of my cat Eddie. I hope that which I am about to apply will help you as much as it has helped me in the very difficult area of "letting go."

Most of us struggle with this concept whether or not it deals with a family member or a past event. "Letting go and letting God" is a well-known precept in Christian circles, but a rarely used philosophy in the Christian's life. It is an easy proverb to preach, but a difficult byword to practice. Who of us hasn't known of an occasion when we ought to have applied this truth, but have found it harder than we thought to make application of it to our situation, maybe a wayward son or a besetting sin that the devil uses still to keep us from serving Him. It is for you, it is for me, that I print these anonymous lines.

> To let go doesn't mean to stop caring,
> It means I can't do it for someone else.
> To let go is not to cut myself off,
> It's the realization that I can't control another.
> To let go is not to enable,
> But to allow learning from natural consequences.
> To let go is to admit powerlessness,
> Which means the outcome is not in my hands.

To let go is not to try to change or blame another,

I can only change myself.

To let go is not to care for,

But to care about.

To let go is not to fix,

But to be supportive.

To let go is not to judge,

But to allow another to be a human being.

To let go is not to be in the middle arranging all the outcomes,

But to allow others to effect their own outcomes.

To let go is not to be protective,

It is to permit another to face reality.

To let go is not to deny,

But to accept.

To let go is not to nag, scold, or argue,

But to search out my own shortcomings and correct them.

To let go is not to adjust everything to my desires,

But to take each day as it comes.

To let go is not to criticize and regulate anyone,

But to try to become what dream I can be.

To let go is not to regret the past,

But to grow and live for the future.

To let go is to fear less and love more.

As I pondered the theology of that simple writing, I thought of Paul's philosophy printed above. They are saying basically the same thing. There comes a time in every life, every relationship, every circumstance, and every situation when it is time to let go. I believe there came a time in the life of my Eddie when somehow he realized that living under the neighbor's back porch wouldn't be sufficient as winter approached. Despite the fear he felt towards the man across the street, he knew he had to let go of his old life existence and embrace the free gift of food and housing offered by that man across the street. It was hard to let go of old habits and patterns, but eventually Eddie did. I feel at times Eddie still struggles with letting go of those old feelings, like yesterday when he came into my office and ate nearly a bowl of cat food only to throw it all up before he got out of the church. Why? Eddie still at times remembers his last meal and the feeling of not knowing when his next meal will come. He doesn't need to eat that way any longer because there will be another meal in just a few hours, but he struggles still (he counts not himself to have apprehended yet). I struggle still with the relationship I have with my wayward son. I have let him go, but when he calls like he did yesterday, I burn to get back into the struggle for his soul. It is then I have to remind myself that "letting go" means just that—"letting go and letting God" work it out in His time and in His way.

The minute I found the words from the unknown author I shared them with my wife. Together we have wrestled with this concept, whether with children or parishioners. There are just some individuals we can't help despite years of trying. I am just coming to a time in my ministry when I can honestly say I am practicing more and more this concept, but will admit I have yet to graduate from the school of "letting go." Like Paul "*I count not myself to have apprehended.*" Maybe it is a life-long contest, but I am so glad to know that others struggle as my wife and I do. The key to my advancement in this area is the truth of the line that said, "To let go is not to enable, but to allow learning from natural consequences." I am an enabler. I believe my generation was cursed with this trait. I have finally learned after many a year that sometimes when you help someone you are not helping, but enabling. We have done it with our kids and our church members. We have enabled them to continue in a destructive action, and we are guilty because we haven't allowed the natural consequences of their actions to teach them and train them that their actions were wrong. We have bailed them out more than once, and, eventually, they have returned to the very action we were hoping to help them out of.

If my cat could learn to "let go," then there is hope for me, and you. I am still working on this, as was Paul, and so are you. It is my wish that you will keep trying because it will be best for us and them when we finally "let them go."

Chapter Eighteen

Confronting the Contentious

"But unto them that are contentious, and do not obey the truth, but obey unrighteousness, indignation and wrath."

—Romans 2:8

Before Eddie came into Precious Pearl's life she had her "moments," but after the black and brown and white short-hair tom came into the parsonage those "moments" happened all the time. Our decision to bring Eddie into Pearl's life has turned Precious Patience Pearl into a contentious feline! Before you think ill of Pearl let me tell you of the stress level of this Maine coon cat since the arrival of "Edwardo the stocker."

From day one Eddie has loved the "Pearl." It was love-at-first sight, and why not? Precious is the most beautiful cat in the world according to my wife. Eddie seems to be attracted to her gorgeous long gray hair and the lovely features of a perfectly fashioned Maine coon. Despite Eddie's affection, Pearl will have nothing to do with this unbridled love affair. After nearly six years of peace and quiet, of the house to herself, Pearl had become a cat of a daily routine. Pearl loves to sleep in; Eddie is an early riser. Pearl loves to nap in the morning; Eddie loves to roam. Pearl loves to eat slowly; Eddie devours his food as fast as possible. Pearl has lost her kitty energy; Eddie is a bundle of strength and loves to play. Eddie tires Pearl out just watching him play with a favorite toy, a ball of yarn, "red dot" (a small laser that projects a bright red dot on things), or a small pillow filled with cat-nip. And then there is the stocking!

Pearl loves to be left alone. She loves a quiet house. For years she had the parsonage all to herself. We had gotten Pearl just before our last child headed off to college. For all those years, the house was Pearl's private domain she developed an attitude of independence and a love of solitude. Precious did tolerate us, but she never loved us having company or strangers in the house.

Yes, the Pearl would tell our guests when she thought they had stayed too long with a loud hiss. And then, unexpectedly, along came another cat into her house, a male cat that follows her around like a puppy dog on a string, an outdoor cat that will not give her a moment's peace when he is around. Pearl got so stressed over our new boarder that she has even started to hiss and growl and bat at us at times. There are times when we pick her up that she lets loose with a death cry that will bring Eddie to her defense even to the point he would attack us. In the early days both my wife and I got claw marks, not from the Pearl (she is clawless), but Eddie who felt we were hurting his beloved. She has never thanked him once because in her mind she thinks he is the source of all her frustration and fears.

Despite Eddie's love, Pearl has yet to return the affection. Eddie now lives with a contentious feline. We often find him sitting and simply staring into her eyes, and, when he gets too close, she slaps him in the face. We had the Pearl de-clawed in kitty-hood, but Eddie still has all his weapons, and they are as sharp as knives! Even in fun he could inflict terrible wounds, but he has yet to strike back no matter how bad the Pearl might provoke him. Somehow he seems to know she really doesn't mean it, or does she? To say our first cat's personality has changed since Eddie came home would be an understatement, but our hope is that in time the familiarity and friendliness of Eddie will turn our contentious cat into a loving cat again. We love the Pearl, but we don't love what she has become. We know that it is our fault and the loving stocking of a cat named Eddie. So what is the exhortation we need to learn from this feline conflict?

Paul writes of the contentious above, and who of us hasn't confronted those that would bring strife into our lives, our families, and the church? *"But if any man seem to be contentious, we have no such custom, neither the churches of God"* (I Corinthians 11:16). In my 36 years (49 now) in the pastorate I have faced off against the contentious. I like the Pearl am a quiet loner by my very nature. I despise strife on all levels, yet there are those that can so irritate that strife is the end result. Solomon must have confronted such people because he writes on "contentiousness" more than any other Biblical writer. Here are a few of his comments and instructions on confronting the contentious:

> *"A continual dropping in a very rainy day and a contentious woman are alike."* (Proverbs 27:15)
>
> *"As coals are to burning coals, and wood to fire; so is a contentious man to kindle strife."* (Proverbs 26:21)
>
> *"It is better to dwell in the wilderness, than with a contentious and angry woman."* (Proverbs 21:19)

"A brother offended is harder to be won than a strong city: and their contentions are like the bars of a castle." (Proverbs 18:19)

"The beginning of strife is as when one letteth out water: therefore leave off contention, before it be meddled with." (Proverbs 17:14)

"Only by pride cometh contention. . ." (Proverbs 13:10)

"Cast out the scorner, and contention shall go out; yea, strife and reproach shall cease." (Proverbs 22:10)

I have found this advice to be true in my experiences. Years ago we were struggling with those in the church that wanted a certain style of music over another. Contention and strife were destroying our fellowship. I tried for years to hold the group together, but it wasn't until I let them go that peace and fellowship returned. My wife and I have decided, however, that we will not be throwing out the Pearl. There is a difference between dealing with cats and Christians. Remember, Biblical instruction is for the church, not the cats in your household. But those cats will at times cause you to find an answer that will help with another matter you might be dealing with in your life!

Chapter Nineteen

The Tyranny of Things

"And he was sad at that saying, and went away grieved:
for he had great possessions."

—Mark 10:22

In a previous article (Traveling Light-*chapter fifteen*), I shared with you that one of the greatest lessons I have learned from Eddie and India is the need to renounce "things." A. W. Tozer calls it "the blessedness of possessing nothing" or "the tyranny of things."

Interestingly, even God call these things "things."

> "And God saw every THING that He had made, and, behold, it was very good. And the evening and the morning were the sixth day." (Genesis 1:31)

The Creator God had made everything to the delight and desire of mankind. Anything and everything which God made was for the blessing and benefit of man. Certainly, in themselves there is nothing wrong with "things," possessions. So what went wrong? Sin complicated man's relationship with things. God's wonderful blessings have now replaced God for most, like the rich young ruler (Mark 10:17-22). Paul said it best to Timothy:

> "Charge them that are rich in this world, that they be not highminded, nor trust in uncertain riches, but in the living God, who giveth us richly all things to enjoy." (I Timothy 6:17)

One of the effects of sin was the pushing out of God and replacing Him with things. Sin causes one to covet "things" rather than the Creator of things. Besides the rich young ruler in the New Testament there is the case of Achan in the Old Testament. Remember, he was the man who seeing the "things" of Jericho coveted them (Joshua 7:20-21) to the direct disobedience of the command of God about those very things. The Bible is full of stories of those that were tempted by "things." I am reminded of Solomon (Ecclesiastes 2) as well. The only person that seemingly knew from the beginning of the tyranny of things was Jesus. He not only preached against them and taught about them, but resisted the temptation of them (Matthew 4:8). Few among us have mastered the theology of renunciation, but we must or the love of things will cause us to walk away from Jesus just like the rich young ruler.

For me, the secret of this theology is "having everything, but possessing nothing," the very opposite of Paul's precept of "having nothing, and yet possessing all things;" (II Corinthians 6:10) I believe that one of the reasons that Abraham was the father of the faithful is this ability to have everything, and yet possess nothing. Abraham was certainly a rich man (Genesis 13:1) possessing many things, yet nothing was off limits to God for him including his son (Genesis 22). All of Abraham's things belonged to God in Abraham's philosophy. Remember, that was the argument of Satan to God over Job. If Satan took away Job's possessions, he would curse God. But when Job lost everything (Job 1-2), he still trusted in God. Why? Job had everything, but he possessed nothing. The rich young ruler had everything and possessed everything. I will be honest with you. There are those that have nothing, but their nothing is still a trap to them because they possess their nothing. I was not raised on the spiritual truth of the renunciation of things. You will not find this theology in many theological text books. Few preachers teach or preach on it. The popular theme today is accumulation; that the possession of things, the getting of things is God's way of blessing you. Granted, God gave to Abraham and Job, but neither of them saw this as God's blessing. God's blessings to these men were both internal and eternal! Why else does it say of Abraham *"For he looked for a city which hath foundations, whose builder and maker is God"* (Hebrews 11:10)? Abraham and Job both had come to the heart of the truth about "the tyranny of things," and so had Paul.

> *"While we look not at the THINGS which are seen, but the THINGS which are not seen: for the THINGS which are seen are temporal; but the THINGS which are not seen are eternal."* (II Corinthians 4:18)

Was not Jesus talking about the same doctrine when he challenged his followers with the following?

> *"Lay not up for yourselves treasures* [things] *upon earth, where moth and rust doth corrupt, and where thieves break through and steal: but lay up for yourselves treasures* [things] *in heaven, where neither moth nor rust doth corrupt, and where thieves do not*

THE TYRANNY OF THINGS 57

break through nor steal: for where your treasure [thing] *is, there will your heart be also."* (Matthew 6:19-21)

Now we know where the heart of this rich young ruler and where the heart of Achan was. We also now know where the heart of Abraham and Job were. Both had learned the way of renunciation. One thought of my Indian friends, one look at my cat Eddie, and I am reminded of this neglected doctrine. It is time the Church of God takes a look at this theology lest we become like the Church of the Laodiceans:

" . . . *Because thou sayest, I am rich, and increased with goods, and hath need of nothing . . .* " (Revelation 3:14-19)

I have become a believer that there is a question we need to asked before any purchase or decision: what eternal value does it have anyway?

Chapter Twenty

Do the Work of an Evangelist

"But watch thou in all things, endure afflictions, do the work of an evangelist, make full proof of thy ministry."

—II Timothy 4:5

WE HAVE ALL HEARD about "the church mouse," but when was the last time you heard about "the church cat?" I have a true story to tell you about my cat Eddie, Eddie, Eddie and the part he played in my very first "church mouse" story in 38 years in the pastorate.

I have been a part of a local church for nearly six decades now. In that time I have very few animal stories that have taken place in a church building. I will never forget the Sunday I attended an Aboriginal church in the outback of Western Australia and found more dogs in the service than saints. I was on a short-term mission trip between my junior and senior year in college. My cousin Bob and I had been "downunder" for nearly a month when our journey landed us at the Cosmo Newbury Mission Station, a million and a half acre sheep and cattle ranch used by the United Aboriginal Mission of Australia to evangelize the natives of the Gibson Desert. When we got to Sunday services that morning, we discovered that the aboriginals loved to bring their dogs to church. I will admit that the dogs of the Gibson Desert were quieter than some of my congregation. I learned in that experience that the house of God is not restricted to just humans.

Nearly three years ago a blind man, Michael Griffin, began attending our church here in Ellsworth. Each Sunday that he is able to come he brings Amanda, his seeing-eye dog, with him. Amanda is a perfect lady in church, and only once in three years have I ever heard her say "amen!" A couple of weeks ago the young people were leaving the auditorium for their downstairs children's church service (the kids stay with us through the singing part of the morning service) when a bark came from halfway back in the sanctuary.

Normally, Amanda stays under the pew that Michael is sitting in, but on this very hot and humid August Sunday Michael had allowed Amanda to lie in the aisle. As Jen Brennan (our children's church teacher) walked by Amanda with the kids in tow, a sharp warning came from Amanda's mouth. Perhaps, Amanda thought Jen didn't see her or was afraid she might step on her, but, whatever, Amanda's first amen was heard. I believe Amanda has been well accepted because just a year before Amanda's arrival another animal had won over the hearts of the people of the Emmanuel Baptist Church.

Because the church building was Eddie's first safe haven after coming in from his outdoor life, he thinks the church is as much his home as the parsonage across the street. Eddie first came inside at the church. His first indoor meal took place at the church. Now, even after six years, Eddie daily comes with me to the church and roams at will around the church. As I type this story into my laptop, Eddie is asleep under the big picture window at the back of the sanctuary. It is nearly three in the afternoon and time for Eddie's afternoon nap before he takes up sentry duty in the backyard of the parsonage, his evening job. At first I thought the people of the church might not like this arrangement, but over the years Eddie has become as much a part of the church as Amanda. Most people who come by the church during the week and don't see Eddie ask about him. I try to keep him away on Sunday and Wednesday because he gets uncomfortable with too many people around, but on the odd occasion he has attended meetings, too.

Whether sitting and looking out the floor to ceiling windows at the back of the church or sleeping in the desk chair in my office, Eddie has made himself at home at the Emmanuel Baptist Church of Ellsworth, Maine. He gets very upset when on Sunday morning I take him back to the parsonage before Sunday school. Even the kids have come to love Eddie and Amanda in the church. It has resulted in show and tell coming to church with everything from a baby goat to a pair of rats coming to church for a visit. Many say I ought to allow Eddie to stay, and I have on the rare occasion allowed him to stay for prayer meeting, but most of the time Eddie is only allowed in the church when it is empty of people, and he prefers it that way as well. Just a few weeks ago I discovered an important reason why I have kept to that rule; now for my Eddie story and another Eddie exhortation.

Often when I am studying in my office Eddie likes to go outside and roam in the deep grass and the small forest behind the church. When Eddie has had enough wandering, he will come to my study window and call for me. On good days I jar the front door open so that Eddie can come and go at his own good pleasure. It was a typical Indian summer day in late October when I heard that distinct meow and I headed for the door to let Eddie in. Opening one of the double doors that leads to the front porch of the church,

I saw out of the corner of my eye Eddie racing around the corner of the church building that faces Park Street. In Eddie's mouth was a small field mouse and like any proud hunter Eddie was coming to show me his kill, or so I thought. Bringing the mouse into the lobby Eddie placed the small creature at my feet. Motionless, the mouse laid deathly still as I rubbed Eddie's back and told him how proud I was of him. Then it happened! Suddenly the little mouse got up on all fours and like a streak ran into the main sanctuary. The mouse was only playing dead and had taken its only chance to escape. The chase was on. I had never chased a field mouse in a church before. Eddie seemed to be enjoying the romp as I tried to catch the elusive creature. Time and time again I thought I had it only to lose it under a pew or behind a chair. Eddie seemed to be getting more pleasure watching me rather than helping. I imagined he was thinking that he had caught it once, now it was my turn. Unable to catch the mouse a second time, it only left when I opened the door and chased it back into the upper parking lot.

I wish I could say that was the only time Eddie brought me a present, but it isn't. Rarely does Eddie kill the creatures (baby birds, baby squirrels, baby mice—he seems to pick on the innocent) he catches, but without fail he always seems to bring them to church. I have come to the conclusion that Eddie is neither a hunter, nor a killer, but an evangelist wanting others to come to church. Is not that the mission we are on? I know well that there is the spiritual gift of "evangelist" (Ephesians 4:11). I also know that I don't have that gift, but according to Paul we all ought to be doing the work of an evangelist, bringing others to Christ. I learned long ago and have recently been rebuked by Eddie that we are all responsible for the bringing of souls to church. We are challenged by Jesus to go into the highways and hedges and compel them to come in. If Eddie can roam the fields around the church for mice and when finding them "bring them in," why can't we?

Chapter Twenty-One

The Need to Escape

*"Deliver me in Thy righteousness, and cause me to escape:
incline Thine ear unto me, and save me."*

—Psalms 71:2

It is Thursday morning, and I am still pondering a devotional I shared with the Wednesday prayer meeting group last night. Over the last few years I have not had a traditional Bible lesson at our weekly prayer meeting. We have decided that prayer meeting ought to be more of a ministry than a service so we have cut out all normal activities like singing, preaching, and teaching to give ourselves to prayer and sharing prayer requests. The dozen that come see this as a vital ministry to the church family and our extended families around the world. (We have mission outreaches on all five continents, young people in the armed services, and college/career kids scattered around the county.) Because of my love of writing, however, I have taken it upon myself to write a devotional for each prayer service, a handout sheet that I hope will challenge those who come. This year I have been sharing a series of devotional on "morning meditations." As Eddie and I settled in for our morning devotions in our prayer room at the back of the church, I share with you what I wrote for the prayer warriors of the Emmanuel Baptist Church of Ellsworth, Maine:

> Sometimes I need to escape. Sometimes I feel the city has made me its prisoner. Surrounded by the houses and the businesses of this small coastal city, I get closed in both in body as well as in soul. Sometimes I need to simply run away to the country where my surroundings are open and my eye sees nothing of mankind, manmade, or his madding walls. I need God-made, God's country; I need to escape to home. I never felt like this when I lived on the family farm of in Perham, Maine (a little

hamlet in the Aroostook River valley of northern Maine). I can never remember a case of cabin fever there, despite the long, cold winter days that lasted sometimes a third of the year. Even in the worst of weather I got out and about to a world of quiet and solitude. I need today to escape as I once did as a boy on a morning jaunt into the hills. I need to once again "... *lift up mine eyes unto the hills, from whence cometh my help. My help cometh from the Lord, which made heaven and earth.*" (Psalms 121:1-2) Yesterday, I strolled away from the farmhouse I called home to climb a hilltop that has always cast its shadow over my barnyard. I use to escape to that hill and its woody slopes whenever I could. The moment I would start climbing I would enter another world, a world void of family and friends, a world without man's devices and deadlines. No matter how the farm or the farm boy changed from year to year, that hill and its surrounding forest stayed the same, just like God (Hebrews 13:8). Perhaps, that is what I love most about the country versus the city. The city is always in constant change while the country stays the same. When one escapes to that hilltop, one moves into the realm of the unchanging. The birds on that hilltop have never learned a new song because the old ones have always been good enough. The wildflowers that bloom there in spring have never changed colors because they are already painted with the best of hue. Modern, manmade colors have yet to invade the prism of colors cast at creation by the Master painter. On that hilltop in my childhood the grass was ever-green and the dandelions were always yellow! I have always found great peace in slipping into something that stays unspoiled, just like it was, and forever will be—God's things versus man's things. Perhaps that it why I wear the same style of clothing, part my hair the same way (what there is left of it), and enjoy going back to the same fishing hole year after year. When I escape, then and now, I want to escape to the familiar. Long ago I stopped seeking a new vista, a new wife, a new calling. I am afraid that I find great comfort in the same ol', same ol' things. While others have gotten tired of God, His Son Jesus, and the Church, I haven't. We live in a land that is going crazy with the imported "faiths," the new "religions," and modern "worship." I still enjoy the old-time religion, the classic hymns of the Church, and "the faith of our fathers." But sometimes in the bedlam of Broadway, I forget that there is such a world still out there. I sometimes get captured by a society that cares little for the sanity of the soul. Granted, to move from one world to the other, to escape from here to there, can be a shock to the system, but I believe it is worth the chance of a heart attack to rest awhile in the sameness that is found in creation and the Creator (Psalms 19:1-2). We have almost lost in this world of constant motion the ability to escape. To walk and meditate is a lost art, and the woods and hilltops that once brought us great relief have been covered over with housing developments and strip malls. The natural, soothing sounds of the woods have been driven away by the noise of car and truck and vehicles that blast the sound of silence from the roadside. On occasion I still do hear the faint sound of a singing bird, but no matter the momentary pleasure because I know that it will never last unless I escape to a place where man can't be found, but God can.

I wrote that a number of years before Eddie arrived in my life, but now that I have been reminded of these thoughts I think it would only be proper to leave this computer and take Eddie for a walk into the backyard. (His love for the out-of-doors is only matched by my love.) I know God will be there, but just maybe we will hear a singing bird or watch a squirrel gathering nuts and be transported back to a time and hilltop where one can "see forever."

Chapter Twenty-Two

Training up a Child

"Train up a child in the way he should go: and when he is old, he will not depart from it."

—Proverbs 22:6

I know of dogs and horses and many other animals that can be trained, but I am still amazed that there is a cat on this planet that could and would be trained!

I had always believed that cats were arrogant, independent, and aloof by nature, or at least the cats I have known. For that reason and more I have been a dog-lover since my boyhood. I love anything that is obedient. Obedience is a top virtue in my book—human or animal. That is why when a little white, black, grey, and brown waif came into our home, I didn't think at first of even trying to train the newest member of the Blackstone family. But it was Eddie's dog-like characteristics that first turned my apathy into affection. In time I began to notice that Eddie quickly knew his new name (who knows what his original owners called him). His full name is Eddie, Eddie, Eddie, but over the years a variety of nicknames have become attached to this tomcat with the enormous brown goatee. Each of his names can be used singularly. Eddie repeated rapidly will call him from across the street, the yard, or the neighbor's lawn. Edwardo is his formal name only used on special occasions, and "the lad" is my personal name for him. He comes to all now almost without exception.

It wasn't long into our relationship that I concluded that Eddie had a dog's spirit wrapped up in his cat heart. He was unusually alert like a guard dog and very attentive, possessing a great amount of teaching ability. Very soon Eddie dispelled all my misgivings and apprehensions about proud cats. Time was revealing just how quick and intelligent my cat was, and, besides this, he was very trainable. Like a dog Eddie comes to a whistle I have created just for him. Besides that special call Eddie is learning to come to another special sound just understood by the members of the Blackstone family. In my young adulthood I learned a creative whistle while attending college. It was our society whistle created so we could contact a fellow brother in a crowd. Over the years I taught that whistle to my wife and kids so that we could always find each other in a crowd. Both my kids are in their thirties, and they still respond to "the whistle" as do I and my wife. Last night Eddie came to me for the first time using just the sound of that special call. However, I still believe Eddie's greatest accomplishment and in my opinion greatest achievement is this.

Eddie loves his treats—special bits of cat food with a big flavor of salmon. When my wife first bought Eddie's treats, I had decided by then that Eddie could be trained. It wasn't long before a simple shake of the treat container would bring Eddie running. I have often used that sound to bring Eddie home at night or to find him when I don't know where he is. The sound is enough to bring Eddie home from wherever because to Eddie treat time is the best time of the day except perhaps our devotional time in the morning (more later). I was soon teaching Eddie to sit on the arm of my recliner before he could get a treat. Once he become patient enough I taught him to raise his paw and touch the container (a very special container) before I gave him his treat. Then he would have to shake my hand before I put the treat in his mouth. It wasn't long before I had Eddie acting like a dog waiting for a bone treat. Eddie even will take the end of a string and carry it into another room as I try to pull it back. Our version of "tug-of-war" is another favorite play time as well as something I have trained him to do.

Nearly seven years into our relationship, Eddie and I have come to quite an understanding of each other. I have learned to talk a bit of felinese, and he has learned some simple commands that allow us to communicate and react to each other quite well. Whether sitting at his spot in the kitchen for supper or his special meow just before he heads up stairs for bed, I can see that over the years Eddie has taught me to respond to what he wants as well. Sometimes I wonder who is really training who.

It Eddie's willingness to learn that has brought a new reality to the classic proverb printed above.

One of the problems facing my generation when it comes to their kids is the inability "to let her go." For some reason we want to hang on even after we have taught them to live and work and be on their own. Part of training up a child is to know when to let go. I have come to see that one of the greatest mistakes of parenting is hanging on too long at the back of the bike. As I said to my wife the other day, is the problem more that we think we need them than they need us? We know all about training and for most of us we have loved the responsibility and power that comes from holding onto the bike. The pride that comes in seeing them riding, achieving, accomplishing, but what happens when the training wheels come off and they no longer need us to balance them, hold them, and be there to catch them lest they fall? One of the reasons I believe that my kids' generation seems to have a hard time leaving home, letting go, isn't them, but us. You must let go to let go. You must walk away and turn away and let them ride on their own, even if they fall. If I can do that with my cat, why can't I do it with my 34-year-old Army son or my 31-year-old seminary student?

Chapter Twenty-Three
Constant Companionship

"...and He hath said, I will never leave thee, nor forsake thee."
—Hebrews 13:5

THE SLEEPING ARRANGEMENTS FOR the parsonage of the Emmanuel Baptist Church of Ellsworth, Maine, are pretty well defined now. There was a time, however, when the "Emmanuel Bed and Breakfast was full." When this remembrance of Eddie, Eddie, Eddie occurred, my daughter Marnie, was home after a year of missions work in the eastern European city of Bratislava, Slovakia. At the same time my mother-in-law, Opal, was living with us while her new rent was being prepared. Opal had just moved to Ellsworth after living her entire life in Aroostook County (Maine's northernmost county). Needless to say, there was need for double occupancy especially when you add to the list of residence two totally different cats.

Opal occupied the cot in the craft room. Coleen and I slept in the master bedroom. Marnie was back in her old room, what is now our spare bedroom. Pearl loves to sleep wherever. On certain nights she loves to sleep with Coleen with her back up against Coleen's pillow. When Marnie is not home, she usually sleeps on the quilt at the foot of Marnie's bed. Eddie on the other hand loves to start the night out on our bed and will remain there if I am his only bedmate, but the minute Coleen comes to bed he finds other sleeping arrangements. Pearl will never sleep with Marnie, but Eddie came to enjoy the companionship when Marnie was home. He also came to like a certain teddy bear named Frederick.

Marnie has never slept alone. When she was just a baby she was given a rabbit-blanket that she kept in her possessions through her childhood, teenage years, college, and she even took "Bunny" to Africa twice and, of course, to Europe. Now "Bunny" is getting his masters at Dallas Theological Seminary with Marnie. I can't exactly remember when Frederick became

Marnie's bedmate, but this brown bear has been in or on Marnie's bed for over two decades now. The well-worn bear soon became a fascination to Eddie, more than we could ever imagine.

With the Pearl and Eddie not getting along, it was not surprising and quite understandable that Eddie wouldn't rejoin us in our bedroom, especially those nights Pearl decided to sleep with us. A few problems arose, but as time passed Marnie and Eddie worked out the best way to co-habit the same space at night. It was cute watching them sleep together, but this sleeping arrangement did result in a very strange and unusual event that after all these years we are still trying to figure out!

Marnie was the first to notice this strange happening. The first time it happened it was just an ordinary night like so many before it. After a bit of reading (Marnie has always enjoyed reading before she goes to sleep), Marnie settled in for a good night's sleep. Just before she turned off the light she checked to see if all her "boys" were resting. Sure enough, there was Eddie at the foot of her bed sleeping peacefully on her quilt. Next to her was "Bunny" and "Frederick" so off went the light. It was an uneventful night (Marnie has been known to sleep walk on occasion so they are not all uneventful) until Marnie woke early the next morning (Marnie was working for the local YMCA at the time and was the first off to work). She noticed that Eddie was missing which is not strange because Eddie gets up with the sun and is usually waiting at the front door to be let out by the first person that gets up. Marnie showered and returned to her bedroom and soon discovered that someone else was missing—Frederick. Finishing getting ready, Marnie headed downstairs wondering what had happened to Frederick overnight. When she arrived in the living room, all her questions except one were answered. There in my chair was Eddie fast asleep, but lying beside my chair was Frederick. How had the old, over-stuffed animal made the trip from Marnie's bedroom to the downstairs living room?

To this day it is a mystery, a mystery that has been repeated at least a handful of time more. In a logical reasoning of the facts there seems to be only one clear answer—Eddie took Frederick downstairs with him to keep him company until the rest of us woke up. But that explanation opens up another question, how? This teddy bear is just about the same size as Eddie, and though not heavy the logistics of pulling that bear all the way downstairs would be something to see. Something none of us has seen as yet, and still Frederick has shown up downstairs after starting the night upstairs on numerous occasions. Perhaps Eddie just likes the companionship of Frederick, or, perhaps, we have before us another Eddie Exhortation!

Most of us remember the promise of Jesus' presence given to His disciples just before He ascended on high (Matthew 28:20). His constant companionship is a vow He made to any that would believe on Him and follow Him (Hebrews 13:5). The division between us was removed when the veil was torn open (Matthew 27:51), and nothing, absolutely nothing, can separate us any longer (Romans 8:38-39). In our original form we were created for Him. The great church father Augustine once wrote, "**Thou hast formed us for Thyself, and our hearts are restless till they find rest in Thee**." Revelation 4:11 seems to verify this theology so why wouldn't God promise constant companionship to those He loves? If a simple creature like Eddie craves companionship (mine more than Frederick's), then the human soul must. Some of the great stories of the Bible reveal this truth. The most amazing fact about the wilderness tabernacle of the children of Israel was that Jehovah God was there, a living presence within the veil, and then to think that that same Presence took on flesh to literally dwell among us (John 1:14)? I love how A. W. Tozer put it: "*The world is perishing for lack of the knowledge of God and the Church is famishing for want of His Presence.*"

In the Old Testament it was called the "shekinah," the Presence, but in the New Testament it is called the "Spirit," the promised Presence of Jesus to the Church (John 14:16). I can honestly say that in the last seven years of my life, since Eddie came into my life, there has not been a single person, family, or friend that has been in my presence more than Eddie. And it has been Eddie who has drawn me back to a more consistent daily communion with my Lord and Saviour Jesus Christ. Each morning Eddie will not press on with his day until we go out back in the church building and have a quiet time, just him and me. I have started to see that he wants to be with me just like I believe Eddie wanted Frederick to be with him. Companionship is a powerful emotion, and that energy ought to be drawing us daily into the presence of the Almighty. Amen and Amen!

Chapter Twenty-Four

Apprehending God

"O taste and see that the Lord is good: blessed is the man that trusteth in Him."

—Psalms 34:8

HAVE YOU EVER OWNED a cat that followed you around like a puppy? I never did, nor have I seen it in other people's cats until Eddie, Eddie, Eddie came along. Eddie is more my shadow than any other person, including my wife.

The minute the morning sun turns our Ellsworth neighborhood into dawn, Eddie is by my side wanting to go out. Without fail, when I finally open the front door to the porch to head for my office across the street, Eddie is waiting for me on the top step. As I leave the porch for the walkway that leads to School Street, Eddie is by my side walking step for step with me. Oh, he does stop on occasion so that I will rub his head, but rarely does he leave my side until we arrive at the side door to the church. Some days he will stay outside to check around the church, but ninety-nine times out of a hundred he will walk into the building with me. He will follow me into my study to check the answering machine, and, if there are no urgent needs, I will go out back for a few quiet moments of meditation and reading my Bible before my day begins. Sure enough, Eddie will join me as he follows me to a recliner in the back corner of the upstairs classroom. Once I sit down Eddie will jump up into my lap for a few minutes of rubbing and patting and loving. This is pretty much our morning routine now.

The rest of my day, if it is a study day or an office day will find Eddie within sight of me. Where I go he does, downstairs or upstairs, indoors or outdoors, and, yes, to certain places he will ride with me in the church car (my wife's office, my mother-in-law's house, to pick up the mail, to get gas). That old popular song, "Me and My Shadow," has been running through my mind recently as I sometimes wonder why Eddie has become so occupied with being near me. If I am in my study at the computer, Eddie is sleeping in my other office chair waiting our return to the parsonage. If I am in the bedroom getting ready for work, and he hasn't been let out yet (like on Sunday mornings), Eddie can be found in the hall at the top of the stairs waiting patiently for my descent. At night when I am watching television, Eddie curls up in my recliner beside me or on me, and other nights he settles in next to my chair. Occasionally, Eddie will even watch television with me. He really likes action movies. I even have a picture of Eddie watching a Red Sox baseball game. Where I am Eddie wants to be.

If I should decide to go to bed early for some reason, Eddie is not far behind. I enjoy reading before I go to sleep, and without fail Eddie will be there washing himself before he falls off to sleep. Recently, I have been staying up a bit longer than usual so Eddie often beats me to bed, but, sure enough, when I ascend the stairs and get into the bedroom, Eddie is already there waiting my arrival. Eddie loves the out-of-doors, and he especially loves it when I am doing yard work or working in the garage or basement. Eddie isn't far behind no matter where I am or what I am doing. It is often these small adventures I remember best when I think of "my shadow and me." Granted, there are times when Eddie will go off on his own to explore the priest's house (the local Roman Catholic priest lives across the street from us and has a cat named Sheridan) or the backyard of our other neighbor (they have a dog by the name of Max), but more often than not Eddie is content to stay where I am.

God speaks through the world (Psalms 19:1-2) just as much as he speaks through the Bible (II Timothy 3:16-17). He will manifest Himself whenever and wherever His people need Him, and this is why the Word of God speaks of "tasting" and "seeing" and "smelling" and "hearing" and "touching" God. God has not only given us our five senses to interact with the natural world, but also so we can interact with Him. Faith (Romans 10:17) enables us to function within the realm of God using the very elements that allows me to interact with my cat Eddie. The spiritual world is as close as the nature world enclosing us and embracing us and enabling us to recognize and relate to the Almighty. The basic problem with most is that the visible becomes a handicap of the invisible (II Corinthians 4:18), and the temporal becomes a problem for the eternal. This shortcoming has been inherited by every member of Adam's race. Again, I like A. W. Tozer on this: **"The object of the Christian's faith is unseen reality!"** Surely by now in your Christian walk you must realize that the greatest "unseen reality" is Christ (I Peter 1:8-9).

I now have a new Eddie-consciousness after our six-year relationship. Our time together has allowed me to almost predict his every move and where he can be found. It is mid-afternoon as I finish these thoughts. If I get up from my computer, I know I will find Eddie in a small sunny place by the side door of the church. It is where the afternoon sun shines in the door window, and a place where Eddie is sure to know when I leave the building. Oh, that we would have a new God-consciousness as the Psalmist in the verse printed above sings about to "taste" and "see" the goodness of God that the things of God will become more of a reality than the things of earth. Do you know where your God is right now?

Chapter Twenty-Five

A Lesson from a Gadabout

"Thou tellest my wanderings..."
—Psalms 56:8

Do you know the term "gadabout?" Webster defines this unique word as "one who roams about in an aimless or restless manner; going about seeking fun and excitement." We might use the term "wanderer" to describe such individuals. Recently, I was reminded of a short story I wrote many years ago. I was writing a book on the country creatures I met in my boyhood. I wrote this about a cow we once had on the homestead, and the Holstein caused me to take a second look at the gadabout that now lives in the parsonage, a cat named Eddie. This is what I wrote:

> Every farm must have one as does, seemingly, every family and church. I am talking about that restless animal, or that restless soul, discontented, always looking beyond their boundaries, wishing they could see what is on the other side of the fence line, the pasture, the church—a "gadabout." She was very beautiful in her white and black coloring. She had a strong will and a pair of well-set and bright eyes. She was cleaner than most of her cousins and gave an abundant supply of milk. She bore sturdy calves, but without fail, if not in the barn when she gave birth, we would have to hunt for her calf in early morning dew in some forest area of the homestead. Despite her admirable attributes and her attractive appearance, she was restless, a fence wanderer, a Holstein gadabout. If there was the slightest chance to get out, she would take it. If the current on the electric fence wasn't strong enough to hold her in, she would walk straight through it. She traveled the miles and miles of Blackstone fence line to find a weak point, and, if she did find such a spot, it wasn't long before we would get a call from one

of our neighbors informing us that the cows were out. She would never go it alone, but would persuade her companions that the grass on the other side of the fence was always greener and fresher and more plentiful. She would lead others astray as she went astray. She was always looking for a loophole or a down fence post to aid her escape and the release of her sisters. It wasn't that she lacked pasturage. It wasn't that she was not cared for properly. When she was giving milk, she got extra grain and extra hay. There was no better grazing in the whole of Perham and yet out she would get. Some might say it was freedom she sought, yet there were no animals more free than the Blackstone herd. The farm numbered 720 acres with over two-thirds that number being pastureland and forest land. She had acre after acre to roam, wander, and stretch her legs. Granted, we did fence her in, but she was enclosed on the best land in Perham. Ask anyone! Yet she was constantly getting out, roaming whatever field and forest she could find that was different from the fields and forest she lived in. Our "gadabout" had an ingrained habit of discontentment. Despite the good feeding she had, I would often find her feeding on the bare, brown, burned grass in our neighbor's field or lawn. No matter how many times we would bring her back, she would try to return to that forbidden fodder. Maybe she got a taste for the tasteless; maybe her taste buds liked brown instead of green; maybe she savored the escape more than she savored enough. If I remember clearly that last autumn of her life, my father and grandfather were deciding which cow would be sacrificed for our winter's meat and that "gadabout" was chosen. She was more use to the farm dead than alive. Over the years I have wondered just how many wandering souls are sacrificed simply because they are a troublesome gad-about.

Eddie is a gadabout in the basic sense of the word. He loves to wander and roam, and I believe it is because he is looking for something. The difference between my childhood gadabout and my adult gadabout is found in the truth of the verse printed at the beginning of this article. Not every wandering is because of the nature of the wanderer; "prone to wander, Lord, I feel it." There is another kind of wandering, a wandering caused by others affecting your situation. Paul described this group with these words:

> *"(Of whom the world was not worthy :) they wandered in deserts, and in mountains, and in dens and caves of the earth."* (Hebrews 11:38)

Question: Was Joshua and Caleb's wandering because of a restless and aimless spirit? I believe the answer is no. They wandered for forty years because of the choices of others. I believe it is such people as this that the Psalmist is talking about when he writes:

> "Thou tellest my wanderings: put thou my tears into Thy bottle: are they not in Thy book." (Psalms 56:8)

Eddie's wandering nature came about because he was abandoned as a kitten, and he had no other choice but to wander.

I believe we have before us two wonderful lessons from cow and cat. My memory of that homestead cow teaches us the dangers of being a wanderer in the well ordered things of God. Check out Hosea 9:17 and Jeremiah 48:12. The wise man Solomon gave us this proverb in his classic recording of his wanderings in Ecclesiastes 6:9: *"Better is the sight of the eyes than the wandering of the desire: this is also vanity and vexation of spirit."* If God watches the sparrows when they fall (Matthew 10:29), He knows when a kitty is left on School Street to fend for himself. God watched the wanderings of that simple tom and eventually led him to me for keeping. We, too, have periods in our life where we have been abandoned by others. You know of your wanderings better than me, but know this. We have a caring and loving Heavenly Father that watches our wanderings and records them in His book. Like Eddie He will one day bring you in from the cold, if He hasn't already done it? All I ask is that you take time to remember, and I know for many of you a smile is already coming on your face.

For those of you who are still living an aimless and restless life, I leave you with this warning. Maybe you have known no other life than the "gad" life, being a gadfly (a person who annoys and irritates others), being a gadabout. Before you are sacrificed may I direct your attention to these words from Jesus?

> *"Come unto me, all ye that labour and are heavy laden and I will give you rest. Take my yoke upon you, and learn of me; for I am meek and lowly of heart: and ye shall find rest unto your souls. For my yoke is easy, and my burden is light."* (Matthew 11:28-30)

There is another kind of life other than the "gad" life. You can be free from the restlessness you feel if you turn your wandering ways over to Jesus' direction.

Chapter Twenty-Six

The Victory that Overcomes the World

"For whatsoever is born of God overcometh the world: and this is the victory that overcometh the world, even our faith."

—I John 5:4

I REMEMBER WHEN MY world was just the size of Perham, Maine, my hometown. I grew up in the 1950s and 1960s. I rarely left that small hamlet and for most of my early years we rarely drove more than twenty miles out of town. As I have grown my world now includes most of the world. I have had the privilege of traveling halfway around the world to Australia. I have been to France, England, and India, and, of course, Canada. Could I share this Eddie Exhortation that came to me when I considered one day Eddie's world?

Eddie's world includes basically one city block in Ellsworth outlined by the streets of School, Park, Garden, and Birch. In the six years I have watched Eddie roam I have not seen him outside that boundary. The parsonage does lie on the other side of School Street, but once again I haven't seen Eddie explore beyond the triangle that is School and State Streets. The only buildings within Eddie's world is an accountant's office at the corner of Garden and Birch with a nursing home (Colliers) across the street, a residence on the corner of Garden and Park that included a large barn with the church building across from that, the local Catholic priest's home on the corner of Park and School with a small detracted garage, and a family home on the corner of School and Birch, Eddie's first home. Behind each of these dwellings is a small wooded area making up the block. When Eddie is outside, he spends most of his roaming time in this small area.

Every world contains plants and people and pets. Eddie's neighbors are a housebound cat named Sheridan, the priest's cat, a three-legged dog named Max owned by the couple that bought Eddie's original home, an old male cat named Willy, a transplant from Florida, a family of squirrels we

THE VICTORY THAT OVERCOMES THE WORLD

call the "brothers" who have created a home for themselves in our brush pile, a flock of ravens we call "the boys" who fly in and out of the neighborhood depending the season, a huge tomcat we call Big Grey, the neighborhood bully, and a seasonal woodchuck we call "Woody." Add to this list a multitude of birds, including seagulls, field mice, and insects and you have Eddie's world and all that is within it. Granted, the busy street of School will bring a daily supply of cars, motorcycles, trucks, and delivery vans into Eddie's world, but he is very careful to draw a wide birth around every stranger or strange vehicle that invades his world. Eddie seems to believe in the old adage from James: "*...know ye not that the friendship of the world is enmity with God? Whosoever therefore will be a friend of the world is the enemy of God.*" (James 4:4)

Despite the fact that Eddie keeps his distance from all the creatures named above, I believe Eddie also has the philosophy of Glyn Evans: "**I must not deny the therapeutic influence of the world. . .for the world offers me an opportunity to toughen my spiritual fiber if I use it properly.**" Over the years I have observed Eddie quietly overcoming all those that would call our neighborhood home. I still remember Eddie's first confrontation with Max (more later), with Willy (more later), and with Sheridan (more later). Eddie seems to have the strategy of the children of Israel and their tactics in Canaan. The God-inspired plan for the conquest of Canaan was simply *"little by little"* (Exodus 23:30). I am convinced that this is still the best strategy to this day as we contest with our world. Jesus didn't hide himself away from the world, but daily challenged its means and methods and messages. Unlike the Pearl, Eddie must be on the alert every day, every time he ventures out into his world (a recent fox sighting verifies this important trait). I am afraid if we allowed the Pearl to stay out even once we would lose her. She has lived a sheltered life, and the world would quickly destroy her. Eddie on the other hand has been daily, little by little, learning how to overcome Big Grey, busy city traffic, different weather, and strange people.

I now see my cat doing that in his world, but am I doing that in my world? I will admit that I am a home body. I love peace and quiet. I am a loner by my very nature so I don't mind spending my day all alone. Eddie has rebuked me to get out more. Even my wife chimes in every once in a while that I sometimes keep myself so isolated that I don't even know what is happening in Ellsworth. That is why India has been so good to and for me. It has forced me to confront my world, to "dare" and "provoke." Like Evans I have discovered that victory, overcoming the world happens in the small daily battles, "little by little." With each solo into the dangerous world I am strengthening my spiritual will and muscles. With each battle against the enemies that inhabit my world I am developing the skills that will be needed for tomorrow's battle!

I still remember the first time I saw Eddie take on Big Grey face to face. Despite being half his size, Eddie took the offensive and chased the neighborhood bully under our garage. As I have mentioned before, we are to stand up to the devil. It is sin that we should flee. Matthew 16:18 suggests that the Church of God ought to be the aggressor, not simply a defender. Where Eddie learned this I don't know, perhaps by instinct (God given). All I know is that the more I watch him in his world I have a lot I can adapt to my world. Does Eddie have faith? Not in the purest sense of the word, but he is overcoming his world, and according to John it is "faith" that overcomes. Since India I have turned over a new leaf in my battle in "this present world," and the Good Lord has placed within my sight a daily illustration of just how I ought to fight, whom I ought to fight, and when I ought to fight. John H. Yates wrote of this in his classic church hymn, "Faith is the Victory."

> Encamped along the hills of light, ye Christian soldiers rise,
> And press the battle ere the night shall veil the glowing skies.
> Against the foe in vales below let all our strength be hurled;
> Faith is the victory, we know, that overcomes the world.
> His banner over us is love, our sword the Word of God;
> We tread the road the saints above with shout of triumph trod.
> By faith they, like a whirlwind's breath, swept on over every field;
> The faith by which they conquered death is still our shining shield.
> On every hand the foe we find drawn up in dread array;
> Let tents of ease be left behind, and onward to the fray;
> Salvation's helmet on each head, with truth all girt about,
> The earth shall tremble beneath our tread, and echo with our shout.
> To him that overcomes the foe, white raiment shall be given,
> Before the angels he shall know his name confessed in heaven.
> Then onward from the hills of light, our hearts with love aflame,
> We'll vanquish all the hosts of night, in Jesus' conquering name.
> Faith is the victory! Faith is the victory!
> O, glorious victory that overcomes the world!

Chapter Twenty-Seven

An Appointment with the Almighty

"And they heard the voice of the Lord God walking in the garden in the cool of the day . . ."

—Genesis 3:8

A FAMOUS PREACHER OF the Keswick group by the name of George B. Duncan once said this in a message: "***I have a date with my boys just like I have an appointment with anyone else; and when something tries to break in on that, I say I have an appointment!***" Is it not more important, not to break an appointment with the Almighty?

I have used the same argument as Duncan with dates with my wife and other meetings in which something or someone tries to break into my appointment book. The sad truth is that what I have used for my wife and children and other friends I rarely use for God. For most of my life I have tried to keep a regular devotion time, a quiet time where I read God's Word, pray and meditate on the things of Christ. The tragedy is that when something or someone needs my attention during that special time, I have more often than not sacrificed my time with God for them. I was rebuked recently by my cat Eddie over this very issue. Eddie and I have a routine now, a regular time in which he gets up on my lap, and I rub his head for a period of time. He loves it and the purrs are a sweet and soothing sound to my ear. I must admit I have learned to enjoy these times as well because they are very therapeutic in nature. I have become convinced that more troubled people would be cured of their mania by simply getting a cat. Cats can be very calming and comforting, and I have found them to be very challenging as well.

We live in a time where the demands of life have pretty much driven most of us crazy in one form or the other. The rat race of life can best be slowed with taking time out for God. Was that the purpose of God meeting Adam and Eve in the cool of each evening? Was the Almighty sharing with them a secret to living in this old world? Even before the new world grew old, the Lord God was meeting each day with His crowning creation. What was needed then is certainly needed now. Today we are tied up in so many knots that bind us and hold us in the pressure cooker of modern living. We need a release, a renewal time, and a rest away from schedule, work, and life. A walk in the cool of the evening with the Almighty ought to be in every appointment book, but is it? It has been in my book for years, but just because the appointment is there doesn't assure it will be kept.

Vance Havner once said, "**If you cannot untie the knots, cut them.**" This is very good advice for those of us who have allowed everything and everyone to come ahead of our appointments with God. Most of us have been short-changing our time with God for what? A little more money, a few more friends, a bit more praise from others? Let us be honest. We feel more comfortable saying "no" to God than anyone else. We find it easier to cancel an engagement with the Almighty than we do our wife, our son, a co-worker, don't we? And now I have this cat called Eddie who is a part of this list of others that stand sometimes between me and my meeting with the Almighty. I reason and rationalize that God will understand, and He does, but I am the loser just like Adam and Eve were the losers in the garden, just like Thomas was the loser in the upper room when he failed to meet with Jesus after the resurrection. Think with me for a minute. Can we really believe that to miss an appointment with the Almighty could in any way be profitable or that a meeting with anyone else other than God would be more valuable?

I am rebuked by the thought that I might spend more time with my cat than I do with my Christ or that I talk more to my cat than I do to God, and I know what is true of me is true of so many other saints who have gotten so caught up in the ways of the world that we have forgotten the most important appointment of all is with the Almighty. When was the last time you penciled in the Lord God into your appointment book? When was the last time you punched in Christ in your Blackberry and kept the appointment? I am more faithful to Eddie's time than Emmanuel's time and for that I stand ashamed and embarrassed as a preacher of the Gospel. Granted, I have justified these laps of conscience for years by reasoning that I was meeting others ahead of God because I was doing the Lord's work. When did we come to think that God's work was more important than God? That our time spent in service to the Lord was more important than time spent with the Lord? Most of God's servants have fallen into that wicked trap of the devil.

Surely, this is the lesson from the most famous housewife of the Bible. Martha was "*cumbered about much serving*" (Luke 10:40), and it was left to her sister Mary who "*hath chosen that good part*" (Luke 10:42). Sitting at the feet of Jesus is an appointment we all ought to keep. Despite the busy life we lead, nothing should interfere with that time. Granted, it does, but we need to make it a priority to change it. Instead of giving Eddie all my quiet time, I have used this little feline to remind me that my first hour of the new day is God's. I try not to bring conflicts into this time, but have chosen a time that will result in the least number of interruptions.

Years ago a man by the name of Paul Rees was speaking at a conference in which he recalled an illustration from the life of a bishop from India. As the story goes the bishop was approached by a lady who said, "Bishop, I have sought a deeper experience with God all these years, and I don't have it. I have read books. I have read what to do and all the rules, but I am nowhere yet. Does God have favorites?" The old bishop is reported to have replied, "No, my dear, God does not have favorites. But He has intimates!" Is not that what the Lord was establishing in the Garden of Eden, an intimate time, an intimate relationship with Mary, and what He wants with Thomas and us? There is only one way any of us can develop an intimate time or relationship with the Almighty and that is by keeping our appointments with Him.

Chapter Twenty-Eight

Listening to a Quarrel

"Forbearing one another and forgiving one another, if any man has a quarrel against any: even as Christ forgave you, so also do ye."

—Colossians 3:13

THE EARLY MORNING NOISE was so loud that it woke me. I rolled over trying to ignore the racket going on outside my upstairs bedroom window, but I couldn't find sleep again. I knew deep down what was happening, and I knew there was nothing I could do about it. I had witnessed their longstanding argument many times before. I had listened to their quarreling and complaining and fighting, but this morning it seemed that blows would soon happen, that each side was about ready to physically strike the other, so I got out of bed and took a look out the window located just above my bed into the backyard of the parsonage of the Emmanuel Baptist Church. Sure enough, in a tree across the driveway was a neighborhood raven, one of a group of about seven very opinionated and arrogant birds. On the ground under the tree was a coastal seagull that periodically invaded the neighborhood in search of a quick meal. Like the Hatfield's and the McCoy's, these natural adversaries were stirring up a storm of sound that had gotten the dogs of the neighborhood barking, and there in the opposite window was my cat Eddie watching the commotion with a strange smile on his face.

As I listened, this contest of caws and squeaks increased into a war of words and a war of wings. It wasn't long before I saw ravens and seagulls flying in from all directions. I lost sight of the two birds that had started the fight because the driveway and the branches of the trees were soon filled with allies of each side. It was a calm, clear morning in the city with barely a breath of air to deaden the titanic struggle that was unfolding. There seemingly was nothing I could do to break up this major quarrel despite yelling a couple of times out the window. I thought about sending Eddie after them, but I thought better of the plan because of the sheer numbers of large birds now in the backyard. It was then I noticed a change as a major assault from downtown took place. The reserves of seagulls flying in from Union Bay began to outnumber the smaller raven's ranks. The seagulls were even strafing those sitting in the spruce trees by the garage. As the struggle for the high branches continued, I looked around to see what might have started this mini-war. It was then my eyes caught sight of something lying on our graveled driveway. There, halfway up the small incline leading to the garage, was a large patch of cookies scattered on the ground. Now I knew what the "war of the birds" was all about. My wife had gotten up early that morning and decided to discard some old cookies.

Coleen often feeds the birds with leftovers of moldy bread or stale cookies. Coleen's affection for birds stops, however, with seagulls. She thinks they are a very dirty bird, and she hates dirt! Her intent that morning was to feed "the boys," what we call the raven family that lives in our neighborhood. Besides getting rid of week-old bread and hard cookies Coleen loves to watch what our cats do at the gatherings of the birds. Coleen's breakfast is a feast for any who finds it first, and more often than not it is the ravens that are there first. On average the seagulls stay downtown near the Union River, but on this particular morning they had sent a scout up town, and the minute the first raven spotted the free breakfast so did a sharp-eyed gull. As I watched, what was ironical about the whole affair was that while the seagulls and ravens fought over who would eat first, the swallows and sparrows were peacefully enjoying breakfast together.

As Eddie and I watched the event unfolding in the backyard, I understood why Eddie had a smile on his face. My wife and I have come to the conclusion that Eddie, like the Pearl, is more of a bird-watcher than an eater of birds even though Eddie has returned home on occasion with a small bird for lunch. A few pieces of spoiled bread or cookies is all it takes for Eddie to enjoy a good quarrel. And then it hit me that I, too, over the years have been a witness of a few church quarrels over similar insignificant things. I still remember the great debate and eventual quarrel over the color of the new carpet we were to put into my second church sanctuary. I have heard of quarrels over the size of a building project, the shape of the stairs leading into the church, and of all things what would be served at an Easter morning breakfast. The members of the Body of Christ have quarreled over just about anything and everything in its very long and stormy history. Just the other day I was talking with a pastor friend, and he was sharing with me the latest quarrel in his church. How strange it must seem to the Holy Spirit as He resides in us that in His eternal history there has never been a quarrel in the Godhead, but constantly He is witnessing quarrelling among the brethren. The Biblical word used in the verse that highlights this devotional is used for the concept of blame or complaint. Rare is this word in the Bible and besides the Colossians verse, the word is only found one other place in the entire New Testament:

> "Therefore Herodias had a quarrel against him, and would have killed him; but she could not." (Mark 6:19)

This was, of course, the conflict between John the Baptist and the queen over John's condemnation of the unlawful marriage of Herodias and Herod (Mark 6:17). I think if the seagulls and ravens of Ellsworth could kill each other over a few old cookies they would, but this illustrates just how dangerous quarreling can get.

The key in my opinion to this issue is the word "forbearing." (Ephesians 4:2) It is a powerful word in the Bible, but rarely proclaimed today. It simply means to tolerate in others what we can't tolerate in ourselves. There are seagulls and ravens in every church or at least in the churches I have pastored in the last 39 years (49 now). As long as the church is made up of human beings, there will be conflicts and quarrels, but, if we take the Biblical example of Christ and the teaching of scripture, then we ought to be able to resolve these quarrels quickly because what is quarreling to some is entertainment for others. It is a sad state of affairs that a pair of cats would find funny what a group of birds would find so serious, and while the seagulls and ravens fight the sparrows and swallows feast on!

Chapter Twenty-Nine

Learning to Listen

"And the Lord came, and stood, and called as at other times, Samuel, Samuel. Then Samuel answered, Speak; for Thy servant heareth."

—I Samuel 3:10

I HAVE COME TO the conclusion that one of the most difficult tasks to learn is listening. Just last night I was rebuked again in this matter when it took my wife three attempts to get my attention as I watched television. (The Red Sox were playing, and, if they won, which they didn't, they would have clenched the wild card spot for the fall baseball playoffs.) I hate to admit it, but I am very hard of hearing when it comes to a secondary voice trying to get through to me when I am focused on something else. My wife is often a victim of my inattention, but so is my God. How often I have missed His "still small voice" because I have had my mind on something else. Once again, it has been my cat Eddie that has reproved me of the need to sharpen my listening skills, not only for the benefit of my lady (Coleen), but also my Lord (Christ).

Eddie is at the top of his game when it comes to knowing what is going on in his world. His eyes are always alert to anything that might be dangerous. Just yesterday as we crossed the street from the parsonage to the church, he stopped at the edge of the road to see if any traffic was coming, and there was. Just like he should, Eddie waited for the car to pass before he attempted to cross the lane. I never taught him that. He has always been careful when crossing the street. What his eyes don't see, his ears hear. Long before he sees something his ears pick up the sound. When we are in the church alone, the slightest strange sound will provoke Eddie to check out the noise. To this day I can call Eddie from wherever he has roamed because I believe he has tuned his hearing into my voice, whistle, or call. Eddie has learned to listen, but have I?

Without a doubt the Bible teaches clearly that our God has a speaking voice, a distinct voice, a recognizable voice. I love the story in which our key verse comes from. The story of the boy Samuel and the priest Eli is the story of a man of God teaching a child how to listen to and for God. Granted, at first even Eli didn't know what was happening, but eventually he realized that God was trying to communicate with small Samuel. Samuel's first problem wasn't that he didn't hear God, but he had failed to recognize God's voice. Once he knew who was speaking he was quick to listen. Samuel had been taught to listen to the "still small voice" of God, the same voice Elijah heard on Mount Horeb (I Kings 19:12). There is nothing more personal than conversion between two parties, and when one of those parties is the Almighty God, then you have a very special communication happening. And what Samuel learned, I have become convinced that you and I can also learn.

If you believe the Bible as I do then you know that our eternal welfare depends on our learning to listen to God's Spirit. Unless we hear the Spirit of the Lord we will not be convicted of our sins and know how to believe on Christ for our salvation. The tragedy today is that we are not training our ears to hear, but those ears are being distracted by other sounds. I love the way the Apostle Paul described the danger of this lack of hearing in the last days:

> *"For the time will come when they will not endure sound doctrine; but after their own lusts shall they heap to themselves teachers, having itching ears; and they shall turn away their ears from the truth, and shall be turned unto fables."* (II Timothy 4:3-4)

The problem with this age is a hearing problem. Jesus rebuked His generation for the very same fault, *"And having ears hear ye not?"* (Mark 8:18) Most of us are far too stubborn and selfish to give much attention to God. As A. W. Tozer said many years ago, "**This is definitely not an hour when men take kindly to an exhortation to listen, for listening is not today a part of popular religion.**"

Yet I am rebuked and reproved by the simple reality that a cat pays more attention to me than I do to its Creator; that I pay more attention to the simple meow of my cat, the still small voice of Eddie, than I do to the "still small voice" of God. In the time it has taken me to punch these thoughts into my laptop computer Eddie has called on me at least three times to do something for him. First, it was to put a few more morsels of dry cat food in his dish. Then it was to pick him up and love on him for a few moments. (Eddie is very affectionate that way. Rarely does a day go by that he doesn't come to me a couple times in the day for some rubbing and patting and loving.) Finally, I have just returned from opening up the front door so that Eddie could go out and roam a bit. Each time I heard his small cry I knew what he wanted. If I can learn to listen and respond to a tomcat, then I must have the ability to respond to God. They tell me that the most often used phrase in the Bible is *"Thus saith the Lord!"* God is in continual speech, and His voice fills the world, but how many of the over seven billion people (I think it is over eight now) are listening? If I have learned anything about this topic, it is that God will not butt in, or yell, or interrupt. He is patient to wait for us as He did Samuel and Elijah and the countless others in the Bible to which He spoke directly. Whether through His Word (John 1:1) or His Spirit (John16:8-11) or the world He created (Psalms 19:1-2), the eternal Godhead speaks to us in a familiar, friendly voice. Since the first days when He gave man the ability to speak, He also gave man the ability to listen, and I believe He also gave us this admonition:

> *"Wherefore, my beloved brethren, let every man be swift to hear, slow to speak . . . "* (James 1:9)

Chapter Thirty

Appeasing the Lion

"Notwithstanding the Lord stood with me, and strengthened me that by me the preaching might be fully known, and that all the Gentiles might hear: and I was delivered out of the mouth of the lion."

—II Timothy 4:17

Paul might have been speaking literally of lions in this verse in relationship to the historical truth that the Romans did feed Christians to the lions in celebration of their famous "games," but I also believe that he might have been referring to the devil *"as a roaring lion"* (I Peter 5:8). Which either side you take on this verse, there is a wonderful truth that deliverance is ours from either, but how? That is why we never have to appease the lion because his roar is just sound and his threat has no teeth. We have nothing to fear from our adversary if we place our trust in God. He is a paper tiger at best!

In previous articles I have mentioned that my cat's archenemy is a neighborhood tomcat we call "Big Grey." Shortly after Eddie's and Big Gray's first confrontation, I wrote this memory:

> Have you ever thought what your cat might be thinking about when he is sleeping? I have, and I think I know what Eddie dreams about when he is having a nightmare. He is transported through time and space by way of his feline fancy to a time when he is sitting patiently by the back door of the parsonage to be let out so he can romp and roam in the backyard. Deep in his memory, however, is an encounter that still haunts him to this day. He still sees in his mind's eye the patch of fallen feathers near the garage. Small in nature he reasons that they are the remains of a sparrow that was tempted once too often to venture down from the safety of a perch high in the pear tree next to the garage to the killing fields of his backyard. Scattered pieces of bread can be seen near the murder scene so he deducts that

the bird had settled in for breakfast when it was attacked and devoured. Instead of having breakfast he became breakfast, but who could have done the dastardly deed? The tree sparrow must have fallen victim to the evil feline known to Eddie as 'Big Grey.' Because of the ample supply of birds in the active neighborhood, birds by the score have found a home in the bushes, shrubs, and fruit trees of Eddie's backyard. These birds have built their nests in the sheltered places, but often they are found on the ground gathering the leftovers thrown out by the pastor's wife, a great temptation and a dangerous arena inhabited at times by the bully of the block. Eddie learned within a few months of living near the parsonage of the Emmanuel Baptist Church that 'Big Grey' was a relentless hunter. He was a silent killer, stealthy and cunning as well as very crafty. 'Big Grey' often used the protection of the garage to wait his unsuspecting prey to land in the open. Like 'a puff of grey' he would appear and disappear leaving in his wake a patch of fallen feathers. Sharp eyes with swift claws and with slaughter on his mind this killing machine has another pastime, haunting and hounding and harassing Eddie! I, too, have watched him stalk his prey from a distance. Agile as the African lion and as swift as the Indian tiger, this cat is a flash of fury that every creature needs to avoid. Once the attack is over all that is left is a patch of fallen feathers to tell the story of a careless sparrow. Big Grey has retreated from only one opponent since I started watching him a few years ago, and that is my cat Eddie. Why, because Eddie doesn't appease 'Big Grey!'

History tells us that appeasement doesn't work with bullies. Arthur Neville Chamberlain and Adolf Hitler come to mind. The Bible also teaches us the same lesson with such stories as King Ahaz trying to appease the King of Assyria by giving him bribes taken from the Temple of God. What was the result? *"He helped him not"* (II Chronicles 28:21). Instead of turning to God Ahaz sought to appease the kings of Syria *"but they were the ruin of him."* (II Chronicles 28:23) The popular misconception is that if you appease enough your enemy will leave you alone, but they never will. I don't know when Eddie realized this truth, but he did. From the first time Eddie caught Big Grey in his backyard he has attacked him. Oh, Eddie has received a few wounds because of it, but now it is Big Grey that flees, not Eddie. James has told us, *"Resist [not appease] the devil, and he will flee from you."* (James 4:7) Many have come to believe that to give in to the devil will result in him leaving them alone. This is not the truth. He will never leave us alone until he is bound and cast to the bottomless pit (Revelation 20:1-3).

James tells us to resist, and Paul tells us *"neither give place to the devil."* (Ephesians 4:27). I have watched as Eddie maneuvers to get into the best position to chase Big Grey away. We are also not to let the devil get an advantage (II Corinthians 2:11) on us to get a landing spot in our life by which he can invade other aspects of our lives. The Bible is littered with the wrecked lives of those who let the devil get a toehold in their lives: Eve, Esau, Achan, David, Judas, and Demas, to name a few. Giving the devil a chance to get a grip on us could be fatal because he will hang on to the death. We are instructed to attack, not appease. The very armor given to us by God (Ephesians 6:10-18) is for the offensive, not the defensive. There is no protection for our backs in the list so we must take the first step and attack (a preemptive strike) first. Eddie will not even ponder any more when Big Grey walks into his yard. Just a few days ago my wife called for me to go out and get Eddie. Big Grey had come, and Eddie had chased him under the garage. My cat was still tense, and the hair was still standing up on his back when I picked him up. He was in full attack mode, ready to resist and not give even one opportunity for Big Grey to stay!

Unlike my cat, the carnal nature of most of us is to appease. We hate confrontation, the pain that comes from a fight, and the struggle that is often the result. It is easier, or so we think, to appease the lion, appease the sin that so easily besets us (Hebrews 12:1), appease the self in us that wants only the easy road. Appeasement is the habit of a lazy saint, not a loyal soldier of Christ (II Timothy 2:3-4). I have written about my little sentinel and his faithfulness in guarding his territory. We have a territory to watch over, and we can't allow sin, self, or Satan a foothold. Like Jesus we need to learn these five little words: *"Get thee behind me, Satan."* (Matthew 16:23) If my cat can live this way, why can't we? It is not the cat in the fight, but the fight in the cat that counts, and the same is true of the saint.

Chapter Thirty-One

Hospitality

"...given to hospitality."

—Romans 12:13

Ever since Eddie, Eddie, Eddie came into my life a few years ago I have tried to keep a journal of the activities of my feline friend. My wife has already made me a scrap book of pictures highlighting Eddie's first years with us. As I write, I am doing "a day in the life" of Eddie with pictures of his daily activities to be placed alongside these exhortations. Recently, a new friend has come into Eddie's life, an elderly tomcat from Florida by the name of "Willy."

My wife and I have lived at 50 School Street in Ellsworth, Maine, for over 21 years now. Over those years only one neighbor has stayed the same, Mrs. Harriman, the neighbor on the downtown side of the parsonage. All the other homes around us have changed residents at least once and some two or three times. Over the seasons of change we have tried to get to know our new neighbors the best we could. Some we have gotten to know quite well while others have come and gone before any relationship could develop. One of the longer relationships was with Barbara Stratton, an old maid who lived behind our home and to the front of State Street. Eventually Barbara's health grew poorly, and she was forced to move into a local nursing home until her death. With her passing her home was sold to a family that had moved up from Florida and with them came the family pet, a playful and sweet-spirited feline without a voice. (Willy can open his mouth and appears to be crying, but nothing seems to come out. It is actually very cute especially when he is asking for a treat.)

What makes these new neighbors so different is the fact most people leave Maine to move to Florida. This is the only family I know that has reversed that truth. Over time they have been able to remodel the small, three-room bungalow into one of the prettiest houses on the block, and it wasn't long before Eddie and Willy became friends. Despite the fact that Willy is about the same size as Big Grey who is twice the size of Eddie, there has been no conflict between the two. Unlike Big Grey Eddie seemed to sense a different spirit in Willy. Was it because Eddie was respecting his elders? Willy is a much older cat? I can't tell you the difference, but I know that Willy and Eddie are friends while Big Grey and Eddie are enemies. The other interesting thing is that Eddie actually made the introduction and has shown admirable hospitality in the process.

Coming home one day from visitation, I noticed Eddie watching something very carefully from the back porch. Often I find Eddie staring at something, but more often than not I have a hard time seeing what Eddie is keeping an eye on. On this afternoon, however, it wasn't difficult because he was hard to miss. There under the pear trees was a large cat with similar marks as Eddie, just much bigger. Instead of chasing the cat away as he does with Big Grey, Eddie seemed to be enjoying the company of this cat. At first we thought Willy was a female cat. My wife even started to call him "Flo" after Florida, but we soon learned he was not a she, but a he. Willy seemed to be very careful around strangers and at first would run when we came near, but in time we found Willy and Eddie lying together in the backyard. Willy is a long-hair like Pearl, but with a sweet nature like Eddie. Over the year Willy has been around he has become our third cat. (We say we have an indoor cat named Precious, an outdoor cat named Eddie, and a porch cat named Willy.) No, we haven't taken him in because he has a nice home, but he often spends his days on our front porch where we give him a treat or two. Eddie has accepted this arrangement even if the Pearl hasn't. Willy has only been in the parsonage once, but most of the time prefers to remain on the porch. I have been proud of my lad for the hospitality he has shown this stranger from out of state, an attribute taught clearly in scripture.

Paul instructs us to be *"given to hospitality."* The Greek word used here is "lovers of strangers." I learned very early in my training that a man in my position was required to be hospitable (I Timothy 3:2). It should be a characteristic, a requirement for the pastorate according to Paul (Titus 1:8). Interestingly, two of the four times the word is used in the New Testament, it is in the qualities listed for the pastor. I have been blessed all my life with this attribute. I give my parents and grandparents credit for first showing me this quality by example, and then I believe through the Person of the Holy Spirit I was empowered with the nature to "love strangers" (even a strange cat called Eddie). What saddens me is that there are so many Christians today that don't share this same belief. We have more following the example of Diotrephes (III John 9-11) than Demetrius (III John 12-14). In the same book that these two believers are contrasted John writes this to another wonderful Christian by the name of Gaius:

> *"Beloved, thou doest faithfully whatsoever thou doest to the brethren and to strangers; which have borne witness of thy charity before the church: whom if thou bring forward on their journey after a godly sort, thou shalt do well: because that for His name's sake they went forth, taking nothing of the Gentiles. We therefore ought to receive such, that we might be followhelpers to the truth."*
> (III John 5-8)

Follow helpers are hospitable people, people like Gaius and cats like Eddie!

Besides Paul and John, Peter puts his two cents worth of instruction in on this topic when he wrote this in his epistle: *"Use hospitality one to another without grudging."* (I Peter 4:9) If a simple feline can show hospitality to a strange cat from Florida, can welcome him into the neighborhood and share his food with him, why can't we? There was a time in America when we were known as a nation of hospitable people. Friendliness to strangers was a hallmark of our land. Granted, I know that we have been burned and hurt by some that have taken advantage of our open borders and free travel, but nothing should distract us from living in a hospitable way *"one to another"* without grumbling. I like the Living Bible on this: *"Cheerfully share your home with those who need a meal or a place to stay for the night."* Each time I take a handful of cat treats to the porch and give them to Willy and I watch as Eddie says nothing, I am reminded of this exhortation: *"Be not forgetful to entertain strangers: for thereby some have entertained angels unawares."* (Hebrews 13:2)

It is time we revive again the ministry of hospitality in our churches and in our homes. Surely, we can't allow a cat to behave better than a Christian, can we?

Chapter Thirty-Two

The Doctrines of Devils

"Now the Spirit speaketh expressly, that in the latter times some shall depart from the faith, giving heed to seducing spirits, and doctrines of devils."

—I Timothy 4:1

I HAVE COME TO believe that I am living in *"the latter times."* Paul's description to Timothy of these days mirror what is going on in my 21st century world! When you study the topics mentioned here (for there are many, many more)—hypocritical lying (the politicians have this one down pat), seared consciences (the pornographers have this one covered), forbidden marriages (the priests have this one by rule of Rome), and abstained meats (PETA is the promoter of this one)—note that they are proclaimed by *"seducing spirits"* and they are called *"doctrines of devils."* I would love to expound on the first three, but only the last one can I apply to my cat Eddie, Eddie, Eddie.

One of the reasons I have become so attached to my neighborhood stray is the simple fact that Eddie is all male. There is nothing female or feminine about "Edwardo." He is a perfect man's pet. Ever since my wife and I have been adopting cats, we have pretty much gravitated to females primarily because of my wife's love of cats and her desire to make them all indoor cats. My wife loves her cats to be purring and playful, cuddling and carefree, long-haired and loving, petite and pretty, and manly characteristics are far from any of these qualities. When Eddie came into our lives, we discovered from day one that he was completely opposite to Coleen's ideal (Precious Patience Pearl) and more like the pet I have been looking for since I lost my boyhood dog, Rover.

The first sign I had that Eddie was my kind of cat was the moment I realized that Eddie was a meat eater. I am a meat eater by my very nature. Just yesterday I had one of the finest lunches I have had in years. One of my deacons shot a moose on Monday. On Tuesday he brought me back a few small pieces of the tenderloin, and on Wednesday I cooked them up with lots of butter and had them for lunch. That was my lunch, just meat. Perhaps my favorite meal of all is a meal of just meat. Last winter, I went to visit my daughter in Texas for the first time. (Marnie is in her fourth year at Dallas Theological Seminary working on her masters now.) While there we visited a couple that calls Maine home in the summer. One of my desires while in Dallas was to visit a traditional Texas roadhouse barbecue. My friend Dale and Margie Braley took us to the Southside Market for lunch. When I got to the counter, I asked the waiter for a piece of every meat they serve. At first he didn't seem to understand my order, but eventually the owner overheard our conversation and stepped in by saying, "I know exactly what he wants!" I didn't want to fill up with side orders. I wanted to try each and every one of their barbecue meats. That day I made a meal on nothing but some of the best barbecued meats I have ever eaten. Half way through the meal the owner returned and asked if my party would like to have a tour of the roadhouse. My friend Dale said to me, "I have been coming to this place for 30 years and have never been asked to have a tour, but I know why the owner has asked us. You are the first customer he has had that asked for nothing but meat!"

I was raised on a farm in northern Maine where meat was a part of every meal. We raised most of our own meat, chicken, beef and pork. I loved catching brook trout in the local creek and shooting partridge in the forest behind our house. My dad would kill a deer just about every season so meat was a part of my daily diet from the beginning. I knew that I would love Eddie the first night he sat begging by my dining room table chair asking for a scrape of meat from my plate. The sparkle in his eyes after I placed a small piece of chicken in his mouth resulted in an instant bonding. My cat was a meat eater; whether a slice of ham, a chunk of chicken, or a piece of hamburger, Eddie is always rewarded for his extended paw with a slice of meat. What I eat Eddie eats. He even likes pizza (meat pizza with plenty of cheese)! He comes running every time meat is on the menu, and when he is outside, he doesn't pass up fresh meat either.

Over our seven years together Eddie has brought home both fowl and rodent. Each and every time he lays some creature at my feet, it is almost as if he is saying "aren't you going to try some?" He doesn't need to hunt any longer because he gets all the food he wants to eat, but I think the thrill of the hunt is still a joy to him. All I know is that my pet Eddie believes in the instruction of the apostle Paul.

> "... *meats, which God hath created to be received with thanksgiving of them which believe and know the truth. For every creature of God is good, and nothing to be refused, if it be received with thanksgiving: for it is sanctified by the Word of God and prayer."*
> (I Timothy 4:3-5)

Granted, I am still working on thanksgiving and supplication with Eddie, but the precept is very clear. One of my favorite reality shows on television is "Bizarre Foods" with Andrew Zimmer. This program follows the exploits of a man that travels all over the world just to eat strange foods. I have only once seen him put something in his mouth and spit it out immediately (it was a fruit). I believe this man has eaten every meat known to man, and it always amazes me what mankind eats. I might not eat what they eat or what Eddie eats (Zimmer has because I have seen him eat rat and every rodent known to man), but both Eddie and Andrew are right in eating any creature. Again, I don't know if Zimmer always prays over his meal or if he is thankful, but I do know that one of the doctrines of devils being promoted today is to "abstain from meats!"

Up until I met Eddie I was always one who hated to see a pet beg at the table. I had witnessed it in other homes and was quick to judge and condemn those that allowed such practices. Anyone to allow such behavior was simply wrong, crazy, and without proper manners. Like with those that judge others (legalists) on unproven laws, I had been guilty of overstepping my bounds. I know that my family thinks that I am now a hypocrite since Eddie has come into the parsonage. Almost from the start I caught myself slipping my new friend a piece of meat under the table. At first I tried to hide my behavior, but now I don't even care. I only care about Eddie. I can't seem to resist those big, begging eyes, that soft pleading paw, and that long supplicating stare. No matter what, I must share my meat with my meat eater, and now I know that I have scripture on my side. I have been preaching against *"the doctrines of devils"* most of my life, and now I have a practical way of illustrating the truth of the Bible in regards to the truth about eating meats. The doctrine is simple. Eating meat is proper and right in the eyes of God.

Chapter Thirty-Three

The Creator-Creature Relationship

"Be thou exalted, O God, above the heavens; let Thy glory be above all the earth."

—Psalms 57:5

By now you have noticed that I have come to believe that ever since my cat Eddie came into my life that I have had a different relationship with the Almighty. Despite the fact that our relationship began over fifty years ago (64 now) and changed and matured over these years, it has only been in the last four years that relationship has dramatically been altered by the events I am sharing in this book. Much of the change started in India and my second trip there in two years only helped (at the posting of this devotional on the church website I am heading for my fourth trip to India, and now I have taken six), but, when I returned to Maine both times and to my cat, the insight into the Person of God I so often missed before has become very clear.

Who better to teach us of this Creator-Creature than a simple creature like a cat? Did not Jesus, when He was trying to teach His disciples who was the greatest in the kingdom of heaven, place a child in their midst? (Matthew 18:1-3) Not just any child, but "a little child." We adults think we are too old, too mature too wise to learn from anything small or young. I still remember the day I found this exhortation in Timothy. I was a young pastor facing complex and complicated church matters with members that were my parents and grandparents ages. They were looking at me as a kid, and I felt like a kid, that is, until I read this: *"Let no man despise thy youth. . ."* (I Timothy 4:12) and then I found this: *"Let no man despise thee"* (Titus 2:15). The more I read my Bible the more confident I became that I could help despite my young age (22 years old). It was also at that time that I discovered Elihu, my first Eddie.

One of the popular misconceptions in the story of Job is that only three friends showed up to "comfort" (Job 2:11) Job. Unless you read through the entire book you will miss Elihu (Job 32:1-3). *"Now Elihu had waited till Job had spoken, because they were elder than he. When Elihu saw that there was no answer in the mouth of these three men, then his wrath was kindled."* (Job 32:4-5) In my early years as a pastor often times I was the youngest member of the church and still the pastor. When I was the youngest man on the deacon board, or any other board, I took great comfort in this speech by Elihu:

> *"I am young, and ye are very old; wherefore I was afraid, and durst not shew you mine opinion. I said, Days should speak, and multitude of years should teach wisdom. But there is a spirit in man: and the inspiration of the Almighty giveth them understanding. Great men are not always wise: neither do the aged understand judgment. Therefore I said, Hearken to me; I also will shew mine opinion."* (Job 32:6-10)

I was never silent again no matter how senior my deacons or how old my church members.

In the old sailing ship days the master of the ship got his bearings by "shooting" the sun by day and the stars by night. Is there anything in our world greater than our sun? Yet at night the smallest star can give more help in direction than the sun because the sun is not there. It is the same with a small light at night. That same light in the day wouldn't even be noticed, but at night it is a beacon worth following. I still love to sing that grand old song "Let the Lower Lights be Burning" by Philip Bliss:

> Brightly beams our Father's mercy
> From His lighthouse evermore,
> But to us He gives the keeping
> Of the lights along the shore.
> Dark the night of sin has settled,
> Loud the angry billows roar;
> Eager eyes are watching, longing,
> For the lights along the shore.
> Trim your feeble lamp, my brother,
> Some poor sailor tempest-tossed,
> Trying now to make the harbor,
> In the darkness may be late.
> Let the lower lights be burning!
> Send a gleam across the wave!

> Some poor fainting, struggling seaman
> you may rescue, you may save.

More often than not we get our moral bearings by looking at God, but at other times He allows one of his smallest creatures to do the guiding. We have already written of Balaam's donkey in this book and other Biblical creatures that God used to instruct, direct, or teach His followers. I am simply saying I now see that the Good Lord in His wise providence is using a cat called Eddie to instruct, guide, and teach me through our Creator-Creature relationship.

In our pursuit of conforming into the image of Christ (Romans 8:29), it is necessary for us to open up all our senses and relationships to the possibility of hearing from God as He uses our total personality to mold us. Part of my personality is the love of Eddie. We have already dealt with the unlikeness of me having a relationship with a cat, yet here I am halfway through writing a book on what I have learned about the Almighty through my experiences with Eddie. If anybody is surprised by this it is me, yet there is ample proof, at least to me, that God is using a small creature to teach me more about our Creator. I have a long ways to go, I know, but my perfection and God's holy intention to make me like His Son will one day be partly because of a cat named Eddie.

Chapter Thirty-Four

Adopted

"For ye have not received the spirit of bondage again to fear; but ye have received the Spirit of adoption, whereby we cry, Abba, Father."

—Romans 8:15

As I meditated this morning, a number of adoptions flooded through my mind. In the church I currently pastor, a young couple I married over ten years ago is within two weeks of adopting a precious little girl. After losing a number of children that never came to term they decided if they were going to be parents then adoption was the only course of action left to them. Nearly a year ago she came into their lives when she was just a few days old. The church family has already adopted this child, and our prayer is that nothing will happen that would block this adoption. Then I thought of the only adoption I know about in my family. A number of years ago my mother's younger brother (the reason I was thinking about him is because he just had his homegoing to heaven a few week ago) adopted a child they called Billy. Billy is my only adopted cousin. Over the years I have known of others in my churches and communities that have made the choice to adopt. Even my wife and I pondered this method of ministry when in our early married years had difficulty in getting pregnant, but eventually Scott and Marnie (and between them we lost another child Cherith Bevan) came along so we didn't have to adopt. As I prayed and thought on this wonderful truth, another adoptee jumped up in my lap.

Eddie, Eddie, Eddie is my only adoption. Seven years ago I began to notice the stray foraging for food around the Emmanuel Baptist Church property. Within four months my wife and I made the decision to take the tomcat into our family. The vote was two to one in favor (our cat Precious Pearl voted strongly against the adoption) of making Eddie a part of our family. For us the process was simple because there were no objections from Eddie's previous owners. He quickly became a member of our family, and we have loved him and cared for him ever since. As I thought on these things, I was reminded of the marvelous Biblical doctrine of adoption I had taught just last Sunday. One of the most overlooked theologies of God's Word, adoption is the end result of the wonderful truth of predestination (Ephesians 1:11).

I had just started a new study in my adult Sunday school class on the "Big Words of the Bible." My first "big word" was predestination. I had decided to do each word with this simple outline: meaning, a definition of the word; method, God's way of expressing this truth; means, how God works this truth out in our lives; me, the personal application of this truth; and message, the spiritual challenge. I have come to believe that predestination is the pre-determined, foreordination of God (Jeremiah 1:5). This can happen because of the attribute of God by which He is able to know before the creation of the world how things will turn out or foreknowledge (Romans 8:29-30). This results in "election" (I Peter 1:2), the sovereign act of God's grace whereby from all eternity He chooses in Christ Jesus for Himself and for salvation all those who He foreknew would respond positively to His grace (Romans 11:5 and I Thessalonians 1:4). These wonderful attributes of God affect you and me personally through "the adoption of the believer." In my theological statement I define this doctrine this way:

> I believe that adoption is the gracious act whereby the Father, for the sake of the Son, places new believers into the honored position of sons of God by the Spirit. (Ephesians 1:5 and Galatians 4:1-7) I went on to give my class this message. I believe that God votes "yes" concerning our salvation (II Peter 3:9), but the devil votes "no" on our salvation (II Corinthians 4:4). The deciding and determining vote is ours (Romans 10:13). How will we vote or how have we voted? If we vote "no," then a Christless eternity is all we get in the lake of fire. If we vote "yes," then adoption takes place. Here is the Biblical proof I shared with my class:
>
> 1. THE DEFINTION OF THE DOCTRINE OF ADOPTION (JOHN 1:12)
>
>   a. The Term called Adoption (Galatians 4:1-5)
>
>   b. The Time of Adoption (Ephesians 1:5)
>
> 2. THE DURATION OF THE DOCTRINE OF ADOPTION (HEBREWS 11:39, 40)
>
>   a. Eternity Past (Ephesians 1:5); heart attachment.
>
>   b. Experience Present (Galatians 3:26); living attachment.

c. Exalted Future (Romans 8:23); legal attachment.

3. THE DIRECTION IN THE DOCTRINE OF ADOPTION (ROMANS 8:19)

   a. Deliverance (Romans 8:15 and Galatians 4:4-5)

   b. Assurance (Romans 8:16 and Galatians 4:6)

   c. Inheritance (Romans 8:17 and I Peter 1:3)

Each and every time I see my little friend Eddie jump up in my lap, I am reminded that I, too, have been adopted into the family of God. Eddie's "Abba Father" sounds more like a meow, but I hear "Abba Father." His cry pulls and draws me to him, just like my cry and call draws the Father to me. Like Eddie I was chosen, and like Eddie I now have a new relationship with the Almighty God. Not as God, but as Father! With all the privileges as a member of the family, I now can come boldly before my Father's throne (Hebrews 4:16) and ask of Him without fear or dread, just as Eddie now comes to me. Recently, at my Uncle Sherwood's funeral I watched as Billy took his place beside my aunt as the only son of "Woody" (my uncle's nickname). Not one person of over a hundred people there questioned Billy rights or his sonship. Why; because everybody has come to recognize Billy Barton as Sherwood's legal and rightful son. I hope the day will come for Lilly Grace that the same is true for her. I believe that I now hold the right of sonship with God Almighty, and that I am a "joint-heir" with Christ. Are you? It would be sad that a cat has been adopted, and you are still a stray and far from the joys and privileges of being an adoptee.

Chapter Thirty-Five

Best Friends

"A man that hath friends must shew himself friendly: and there is a friend that sticketh closer than a brother."

—Proverbs 18:24

I HAVE MENTIONED HIM before in previous articles. Of all Eddie's friends, he is his "best friend." I am writing of a neighborhood cat called Willy.

Just a few days ago I was doing some work in the parsonage garage. As I prepared the single car garage for winter (if your garage is like my garage, the months I don't put my car under cover, the space seems to fill up with other things), I watched from afar the actions of two best friends. I couldn't help but stare as Willy and Eddie played in the backyard. Since Willy's coming into our quiet Ellsworth neighborhood, he has become an almost daily figure in our yard, if not on our front porch where we always give him his lunch. Unlike Big Grey, Eddie instantly liked this Florida transplant. At first, I would watch them eyeing each other from across the driveway, but within a short period of time they were playing together like I saw them last Saturday. I have never seen them actually fight though on occasion they will engage in a mock form of combat. Sometimes it is Willy chasing Eddie, but on this forenoon it was Eddie chasing Willy up one of our backyard apple trees. With tails wagging back and forth, the two friends played their game of "tree the squirrel." It was a joy to watch friends being friendly.

For any of us that has had a "best friend" in this life, we can relate to the friendship of Willy and Eddie. In my childhood, when I had time to play in the backyard, it was a cousin named Bob. Bob and I were and still are best friends though time and distance has changed our relationship quite a bit. We are no longer neighbors as we once were, and we no longer get together on a Saturday afternoon to play softball or basketball or to go fishing together. Unlike Willy and Eddie who are in the early years of their friendship,

Bob and I are in our final days. Just how quickly our time has passed came to the forefront recently when Bob had a heart attack on a cross country trip to deliver freight to Utah (Bob is a long-haul trucker from northern Maine). It was a miracle and God's grace that he made it home safely, and when he got home they discovered that one of Bob's arteries in his heart was completely blocked. An operation was out of the question and only through a major life altering change will he get any better. I realized that I had almost lost my only true earthly best friend, and that our playful days in a warm Indian summer sunshine were probably over. (As I post this article on the church website, I have just returned from having my cousin's funeral. Bob died of a second heart attack the day before the fourth of July, 2012.)

Willy and Eddie reminded me today of the importance of best friends and the need to take advantage of every opportunity to spend some time with your best friend. Shortly after Bob returned from his working trip, my wife and I met Bob and his wife Bonnie in Bangor where Bob was undergoing tests on his heart. We spent a wonderful evening together visiting and having supper at a local steak house. The time went by too quickly as we headed back to our home on the coast, Bob and Bonnie headed back to their motel room, and the next day back to their home on the Canadian border in northeast Maine. Like Willy and Eddie on an afternoon on the front porch together, Bob and I talked of days gone by and the hope of a few more together. Unlike Willy and Eddie, Barry and Bob will have no tree-climbing days in their future I am sure, but I am also very sure that for me and my other "best friend" our best days of play and togetherness are still ahead in the glories of heaven!

I am convinced that the friend Solomon writes about in his classic proverb printed above is none other than the Lord Jesus Christ Himself. Did not Jesus tell His disciples?

> "Ye are my friends, if ye do whatsoever I command you. Henceforth I call you not servants; for servants knoweth not what his lord doeth, but I have called you friends; for all things that I have heard of my Father I have made known unto you." (John 15:14-15)

Why did Jesus have friends, because He showed Himself friendly? Remember, His critics said of Him "... *a friend of publicans and sinners...*" (Matthew 11:19). These were not easy people to be friendly with, yet Jesus made many a friend among them. I ask you the question, is Jesus your best friend yet?

Today, as I write this Eddie Exhortation, I can in confidence write that nothing interests me more than God's interests. I have no plans other than those that God plans. I am moved by nothing other than the motivation of God on and in my life. My interests and plans have been polarized with my best friend's interests and plans. Amos wrote long before Jesus' arrival, *"Can two walk together, except they be agreed?"* (Amos 3:3). I don't know why Eddie and Big Grey aren't friends, but they are not. I don't know why Eddie and Willy are, but they are. Eddie will not allow Big Grey to even step foot in the backyard without a fight, but Willy comes and goes as he pleases. Friendship is not an automatic result of two meeting, human or animal, we all know that. There must be more than just a relationship (most employers and employees have a relationship, but few develop into a friendship). There must be something that they can "agree" on. Willy and Eddie have come to that agreement even though I still don't know what it is. In our relationship with Jesus it is the truth that He died for my sins, and why wouldn't that be grounds for an earthly, everlasting friendship?

Chapter Thirty-Six

It's a Male Thing

"(For as yet HE was fallen upon none of them: only they were baptized in the name of the Lord Jesus.)"

—Acts 8:16

For nearly six years the only activities attempted by our cat "Pearl" was playing with string and sleeping. Pearl has never spent more than a few fleeting minutes in the out-of-doors roaming, and as for hunting or "mousing" I don't think she would know what either really was. Things changed dramatically, however, when Eddie, Eddie, Eddie came to stay. Having to survive on one's own causes one to develop the abilities and the skills needed for self-preservation, and one of those talents is the necessity to hunt for supper.

A couple years ago I made my annual trip to Hampton Bible Camp (where this series of "Eddie Exhortations" began, a series as you can see has turned into a book) for a five-day summer camping ministry. While I was there my wife Coleen and my daughter Marnie were treated to a supper of fresh "bird." I had noticed a number of times that summer that Eddie was once again on the prowl. It wasn't that Eddie needed to hunt any longer for a square meal, but his basic instincts and animal drive still beat strongly in his little chest. Actually, just before I left for New Brunswick, Canada, I saw him chasing a small bird off our front porch that opens up onto School Street. His eyes were staring intensely, and his tail was twitching violently as the small bird landed on the porch railing. In a flash Eddie was after the intruder, but the fowl was just a feather faster than Eddie and flew away into the upper limb of our bent apple tree. At the time I didn't even give the incident a second thought because that is what cats do, don't they chase birds? Even the "Pearl" loves to watch birds, but to eat one, God forbid!

As I always do on Tuesday afternoon, I called my wife for an update on the family situation and to share with her prayer requests for the camp. Besides my son's news (my boy Scott had just joined the United States Army and had been accepted into the 82nd Airborne and jump school) my wife said, "Do you want to hear about your other boy?" As I have written, it is hard to explain why of all the cats that has come into our family that I have taken such an interest in Eddie, but I have. He had become a friend, a walking companion, and a world-full-of-stress reliever. Even when I was in India for six-weeks my weekly calls included an Eddie update. So when my wife asked, I, of course, said, "Certainly I would like to hear about Eddie!"

It seems the night before Eddie had had a successful hunting expedition across the street. Normally, in the evening Eddie will cross School Street for the deep grass of our neighbor's backyard. Our neighbor is the local Catholic priest (Scott Mower), and Scottie (as we call him) also has a cat whose name is Sheridan. Sheridan, like Pearl, is just an in-door cat, but Eddie likes to watch and visit with him through a window in the side door to the manse. Often this is as far as Eddie goes if Sheridan is around, but on this occasion Eddie pressed on to his old hunting ground behind the Hurley House. As my wife tells the story Eddie must have found a small bird in his territory and this bird was not as fast or as alert as the other birds in the neighborhood because Eddie returned from his nightly hunt with the bird in his mouth. As my wife put it, "Eddie strutted across the street walking like a proud peacock!" Another custom of our family in the summer is sitting on the porch and swinging in the porch swing in the cool of a coastal dusk. That evening was no exception and was the reason my wife could tell me this Eddie story. At first they tried to ignore meows because neither of my girls enjoys anything dead. But in time they couldn't ignore Eddie any longer as he showed off his prey. Eddie "strutted his stuff" in front of the girls, including the Pearl who often sits in the living room window overlooking the front porch. I am afraid that Eddie's successful hunt was lost on the three females because as my wife explained, "It's a male thing!"

As I recalled this story out of the history of Eddie, Eddie, Eddie, I also thought of the verse I have printed at the beginning of this exhortation. Recently I reread this verse in another reading through the New Testament. It reminded me again of the masculine in the Godhead. Each member of the Godhead is found in the Bible in the male gender. The verse in Acts is of course speaking of the Holy Spirit. One needs only read the Old Testament to conclude if God is pictured in any gender, it is the masculine or "it is a male thing." Perhaps that is why at times it is hard to understand why God does what he does. Certainly a feminine god would do it differently as so many other religions love to say. Just about every other world religion that worships a variety of gods has within that group a goddess, yet there is no such "god" in the Scriptures. Whether the feminist like it or not, whether the liberal "Christians" like it or not, the Word of God is masculine in its very nature, and I write this not because I am a male, but because it is simply a Biblical reality!

I have battled most of my life the concept that only males are called into the pastorate. I know many denominations have opened the pastorate to women, but I simply ask, "Is this Biblical?" We are living in a society that wants to change tradition because of equal rights to all. As I write this article, my home state of Maine is voting on whether or not to change the definition of marriage. (Praise God they voted to keep it between one woman and one man, but would in time fall the liberals and vote to change God's law!) Our governor had already passed a law that would change the definition of marriage to include men with men and women with women. We as a society want to break down all gender issues and make no distinction between the feminine and the masculine. What is tragic is there are some in my State who want it to be like Sodom, and we all know how that ended! When God created, HE created male and female (Genesis 1:27), but those that believe in evolution make no such divisions. Why? I have come to believe that in man's depravity he has decided that he knows best. For me this has nothing to do with "the battle of the sexes" because, if we read carefully, in the writings of Paul he states: *"There is neither Jew nor Greek, there is neither bond nor free, there is neither male nor female: for ye are all one in Christ Jesus."* (Galatians 3:28) Despite this great equalizer there are still God-ordained divisions that must be respected because I have not discovered anywhere in Scripture that God has changed from the masculine to the feminine, and God has not changed the relationship of marriage as being between a single woman and a single man. There are just some things that, if changed, would change the natural order of things. (And they have!)

I know that science can now change the sex of an individual, but does that change the truth that they were either born male or female? I know the voters of the State of Maine have the right to change the definition of marriage, but does that change the ordinance of God? I know the Supreme Court of the United States has changed the time life is conceived, but does that change life itself? Other races and peoples have made their god into a goddess, but does that change the Biblical truth that *"Hear, O Israel: The Lord our God is one Lord?"* (Deuteronomy 6:4) I believe that "it is a male thing."

Chapter Thirty-Seven

Lyra Sojourner Newswanger

"Pure religion and undefiled before God and the Father is this, to visit the fatherless and widows in their affliction, and to keep himself unspotted from the world."

—JAMES 1:27

ONE OF THE GREAT joys of having cats in the parsonage is the entertainment value my wife Coleen and I get when children come for a visit. Kids are instantly attracted to animals, and when you have two totally different cats with two totally different personalities, like we do, it makes for some interesting encounters. A few years ago a young lady visited the parsonage for the first time which in memory has provoked in me another Eddie exhortation.

Our daughter Marnie did her undergraduate work at Lancaster Bible College in Lancaster, Pennsylvania. (Marnie is now doing her graduate work at Dallas Theological Seminary in Dallas, Texas.) While at LBC Marnie became friends with a grand lady by the name of Amy. Amy and Marnie became instant friends and over the years have developed a best friend and a lasting friendship relationship. When Amy married Jared, another college friend, Marnie was her maid of honor, and because of this relationship my wife and I were also a part of Jared and Amy's wedding. Amy had become like a second daughter to us. When Amy and Jared gave birth to their first child, we couldn't wait for a visit because we felt like we had become grandparents.

In the summer of 2006 Lyra Sojourner (named after the famous Christian missionary) Newswanger made her first visit to the "duke and duchess" (Amy's name for Coleen and I) of Maine. We couldn't wait to meet "the most beautiful baby in the world," that is according to her Aunt Mar-Mar (Marnie). When the day finally arrived, Marnie had only told us half the story of this special child. Our only concern was how the cats would react to a baby in the house for a week.

Pearl had in her short life endured a few small people invading her space, but this would be the first long-term stay by any of them. As I have already shared in this accounting of Eddie's exhortations, the Pearl isn't the most hospitable cat in the world. As a matter of fact, she is downright rude when it comes to any company. Despite the tender affection of Lyra, very gentle for a baby, Pearl would have nothing to do with the young lady from Pennsylvania during her visit with us. Coleen and I even got to babysit for a few of those days while mother and father had a mini-vacation on the coast of Maine without a baby in hand, but even throughout that time the Pearl pretty much avoided Miss Newswanger and either stayed in her room or downstairs in the basement. Eddie on the other hand found the newest member of the family quite fascinating and very interesting to say the least.

For Eddie, Lyra Sojourner was the first baby we believe he had ever seen or been around let alone meet. Having been an out-door cat for his first two years of life, babies were a rarity in his world. Now that he had become partly domesticated (I don't think Eddie will ever become completely domesticated), he was enjoying the finer things of life, and one of the finest has to be the visit of a baby girl to your world. Because of Marnie we learned that Eddie does like (except for some reason my wife) the women! From Eddie's first house guest we quickly noticed that he was the complete opposite to the Pearl. Friendly and hospitable, Eddie was a wonderful host to Lyra and her parents. Oh, he had to check Sojourner out, but once he realized that she was no threat to him or us, he, like us, adopted this little girl with an open heart. We would find him on occasion checking the house for her after we put her down for a nap. He never hissed or growled like the Pearl, but always purred lovingly around her the whole time she was with us. We are still waiting for that little lady with the great name to come back for another visit, but the verdict on the first visit is still a split vote between our two cats.

After revisiting that visitation in my mind, I immediately thought of the verse that began this exhortation. I also recalled a wonderful exhortation I had read years before by

James described it best when he defined "pure religion." (James 1:27) It has little to do with visiting a house of worship and more about visiting an orphanage. It has little to do with visiting the church and more about visiting the shut-in, the shut-out, and the shut-away. Didn't Jesus tell us this when he said, "I was sick and ye visited me: I was in prison, and ye came unto me?" (Matthew 25:36) Did not Paul honor Onesiphorus for this very deed?

"The Lord gives mercy unto the house of Onesiphorus; for he oft refreshed me, and was not ashamed of my chains: but, when he was in Rome, he sought me out very diligently, and found me." (II Timothy 1:16-17)

When will we realize that the Christianity that is now is not the Christianity that was taught and practiced by Christ and His early followers then? We have missed the purity of our faith because we have lost sight of two clearly defined areas of the Faith: visitation and abstention. In the visit of Lyra these principles were seen from both the positive and negative standpoints. Pearl shut herself away and wouldn't visit, but she also at every opportunity failed to abstain from showing herself to be without hospitality and her friendliness was lacking. Pearl showed herself to be stained by the attitude and actions of most of the world today. Eddie on the other hand showed himself a perfect gentleman, visiting often, especially when Lyra was fatherless for a few days. Our faith is all about action and activities connected to the weakest among us or as Jesus said, *"The least among us."* (Matthew 25:40) When will we realize that we must put our faith into action and be found visiting and abstaining?

Chapter Thirty-Eight

Harvey Wallhanger

"In God have I put my trust: I will not be afraid what man can do unto me?"

—Psalms 56:11

We all have to learn the lesson of naming our fears. This truth came home to me just a few days ago when I heard an amazing and unique approach of confronting one's worst fear. My wife and I were entertaining our dear friends, Mike and Debra Hangge, at our new cottage in Aroostook County in northern Maine. Last Valentine's Day my father's only brother passed away and left us my grandparent's old home. The 1920s homestead house has become a pleasant get-away place for my wife and me. The Hangge's were the first overnight quests we had invited to our retreat, a place we call Dandelion Cottage (because in the spring the seven acres that surrounds the property are covered with bright yellow dandelions). While eating breakfast one morning Debra began to tell a story that instantly drew my attention because of the name of her chief character, Harvey Wallhanger.

One of the aspects of Eddie's Exhortations is the use of God's creatures to highlight and underline a Biblical concept. The only connection I can make to this story and Eddie is that Eddie enjoys the front porch at the parsonage and many a spider calls that sweet retreat home, but he has never seemingly had any trouble with these spiders. My wife, on the other hand, hates spiders, yes, even fears them, especially the big ones that live on the porch. I have been cleaning out her spider webs for over forty years now and have come to her screams on numerous occasions to kill one of God's unique creatures despite the fact that the Bible actually glorifies them in that they are one of four little creatures that are seen as "exceeding wise" in Proverbs 20:24:

> "The spider taketh hold with her hands, and is in the kings' palaces." (Proverbs 30:28)

Each time I remind my wife of that verse I am rebuked with another Scriptural selection:

> "So are the paths of all that forget God; and the hypocrite's hope shall perish: whose hope shall be cut off, and whose trust shall be a spider's web." (Job 8:13-14)

I like to remind my wife that those verses are speaking of the spider's web, not the spider, but nothing I have tried has helped my wife in her fear of spiders, that is, until Debra Hangge's story.

Come to find out, Deb (as we call her) was also afraid of spiders until she confronted a huge creature that lived on the backside of their garage. Deb is very creative and enjoys gardening. She and her husband (a very, handy handyman) had created a lovely outdoor patio between their back deck and their garage. It took years of planting and rock placement to get the area just right. It seemed, however, that each time Deb would work in the side yard, she would be confronted with this huge spider hanging somewhere off the back of the garage. She tried to ignore it, but each time she went outside her eyes were drawn to that frightful creature, and, sure enough, it was always there. Some would say, "Just kill it!" The trouble with that is that Deb doesn't like killing any of God's creatures, including spiders. She knew of the usefulness of spiders to the environment she was creating in her yard. She was in a dilemma. She was betwixt two, the desire to be rid of the spider and the reluctance of killing the spider. She could have gotten Mike to deal with it, as so many wives do, but Deb decided upon another approach and herein does our story and scriptural application begin.

As Deb shared her story around our kitchen table, she told us that she had read or heard somewhere that one of the best ways to confront a fear was "to name it." One day as she was joyfully working in her new creation, her eyes once again fell on the only thing in her garden that she despised—that huge dangling spider that called her garage home. It was then the bit of advice she had heard came to mind, name your fear and confront it. It was then the spider in the Hangge's side yard become known as Harvey Wallhanger. Deb said that she began to feel better almost immediately as she put a face, a name, a personality to her fear. With any "fear" there is the need to understand it and what better way to understand than by putting a label on it, even if it is a funny name like Harvey Wallhanger. Is not this what John Bunyan did in his classic work Pilgrim's Progress? Many of the characters in his tale were named according to a fear or frustration every

Christian faces on his journey from the City of Destruction to the Celestial City. It is important, however, that we distinguish between a destructive fear and a natural fear.

Do we not admire the doctor that fears disease, the businessman that fears debt, the saint that fears sin, and the fireman that fears fire (Mike Hangge is a fireman)? In our very first Eddie story we wrote of the self-preservation protection granted by God to every animal through natural fear. Even our Lord in Gethsemane taught us that He had to face a fear, and I believe that fear was becoming sin for us Who knew no sin. Why else would he shrink from the cross by asking, *"If it be possible, let this cup pass from me?"* (Matthew 26:39) Nevertheless, once Jesus named his "fear" He conquered it. Instead of a hairy, creepy spider, now there is Harvey Wallhanger. Instead of death, now there is the Father's will. Paul wrote of this in Hebrews:

> *"Who in the days of his flesh, when He had offered up prayers and supplications with strong crying and tears unto Him that was able to save Him from death, and was heard in that He FEARED."* (Hebrews 5:7)

Jesus has given us the example, and Bunyan has given us the concept, and Deb has now given us the method. So what do you fear, not a natural fear, I hope, but a destructive fear that keeps you from doing the will of God? Name it, face it, give it a title, and see it for what it is—conquerable, changeable!

Let us remember that there is no sin in fear itself. If sin happens because of fear, it happens when we fail to trust in the Lord. The Psalmist in the same Psalm as our key verse above says:

> *"What time I am afraid, I will trust in Thee!"* (Psalms 56:3)

Remember, all you are really dealing with is a Harvey Wallhanger!

Chapter Thirty-Nine

A Daybreak Meditation

"But his delight is in the law of the Lord; and in His law doth he meditate day and night."

—Psalms 1:2

A NUMBER OF YEARS ago I wrote the following under the caption of "a daybreak meditation":

> At four in the morning on a cloudless September night the country air can be crystal clear. The whole world lays sharp, still, and sweet in the silver dawn, the stars blink with an amazing intensity and clarity. The moon moves slowly across the dark sky appearing to droop steadily towards its appointed disappearing act off the western horizon. There is an awesome breathlessness in the Salmon Brook Valley just before daybreak. It is harvest time on the Blackstone homestead, but before the potatoes can be dug, the cows have to be fed and milked. These are those sacred, special times I remember most as I think back to my past. Those quiet hours I spend with my dad in the color of early autumn. The multi-colored leaves of fall would soon be a distant image in my mind and a fading memory in my heart, but on this predawn trip to the milking shed there was no sign that the Sugar Woods would not always be draped in orange, crimson, and gold. The wind was somewhere else and nothing stirred, not even the Holsteins in the pasture. There was no bending branches, no tumbling leaves, no chattering squirrels, and no movement of any kind. For one divine moment the world was at perfect peace with itself and a farm boy from Perham. On daybreaks like this there is an overpowering sensation that touches one's soul in stillness, quietness so acute that any sound echoes as if off a canyon wall. The wagging of a dog's tail is like thunder

to your ear, and the moo of a distant cow is like cannon shot. These quiet, morning moments are cherished interludes in the busy schedule of a working teenager. This day would be filled with backbreaking labor, but before the intense work begins the Good Lord seems to know that with such days a delightful daybreak is needed and necessary. Amid the ebb and flow of the shifting periods of my life, this eternal value has remained. I still cherish my daybreaks, and though they don't start at four any more, I still enjoy a quiet, gentle beginning to my day. I am one of those that don't have to rush off to a busy office or noisy factory. As I did with my father years ago, I go to work humbled by the breathless beauty of a gathering autumn. Despite the fact I live in a city now, no country here, our neighborhood is tree-lined and the sounds of passing cars are a block away, most of the time. Those city sights and sounds can't rob me of the blinking stars (though they are faded) and the setting moon. (Is there anything better than a full "harvest" moon?) No man can take away the colorful leaves and the windless morning I step out into. My soul is still humbled for I say still, *"This is the day the Lord has made; I will rejoice and be glad in it!"* (Psalms 118:24) The daybreak is still mine to enjoy.

I still sit at times on the steps of my church beneath the morning star and the setting moon wrapped in the wonder of another wonderful daybreak. As in the days of my youth, I am not alone because now there is Eddie, Eddie, Eddie for my companion. I am blessed that my dad is still alive (he died in 2017, two months before my son), but he now lives 200 miles away. My dog Rover died in my early teens, and the Holstein herd of the homestead was sold decades ago. I have exchanged the wooden platform of the old milking shed (it, too, has fallen and is no more) for the concrete steps of the Emmanuel Baptist Church, but the enchantment of that soft, silver splendor of a golden daybreak is still there as I rub Eddie's head and hear his "amen" to my morning song of praise.

Eddie has brought me back to meditation. It is much easier to ponder on the things of God in the quietness of a morning when nothing stirs but the soft fur of a special cat. As I thought back this morning to my childhood memory of an autumn long since passed, I enjoyed as I did then to the same God, the wonderful God of my fathers, and the marvelous and faithful God of the Bible. As with so much changing in this world, little has changed with my relationship with the Almighty. He is still there to start every daybreak with a new day and an old mission—to prepare to proclaim His word as often as I can. I was very young when I read these words in the book of Joshua:

> *"This book of the law shall not depart out of thy mouth; but thou shalt meditate therein day and night, that thou mayest observe to do according to all that is written therein: for then thou shalt make thy way prosperous, and then thou shalt have good success."*
> (Joshua 1:8)

My pet for my morning walk has changed. My companion for my morning work has changed. My view for my morning wake has changed, but my morning meditation has remained the same. I still wander in my mind to the things of God as seen in the law of God. It has been my meditation all these years, and, if I can make it six more weeks, it will be forty years since I started down this daybreak trail. It is a path that leads me back to the Word of God and what that word tells me to do and to share. I believe I can in confidence write that 99% of every sermon I have prepared over my lifetime was prepared in a daybreak meditation. Even these "Eddie Exhortations," or at least most of them, have had there start in the morning, as did this one. I am writing these thoughts in the fading light of a last fall day, but I thought as I found Eddie visiting Big Grey this morning that before this day was through I would be writing this article. It is done. My final challenge for you is to take time in the morning of a daybreak meditation. You might not be inspired by a cat, but maybe, just maybe, a memory of a past morning will cause you to sing with the Psalmist, *"This is the day the Lord has made, I will rejoice and be glad in it!"*

Chapter Forty

Wonderfully Made

"I will praise Thee; for I am fearfully and wonderfully made: marvelous are Thy works; and that my soul knoweth right well."

PSALMS 139:14

EACH OF US HAS uniqueness to us. I believe that God doesn't create in duplicate, even with twins or triplets. Granted, I have over the years in the pastorate had a few twins (no triplets yet) connected to my ministry. Right now in our Monday night Awana (a youth ministry for 3-12 year olds) we have a couple of sets of twins. Over time I have realized just like others they can be distinguished between by certain characteristics. Sometimes, it isn't visible, but more in their personality or behavior. What the Psalmist writes above is a marvelous insight into the creative nature of God. These thoughts came to me this week as I observed again my cat's distinguishing mark. I wrote about this in a short story I called "a brown goatee":

> Like Precious Patience Pearl, Eddie, too, has a distinguishing mark on the front of his body. The facial feature that drew us to the Pearl was the white collar of fur around her neck. It reminded us of a string of pearls, hence her name. For Eddie that facial feature is a very well defined brown goatee. Though Pearl is not 100% Maine coon cat, she does have enough of the characteristics for us to know that a good part of her heritage is from that classic species of cat. Eddie on the other hand has no such distinctions for us to determine just what kind of cat he is. No doubt he is a mixture of who knows what (though he does have many of the characteristics of the American short-hair), but this lack of family history doesn't take away from the handsome tom he is in his own right. Unlike the Pearl, Eddie doesn't have the classic shape of a long-hair; Eddie is a short-hair with a pot belly (Buddha belly) and an unflattering tail. Pearl has a long

flowing tail that seems to be as wide as she is, while Eddie has a thin tail with a crook on the end, maybe an early injury. Eddie waddles when he walks, unlike the Pearl who is very graceful in her stride, yet in his color Eddie reveals his true nature. His legs and belly are mostly white, a snowy white. This is in contrast to the gray fur that covers his head and shoulders and back. Eddie has mostly white facial hair with gray highlights around his eyes and on the top of his head and ears. The white covers his cheeks and nose and runs upward to his brow. He has the typical cat jaw and facial shape of a tiger cat, but what makes him stand out is the brown goatee under his chin. There are hints and highlights of brown on other parts of his body, but most can't be seen in the dark gray hair and black hair that gives him at times that classic tiger profile. His goatee on the other hand is clearly seen against the white background of his chin and throat, and, oh, how Eddie loves for me to rub his goatee. Eddie reminds me of the beatniks of the 60s. I was raised in that turbulent decade when the goatee was the facial hair of choice for many when a small amount of stubble on the chin was a statue symbol of rebellion and revolt. (I have been noticing that the goatee is experiencing a comeback as I have seen this facial hair on many a young person lately!) Long hair with a goatee was my generation's way of showing themselves different, and Eddie is certainly a different kind of cat. I have never met one quite like him, and his brown goatee sets him apart. Like the beatniks of the past, Eddie is an aggressive defender of his right to go things his way, an independent cat that marches to his own beat, a territorial tom that fights over his own turf, one that is looking to change society, by his free spirit and cavalier attitude. Eddie did come from the other side of the street, the other side of the tracks if you will. He is the opposite of the more refined Pearl in culture and upbringing, but his swagger and style is still appealing to most of us. My wife has come to love his roughness even if Eddie hasn't as yet warmed up to her. My daughter loves his personality, and he hers! (Both are strong-willed and high-strung.) Everybody likes Eddie (including the mailman, the church folks, and the neighbors), but not the Pearl because I am convinced that Precious Patience Pearl only sees Eddie as a beatnik!

What God-given mark sets you apart from the rest?

They say that there is not and has never been two snowflakes the same. In the trillions and trillions of flakes that have fallen in northern Maine alone over the years, that they were all unique and different is hard for me to imagine, yet they say it is so. We serve a God of such diversity that duplication is not necessary. I have just finished an article in a series I am calling "inspiring intercessions." My goal in that project is to share some of the most amazing answers to prayer in my life. The supplication story I just finished compiling was about the birth of my daughter Marnie and the birth defect she was born with. I have come to believe that defect was one of the defining characteristics of my daughter, what made her unique and "fearfully and wonderfully made." Like the man born blind (John 9:1-3), Marnie was born the way she was to manifest the marvelous and miraculous works of God. Granted, we struggled through two years of miserable uncertainty and medical challenges, but in the end God was glorified and His name was honored. We came to praise him for the answers to prayer, His healing hand, and our special daughter. You have figured out by now that I have a special bond and affection for the simple cat Eddie and the joy he has given me over our seven years together. His brown goatee is just a mark that reminds me of God's ability to create diversity and distinction within His creation that will help us understand just how precious and special we all are. To think that God took time to make me different; that God thought enough about me to make me altogether unique from every other human being that has lived on this planet; that in all of us there is a piece of God different than our neighbor. No wonder the prophet spoke of us as God's "jewels!" (Malachi 3:17)

The next time you see that birthmark that you have despised all your life, remember it is God's mark for making you unique and loved by Him. The next time you are reminded of a birth defect that has hounded, and, yes, maybe hurt you all your life, remember it is that defect that God has given you to make you special (Exodus 4:11). The next time you see a God-given "goatee" remember:

> "... .and in Thy book all my members were written, which in continuance was fashioned, when as yet there was none of them. How precious also are Thy thoughts unto me, O God! How great is the sum of them!" (Psalms 139:16-17)

Chapter Forty-One

Protecting a Pearl

*"Again, the kingdom of heaven is like unto
a merchant man, seeking godly pearls:*

*who, when he had found one pearl of great price,
went and sold all that he had, and bought it."*

—Matthew 13:45, 46

By now you know that this series of cat devotionals have been inspired by my cat Eddie. You also know that Eddie is not the only cat living at the parsonage of the Emmanuel Baptist Church in Ellsworth, Maine. Her name has been invoked numerous times throughout this book, and her full name is "Precious Patience Pearl," but more often than not we simply refer to her as "the Pearl." One of the interesting and inspiring aspects of Eddie and Pearl's relationship is the protective manner by which Eddie watches after "our pearl of great price!" I know some have probably already stopped reading because you might think this to be a sacrilege to use Jesus' great parable printed above in this manner, but bear with me for a few more paragraphs, and I think you will understand the application of another spiritual lesson illustrated before me through the actions of a tomcat named Eddie.

One of the very first observations we made about our new cat Eddie was his protective nature, whether our backyard, the church sanctuary, or "the Pearl." I feel Eddie has come to believe that he has been asked into our home and lives to protect us. He spends much of his day now with me at the church guarding the door lest a stranger invade. When we leave the church late in the afternoon, he usually positions himself in the backyard guarding the garage where Big Grey sometimes likes to stay. I have already written of his evenings in the windows or walking throughout the upstairs and downstairs of the parsonage making sure everything is in order, and then there is "the Pearl." The best example of Eddie's guardian nature is what happens if by chance "the Pearl" escapes the confines of our home.

Pearl has never been an outdoor cat. We might on occasion put her in a cat carrier we call "the cottage" and let her breath a bit of fresh air and feel a cool breeze once in a while, but to let her out as we do Eddie, never! Yet on those rare occasions "the Pearl" is at the right place at the right time and the door swings open and she makes a bid for a few moments of kitty freedom. Before Eddie arrived on the scene I use to chase "the Pearl" all over the backyard, front yard, side yard until I usually forced her under something—the porch, the car, the garage, and then I would have to somehow get her out. It took me quite a while to figure out that if I didn't chase her at all, she would stop within yards of the door, and in a few minutes I could simply go over to her, pick her up, and return her to the safety of the house. What amazed my wife and me was the first time "the Pearl" escaped and Eddie was around. Out the door Pearl would go and there was Eddie right on her tail. Even when we put her in "the cottage" Eddie usually camps out somewhere very near as if to guard her. I will never forget the time Pearl got out and immediately ran and hid under our garage. Because there is very little room under the garage it is almost impossible to work your way under it. It was then that Eddie literally followed "the Pearl" and within moments had chased her out through an opening in the back of the garage. Despite the well documented fact that "the Pearl" can't stand Eddie, Eddie believes he has found his one and only pearl. It was then I saw a wonderful application to Jesus' parable of the merchant and the valuable pearl.

There are those who only believe that this parable can be applied to Jesus, the 'Pearl of great price." I certainly believe this, but I have also come to believe that while each verse in the Bible has only one primary interruption, it can have scores of applications. Malachi 3:17 tells us that God considers His children "my jewels," a pearl if you will. Why can't we read Jesus' parable as the merchantman is Christ, and in His eyes we are "the pearl?" Certainly, He sold all that He had and gave His life to purchase us (I Corinthians 6:20). Then upon Himself He laid the charge to keep us and protect us until He comes back for us (Philippians 1:6). I have been impressed over the last seven years just how much Eddie is willing to guard someone that doesn't like him, so how much more will our Guardian protect us because He loves us with a love that it beyond degree. Think with me just a moment about those individuals the Good Lord protected beyond measure, men like Elijah.

Remember what happened after Mount Carmel. God's preacher now had a price on his head. The wicked queen Jezebel was out to get him no matter the cost. The prophet fled the land and wanted to die, but not only did God protect His man from his enemies, but himself from self. God's care for Elijah not only carried over to his physical needs, but his emotional and relationship needs. The isolation had taken its toll on God's minister, so God provided Elisha. I have discovered that sometimes God's protection comes in the form of a wife, a best friend, a neighbor, a deacon, do I need to go on? If the Good Lord can send a cat for a cat, don't you think He can send someone to be with you, and when it takes a while for that someone to arrive God Himself will be your Companion and Guardian? Think of it this way: God is just looking out for His pearl of great price.

Time would fail me to write of David and Jeremiah and Paul and a countless list of others to which the Lord protected and guarded through some very difficult times. Even when they escaped the Lord's will, like Jonah, the Lord was there to rescue His "pearl," to find it again like the shepherd found his sheep and the woman found her coin (Luke 15). There will be none that can harm or hurt His jewel, and, if you are one, then you have nothing to worry or wonder about. He knows right where you are at all times, just like with Elijah, and He will find you where you are and will place you into his treasure bag and bear you on through any valley or any wilderness until He places you as a treasured jewel in His diadem (Colossians 3:4). The classic church hymn written by William Cushing in 1856 says it best:

> When He comes, when He comes, to make up His jewels,
> All His jewels, precious jewels, His loved and His own.
> He will gather, He will gather the gems for His kingdom,
> All the pure ones, all the bright ones, His loved and His own.
> Little children, little children who love their Redeemer,
> Are the jewels, precious jewels, His loved and His own?
> Like the stars of the morning, His bright crown adoring,
> They will shine in their beauty, bright gems for His crown!

Who says that one of those gems isn't a costly pearl?

Chapter Forty-Two

If Animals Could Talk? Maybe They Can.

"And the Lord opened the mouth of the ass, and she said unto Balaam, 'What have I done unto thee, that thou hast smitten me these three times?'"

—Numbers 22:28

A FLOCK OF CROWS (ravens) have taken up residence in my Ellsworth neighborhood. Hardly a morning goes by that I don't encounter them on my short walk across School Street to my study in the church building on Park Street. I learned long ago on the family farm in northern Maine to talk to the crows, and their "caw, caw, caw" has become as familiar and friendly to me as Eddie's "meow, meow, meow." In the late summer, as it is now, rare is the day that goes by that I don't engage in a conversation with the crows as I use to do as a lad in the barnyard of my boyhood when a dog, not a cat, was my constant companion. In my early relationship with crows, however, our conversations were far from friendly.

A distant caw-aw, caw-aw, caw-aw sound broke the stillness of an early morning many (more than many) years ago. Soft and faint at first, the noise eventually grew in volume as a flock of black-feathered crows approached from beyond the Sugar Woods. Soaring into the driveway that still circles my homestead house, the flock of a dozen crows landed as if they were touching down on a runway at a major international airport. They had come for breakfast, to feed on whatever they could find in the busy barnyard that often experienced spilled oats, discarded eggs, and, of course, anything dead which was their favorite dish. This particular morning there was an ample supply so as I watched from the front porch more crows were called in to enjoy the feast lying before them. Chattering loudly among themselves, these new arrivals joined their comrade cousins seemingly ignoring the boy and his dog watching their every move:

When I was a lad crows were a sport, not a source of conversation. I hunted anything and everything that moved and was legal to hunt. I saw these country crows as a target and nothing more. As I loaded my shotgun for another attempt at a shot at the uninvited visitors, I quietly moved through the woodshed towards the open door by the side of the shed. It was then I noticed that the caw-aw, caw-aw, caw-aw had changed to kawk, kawk, kawk, and the entire flock of crows were gone before I could get off my first shot. I had been spotted by the two sentry crows sitting on the clothes line on the lawn located on the other side of the front driveway. As I soon discovered, crows are very suspicious by nature and not easy targets for a hunter's shotgun. As a matter of fact, in my entire childhood I was only successful once in my quest for downing a crow. (I wasn't a good hunter no matter the game and that is why I switched to fishing early in adulthood.) That day I caught a group of crows feasting on some scraps of food my mother had discarded on the manure pile behind the cow barn. I was able to sneak undetected through the barn to the only window in the back of the barn. Through that window I was able to bring down three of the birds before the warning "kawk" could be sounded. As I grew old, I realized the greatest joy of seeing wildlife was not in taking their lives, but in talking to them and listening to them talk. Instead of shooting at them, I began to study them, and I discovered that crows have a well-defined communication system. Expects in the study of crows have distinguished over 50 expressions based on the single syllable "caw." With minor modifications entirely different meanings of the sound can be expressed. So I talk to them as they caw back, and I have found them to be wonderful and pleasant conservationists in a city too busy for small talk. Like with my conversations with Eddie, because he, too, can change his meow into a variety of tunes whereby he can tell me what he wants or wants me to know, the crows now tell me a lot of what is going on in their lives. I have on occasion even heard Eddie talking to the crows from the back porch of the church and have wondered whether he, too, has found it more entertaining to talk to the crows than to hunt the crows.

If the Almighty could open the mouth of Balaam's donkey, why do we doubt that God could not speak to us through the animals (Job 12:7-10) that we come across in our wanderings? I am convinced that Noah talked to the birds he released from the ark (Genesis 8:6-11). Note carefully the first bird that was chosen to fly into the new world. When Jesus instructed us to watch the birds (Matthew 6:26), could He have also wanted us to listen to the birds? If my cat Eddie takes time to listen and talk, shouldn't we, if only to recognize the wonderful truth that if God cares for the birds and provides for the birds, even crows and cats, will He not care and provide for us? (Matthew 6:25, 31-33) One day as I watched Eddie admiring the family of crows on Park Street, I imagined what he was thinking. With his tail slowly moving back and forth and a low, mellow meow coming from his throat, I thought I heard him say, "You are blessed that I am so well fed at the Blackstone house or I might be having you for lunch!" Then I thought I heard him add this spiritual thought: "We both are being fed by the hand of the Almighty through the hand of the Blackstones!"

My wife has been feeding these city crows for as long as we have lived in Ellsworth. Whatever scraps of bread and other things we might have left over has been thrown into the backyard for the crows. It was on the occasion of one such feeding that Coleen noticed a stray cat eating the crow's breakfast that her heart was moved to help that cat, and that cat was Eddie. Eddie doesn't eat crow food any longer, but I think in his own right he understands that it was through that act of helping the Almighty feed the crows that he was fed. When will we realize that it is when we help feed our hungry neighbor that we in turn are fed? Jesus spoke of this in another great sermon when he proclaimed, *"For I was an hungred, and ye gave me meat . . . . . Then shall the righteous answer him, saying, Lord, when saw we thee an hungred . . . . . And the King shall answer and say unto them, Verily I say unto you, Inasmuch as ye have done it unto one of the least of these my brethren, ye have done it unto me."* (Matthew 25:35, 37, 40) A crow is in my opinion one of the least in the bird kingdom, and yet I witness the Heavenly Father feeding them constantly as I travel the highways and roadways of Maine. Roadkill is the crow's best meal! Let us learn this lesson from Eddie and the crow and help our needy brother because the day might come when we will need his help.

Chapter Forty-Three

Give Attention to Reading

"Till I come, give attendance to reading, to exhortation, to doctrine."
—I Timothy 4:13

It is Thanksgiving Eve, and I am in my study at the Emmanuel Baptist Church in Ellsworth, Maine, making preparation for an annual testimonial service. As has become our routine, Eddie and I have made ourselves comfortable in our chairs. I am sitting in an old brown computer chair given to me by a member of the congregation. Eddie is washing himself in my black desk chair given to me by my Sunday school class many years ago. It seems that Eddie and I spend a great deal of time in chairs.

Ever since Eddie came into my life, the church building has been a sanctuary for him. Our routine most days is very simple, just like this Indian summer day in late November. Sitting on the upstairs steps of the parsonage, Eddie waits patiently for me to get ready to leave for church. If not on the inside steps, I will meet Eddie on the front porch steps because I have let him out earlier. Eddie likes to roam a bit in the morning so sometimes he wakes me at five so that he can check out the neighborhood before we head to work. This is more his routine in the spring and summer, but, now it is dark later into the morning and colder, he waits for me to get up to go out.

Once I dress and descend the stairs for the living room, Eddie is at the front door excited to be leaving. Eddie enjoys his new home, but is by his very nature an outdoor cat. He enjoys his freedom to come and go as he wants so to open an outside door for Eddie is sheer joy. Once outside we start down the walkway that leads to School Street. We will not cross until the street is clear of traffic. I had to teach my children to look both ways before crossing, but never Eddie. He already knew the dangers of not checking before he came to live with me. I don't know why or how, but it is entertaining to watch him come to the street, stop, look up and down, and then cross. This morning as we neared the road, a heavy truck came roaring up the street. Eddie ran back to the porch and waited for the all clear before joining me for our short stroll up Park Street.

Periodically along our route I have to stop and rub Eddie's head. This might happen just once or a number of times. When we started this little routine I can't remember, but it is all a part of our early morning time together. Once we get to the side door of the church Eddie is usually ahead of me and waiting entrance. Immediately upon gaining entrance Eddie walks to the study to make sure there are still some cat treats in a bowl by my desk, as well as a bowl of water. Content that he will have something to eat and drink during the day, Eddie will walk through the church to make sure everything is in order. If the treat bowl isn't at its proper level Eddie will remind me of the treat container in the desk. Eddie knows exactly where it is kept, and he will paw the desk until I fill the bowl to his desire. Once Eddie determines that he has enough supply for the day and that there are no hidden dangers in the building, he will settle in. On warm days Eddie likes to go outside so I put a door stop in the front door so he can come and go at his good pleasure. On cold days, like this morning, Eddie rarely leaves the building.

By the time Eddie came into my life, I, too, had developed a morning routine. This includes a few minutes in an upper back room of the church where the ladies of the church have set up a mini-living room (chair, lamp, end table, and couch). It has become a quiet retreat for me, away from the office and visitors, away from the phone. It is here I have my early devotions of prayer and Bible reading. It wasn't long before Eddie joined me, and now each and every time I head for the back room along comes Eddie. I sit in the chair, and Eddie sits in my lap. I have taught Eddie the value of a quiet time, but I haven't been as successful with humans. In our busy world most mornings are spent in a rat's race of getting ready for work or school. Unless one gets up real early, the morning is underway before any time for God is possible. Prayer is important at any time and can be performed at any time, but Bible reading takes a tranquil place, distractions at a minimum, and concentration.

Many years ago the Christian Digest printed this <u>Tribute to the Bible</u> by Billy Sunday. I would like for you to find a quiet place and reread this man's thoughts about the most important book in the world, and then maybe you will take time every day to read the Bible.

> Twenty-two years ago, with the Holy Spirit as my Guide, I entered the wonderful temple of Christianity. I entered at the portico of Genesis, walked down through the Old Testament art

galleries where the pictures of Noah, Isaac, Abraham, Moses, Joseph, and Daniel hung on the wall. I passed into the music room of Psalms, where the Spirit swept the keyboard of nature, and brought forth the dirge like wail of the weeping prophet Jeremiah, to the grand impassioned strain of Isaiah, until it seemed that every reed and pipe in God's great organ of nature responded to the tuneful harp of David, the sweet singer of Israel. I entered the chapel of Ecclesiastes, where the voice of the preacher was heard, and into the conservatory of Sharon and the Lilies of the Valley sweet-scented spices filled and perfumed my life. I entered the business offices of the Proverbs, then into the observation room of the prophets, where I saw telescopes of various sizes, pointed to far-off events, but all concentrated upon the Bright and Morning Star, which was to rise above the moonlit hills of Judea for our salvation. I entered the audience room of the King of Kings, and caught a vision of His glory from the stand-point of Matthew, Mark, Luke, and John; passed into the Acts of the Apostles, where the Holy Spirit was doing its work in the infant Church; then into the correspondence room, where sat Matthew, Mark, Luke, John, Paul, Peter, James, and Jude, penning their epistles. I stepped into the throne room of Revelation, where I got a vision of the King sitting upon His throne in all His glory. Revolutions have raged around the Holy Bible. Nations have been buried, and the geography of the earth has shifted in human strife, but the Bible lives on. The foundations of government are laid in its principles. It is the abiding strength of all efficient law. It is the source of the ideals of all loveliness in the human character. The central figure of this Book is the ideal Character and Teacher of all ages, Jesus Christ. It is read on the Lord's Day in the pulpits of our land. In all temples of Christendom, its voice is lifted. The sun never sets on its gleaming pages. It goes to the cottage of the poor peasant, and to the palace of the king; to the hut of the poor man, and to the halls of the rich. No vessel of war goes to the conflict, but the Bible is there. It mingles in all our sorrows, our joys, and our aching heads and hearts find a soft pillow in its leaves. Men rest their hope on the promises of this Book. It is a source of spiritual energy. The Word of God still endures!

As Eddie lays his head on my lap each morning, I lay my head on the Word of the Lord. Why wouldn't I read it? Why aren't you reading it?

Chapter Forty-Four

And Eddie Makes Ten

". . . the tenth shall be holy unto the Lord."
—Leviticus 27:32

Surely by now you have come to the conclusion that I have fallen in love with my cat Eddie, and that for me he is the ideal cat. Except for my affection for a boyhood dog named Rover, I can honestly say that Eddie is the best pet that has come into my life. Even our dog Cherry doesn't come close to the connection I have to Eddie so when I read the phrase from Leviticus printed above I began to think back in the history of the cats Coleen and I have had over the years.

I was raised on a potato and dairy farm in northern Maine where the cats sometimes outnumbered the hogs and always outnumbered the dogs. With a huge cow barn near my home our cats and the neighborhood cats had a perfect place to start a community, and then there was the huge cow barn on the homestead itself. There were always plenty of cats, if you liked cats, which I didn't. I took after my mother in that way so I never became close to any cat in my childhood. As a matter of fact, I can't remember a single cat ever being named! Nevertheless, shortly after Coleen and I got married cats began to show up in our home because my dear wife has loved any kitty, cat, or tom she ever met. Coleen wasn't allowed but one cat when she was a child so felines began to find their way to our home. There was "Melon," then "Tangie," followed by "Taffy," then "Callie," followed by "Butter," then "Sugar," and a rare male named "Bo-Bo," the only cat our son claimed for his own. "Co-Co" was number eight, a cat we got from the homestead.

It was on one of our visits to see our Aroostook County family that my cat-loving daughter Marnie found a tiny, frail kitten that had fallen out of the haymow and had been abandoned by its mother. The weak meow of the poor kitten touched the heart of our daughter, and she couldn't help herself as she pleaded the cat's case before her father. I can still see in my mind's eye the dying kitten wrapped up in Marnie arms as she begged me to let her bring the kitten home. My brother Jay was smiling and my Cousin Gary was laughing under his breath as we stood in front of the huge barn doors debating the life expectancy of the abandoned animal. The fleabag feline was certainly at the point of death with little hope of survival, but Marnie and her eyes eventually talked me into bringing it home and resurrecting it. It was the biggest mistake I ever made in any relationship I have had with an animal!

Despite the fact we nursed the cat back to health and gave it everything any cat might ever dream of having, the cat never really recovered from that fall as an infant. We kept the pussy for years, but it never recovered mentally from its kitty-hood tumble. We even moved it to Ellsworth with us, but it never became a part of our family or attached itself to any of us. Each day when I would return home from work it was like I had to reintroduce myself to Co-Co. It was always afraid and jumpy. It never came to you or would ever set on your lap. She reminded me of a lot of people who come to church. They come, are there, but they never connect; they never join, and it is as if you have to reintroduce yourself to them each Sunday. There seems to be a lot of "Co-Co" Christians in the Church of God today! Like with "Co-co," after seven years they just go away. Co-Co was our only homestead cat, but in some respects Co-Co never left the farm. Perhaps, that is why I was resistant at first when cat number nine came into our home. Precious Patience Pearl came in the same way as Co-co, in the arms of my daughter Marnie, but the meow of this cat was much better and different.

In reality it was my wife that had fallen in love with the Pearl and used our daughter to break the ice that had formed in my heart about any cat, especially after the disaster of Co-Co. We have all heard the stories of the cats with nine lives, but this story is about nine cats and what I thought would be our last cat. Scott had moved out, and Marnie was on her way to college so no more cats. Despite her change of personality, the Pearl has become a part of our family. She is Coleen's cat without a doubt, and, despite her independent spirit and odd personality, she is loved. For over five years she ruled the parsonage and had the run of our home without rivals. That is, until cat number ten came along, and now I know "the tenth shall be holy unto the Lord."

As I studied this concept in Leviticus, I came to the determination that what is being written about here is the holy tithe, the tenth. You can't read through the Bible without noticing that God requires the "tenth." Jacob promised the Lord a tenth of what he made if the Lord would bring him back home safely. The Mosaic Law requires the tithe. Jesus and Paul taught this precept, but added that we ought to be willing also to give a sacrifice on top of our tenth. We live in a world that fights constantly against the ill of accumulation. We are forever fighting the urge to gather in, to hoard, to collect, and to store up. One of the best ways to be alert to these dangers is to always remember that the first tenth is God's, and to give it back to Him as quickly and as soon as possible. W. Glyn Evans once wrote, "***The soldier who enters a battle overloaded is already defeated.***" Now when I see Eddie, I think again of the Biblical principle of "ten." I can't hold on to anything that already belongs to God or I will soon idolize it. I must hold on lightly to my possessions unless they hold on tightly to me.

Throughout our seven-year relationship, I have been amazed at all the times Eddie has either in his actions or because of his presence taken me to the Bible, and in the Word I've seen something different; an exhortation, edification, an example. How can the recalling of ten cats remind me of the Ten Commandments? Each cat was distinct and different as are the Ten Commandments. I know now that the Good Lord can bring us through unknown paths of thought, but eventually those thoughts will bring us back to Him and His Word. Eddie is far from holy, he is just a cat, but our relationship has provoked in me a greater relationship with my Lord and Saviour Jesus Christ because I believe that not only is a tenth of what I have His, but the rest as well, whether my time or my money or my talents. Granted, do I think Eddie is a special cat, an once-in-a-lifetime pet? Certainly, but what I love best about my feline friend is the spiritual insights he has opened to me by his presence. They tell me that ten is the number in the Bible of completion. Well, if that be true, then Eddie is my last cat, the finisher of a string of cats that have taught me much, both positively and negatively. So, there you have it, another "meow from the manse!"

Chapter Forty-Five

Go Tell that Old Fox

"And He said unto them, Go ye and tell that fox . . ."
—Luke 13:32

I SIT THIS MORNING in front of my computer with my dear companion Eddie, Eddie, Eddie on my lap. It is a cold second day of February, and Eddie is in from his early morning check of the neighborhood. A recent ice storm has covered everything with a thin coat of frozen water, and I have learned that Eddie doesn't like his feet to get wet or cold. Before he left for his quick romp around the parking lot of the church, I warned him to watch out for the fox.

It might sound strange that we have a fox in the neighborhood seeing we live in a well built-up section of a city. Foxes have been a rare sight in my nearly 21 years in Ellsworth, but recently sightings have become more frequent. Just a few weeks ago our church treasurer called after attending a meeting at the church telling me she had seen a fox run across the street between our house and our neighbor's home across the street. Her concern was Eddie. Just yesterday I was studying at my desk when the phone rang. It was my neighbor Mrs. Hart. She works for a local contractor, and she was calling to warn me that she had just seen a fox run across the street from the cemetery to our back lot. A cat lover, she was concerned about Eddie because she knew he spends a lot of time in that vacant field. What was interesting about our conversation was the added fact that she saw Big Gray, the neighborhood tomcat, chasing the fox. Sometimes your enemy's enemy is your friend! Big Gray and Eddie have always been at each other, as you know from previous devotionals, but just maybe Big Gray has an admirable quality?

In the seven years I have had Eddie I have become amazed just how many people in the church and outside the church have taken a shine to my cat. It seems that everybody is looking after the stray that has come to stay.

Our trips across the street between the parsonage and the church has been witnessed by scores of people, and the arrival of a fox has only caused Eddie's friends to become more vigilant in their watching out for his best interest. As Mrs. Hart and I talked, we both have come to the conclusion the reason we have been seeing a fox so often lately is the arrival of chickens to our community of animals. Our neighbors up the street have started raising chickens, and where there is chicken there will be a fox. I learned that valuable lesson on the family farm in northern Maine in my youth.

During my childhood my father raised chickens for their eggs as well as meat. I don't know how many times I saw my father grab his gun and head out to the chicken coop by the back fence. In the summertime we would put the chickens in an enclosed area behind the old below-ground potato house. It was sheltered just enough so the local fox family could sneak up through the pasture unseen. We would know there was trouble when the rooster and the hens began to make a racket loud enough to raise the dead. More often than not Dad would get there in time because the fox had to find a way through the high wire fence that surrounded the enclosure. There was also a hen house that offered some protection. Despite all our precautions, we would find a hen missing every once and awhile. In the wintertime we didn't have to worry because the chickens were safely housed in a room in the back of our cow barn. It was only in the summer that chicken was on the menu. I also learned in my boyhood sometimes cat was also on that menu.

A few years back I wrote this about my memories of the creature called fox:

> On an early morning run to take a man to the hospital in Bangor for a kidney treatment, I saw a red fox lying in the road on Bridge Hill in Ellsworth. As I continued my travels to Bucksport, I had a chance to remember the beauty of a fox in the wild. The sly fox has earned a reputation for cunning and wit, but my early morning fox hadn't figured on the speed of a passing car or truck. The fox was born for the woods. Its timid and cautious nature serves it well in the fields and forests, but the streets and lanes of a busy city can be very dangerous. My encounters with a live fox have been very few, but each one has been memorable. The first such encounter I remember was during a walk down Salmon Lake Road just below my boyhood home. The red streak was just for a moment, but the vision still lingers to this day. I have since learned that probably the fox was out hunting for food for its young. It was the right time of the year for such a hunt, and I suspect she was looking for some mice in the hay fields along that country lane. I was but a distraction from the

mission she was on. I was not a threat, but the fox was taking no chances with the farmer's son. I had no gun, but she was not in a visiting mood. She was on a quest for supper, not an afternoon social call with me! The next encounter I recall was during a hot August evening after a thunder shower had passed through the homestead. We had just finished supper when Rover, my childhood Eddie, began to bark. His warning directed us to the small chicken coup near the side pasture. As I came around the corner of the woodshed, I saw a flash of red heading down across the back pasture. I only got a glimpse but the sight was clear enough. There in the mouth of the neighborhood fox was one of our newly raised hens. Dad wasn't long behind me with his rifle, and just as suddenly a shot rang out, but the last anyone saw of the wily fox was his tail waving "so long, thanks for supper!" The last sighting of a fox in my boyhood I remember took place on a late autumn hunting trip along the apple tree trail looking for partridge. This was a path I often took after school that ran from behind my home along the lower pasture to a series of apple trees in the back corner, up through the lane that led to the Russell Place to a small orchard on the Blackstone/Dickinson line. More often than not I was in competition with the local fox family for the mouth-watering meat of fresh partridge. Making my way quietly through the trail hoping to find a fat partridge sitting peacefully in a lower branch of some tree, I was watching more for fowl than for fox. I had already bagged a plump partridge below the cow barn when I noticed a movement in the bushes. Hoping it was another partridge, I waited quietly for the sound to expose itself. To my surprise it was a hunting fox, but it was I who startled him. Our eyes met for just a moment, and then he was gone.

As I ponder this morning the two recent sightings of a Maine fox in our neighborhood, I recalled Jesus classic rebuke of King Herod recorded in the Gospel of Luke. Herod had put a price on Jesus' head (Luke 13:31), but Jesus wasn't intimidated by the power of that monarch. I know that Eddie didn't understand my warning about the fox, and, just maybe, his archenemy, Big Gray, has placed a fear into that fox that he has invaded their territory. Whichever situation might develop, I am sure that it is important that Eddie learns the lesson we all must learn as clearly recorded in I Peter 5:8:

> "Be sober, be vigilant; because your adversary the devil, as a roaring lion, walketh about, seeking whom he may devour."

With a lion or a fox there are those that would love to eat us. Eddie would be a good meal for a red fox, but I feel we must stand up against the "foxes" of the world just as Jesus did. We must learn and believe that *"greater is He that is in you, than he that is in the world."* (I John 4:4) Is there a danger out there, just like there is a danger each and every time Eddie goes out into his world? The answer is yes, but we can't be afraid to go out into our world because behind some situation or circumstance the devil may be lurking. Let us like Eddie did this morning venture out into our world aware of the danger, but also fully confident that we will not be devoured if we maintain our vigilant lifestyle. So "go tell that old fox" that you are still here, and that you will not be scared or frightened out of your backyard.

Chapter Forty-Six

Home Alone

"...I sat alone because of thy hand..."

—JEREMIAH 15:17

THE DAY OF THE great test had come. My wife and I were going to leave our two cats home alone for the first time. My wife, Coleen, had a speaking engagement in Canada over Memorial Day weekend at a ladies retreat at Hampton Bible Camp, and since Eddie had come into the manse we had never left our two felines home together. This would determine whether or not Eddie and Pearl could co-exist without help. With a huge bowl of cat food and an even larger bowl of water, Coleen and I locked our two cats into the parsonage. Normally, Coleen's mother would watch them, but on this occasion Opal was going with us. We were only going away for 48 hours so we thought it would be safe to leave them for a couple of days. Oh, to have been a fly on a wall over that 48 hours. I can only imagine what happened when Pearl realized she was alone with Eddie, and Eddie realized he was shut in with the Pearl.

Eddie would have instantly started to pace. Eddie is a pacer by his very nature, especially when he's fenced in. I have come to believe Eddie's theme song is that old cowboy classic "Don't Fence Me In!" If Eddie isn't eating, he is pacing. If Eddie isn't sleeping, he is pacing. We have come to believe this character trait is because of the very dangerous life Eddie use to live before he came to stay in the manse. To show you just how alert Eddie is, yes, nervous, I share an event that took place just last night. Coleen and I were watching the PBS show Nature. It is Eddie's custom to lie on my lap in the evening, and normally while I watch television Eddie sleeps, curled up on his quilt. Eddie had just settled in between my legs facing the television. I thought he was asleep as the program started. It was a documentary on wolverines. Actually, filming wolverines in the wild is very difficult according to the narrator, but somebody had gotten some great shots of a large male running through deep snow. The person filming must have been straight on the wolverine because it looked like the animal was running directly into the camera lens. It was when the wolverine filled the screen that Eddie reared up on his hind legs and made a dash for the back of the couch. Both Coleen and I were startled by Eddie's sudden departure. It was then we realized that Eddie must have been watching the television and his worst nightmare was coming to get him! I got up to find my cat trembling in a corner near the pelt stove. His eyes were wide open, and the hair on his back was sticking straight up. You could see the terror on his face, and his whole demeanor was one of shock and fright. I can't tell you what he was thinking, but I can tell you his actions revealed his dislike of wolverines. Because Eddie was abandoned as a kitten and lived for a number of months on his own in a very rough and dangerous neighborhood, he learned very early to be on "red alert" at all times. Even now, years after those days, he is very vigilant, whether crossing the road, meeting strangers, or seeing strange things. I have watched him slowly and cautiously creep up to an odd shape thinking it might be something that will hurt him. I was not surprised by the wolverine episode as it only invoked in my imagination what he must have gone through that first time we left him alone with Pearl that Memorial Day weekend.

This inner fear was confirmed a few weeks later in another example of sheer terror. Eddie was sleeping on his pillow that I place on the corner of a bookshelf that sits in front of my desk at church. Eddie loves his afternoon naps, and, when he is with me in the office, he curls up while I study, or do office work. On this particular Friday afternoon our church janitor, Steve Wood, was in the church doing his weekly cleaning. After he was through, he came in to say hello. Eddie knows Steve well and was unmoved from his perch as Steve and I talked for a few minutes. Just before Steve left he asked if my wife was home as he had something he wanted to show her. Steve does lawn art as a hobby. He creates images out of wood and especially likes Christmas things. His is a typical Griswold lawn at Christmas time. Because Coleen was away shopping, Steve decided that he should show me his newest creation, a three-foot-tall Rudolph the red nosed reindeer with a red light bulb for a nose. Steve went to his truck to bring the lawn ornament into the office. Eddie was unaware what was about to happen. The minute Steve filled the doorway with his rendition of Rudolph, Eddie was gone. I think he thought that he was being attacked by old Rudolph. It was over an hour later that I finally found Eddie in the back room of the church. Eddie has some deep fears that I am just learning about.

During those 48-hours with the Pearl, Eddie would have first checked all the doors and windows to see that no predators could get at him or his beloved. To this day he still paces through the house until he is confident that his environment is safe. Then Eddie would have started to patrol the fringes of the living room or any room where the Pearl would have been sleeping. One of the interesting events in our lives is when Eddie can't find the Pearl. Often Precious Pearl sleeps in her many hiding places. Eddie can't seem to rest until he is sure where the Pearl is sleeping. Once the perimeter was secure and the Pearl was safe, Eddie would have climbed the stairs leading to the upstairs bedrooms and bathroom. About halfway up he would have stopped to check the front porch. There are two large windows on the south end of the living room which allows Eddie to see anyone or anything coming up the walkway. It is his sentry tower. Coleen tells me sometimes when I go over to the church without him that he sits there watching for my return. (What a friend!)

After Eddie would have made sure the downstairs was safe, he would have gone upstairs to check the three bedrooms. Of course, while Eddie was doing this Pearl would have been sleeping quietly and restfully somewhere without a care in the world. The Pearl has never had sentry duty, and she never will. Hers is a carefree life without any fears or frets. Over the near decade we had Pearl without Eddie, we had left Pearl alone often without mishap or trouble. Pearl was always glad to see us return it appeared, but she was never concerned with staying home alone. She is like the two monkeys—see-no-evil and hear-no-evil. Pearl, unlike Eddie, has no frustrations when she is alone.

After finding the house secure, Eddie would have checked out the food supply. Again we believe this phobia comes from his days alone in the neighborhood not knowing where his next meal was coming from. Since Eddie has come into the manse, he has literally eaten us out of house and home. He appears to have a hollow leg, if not four! When his soft food is gone, he seeks more food from the hard food dish. He is always looking to me for a handout, and more often than not I give it to him. We call them treats. Something the Pearl will never think of doing, too un-lady-like. In the corner of the kitchen near the dryer is a huge crock pot which can hold about ten pounds of cat food. In it Coleen keeps the cat's dry food. It is funny to watch Eddie when we open the lip to either fill it or take from it to fill the dry food dish across the room. It is as if he is thinking it is the mother-load of reserves, and it is ALL his. I suspect Eddie checked it out a time or two just to make sure he had enough food until we returned. On the other hand the Pearl wouldn't have given the food supply a second thought because she has always had enough.

Her only complaint would have been that she wasn't getting her daily supply of 'fish and shrimp', her most favorite soft cat food.

The last great difficulty for our cats, home alone, would be the reality that Eddie wouldn't be going outside. Eddie still loves his freedom to roam despite the dangers that still exist in the neighborhood. He loves the woods behind the church and the yard behind the parsonage. To explore his world is his first love, with the Pearl his second, we think. To be shut in for two days would have been hard on him, but even harder on the Pearl. She still believes in a one-cat world. Her biggest frustration would have been shut up and alone with Eddie. And there is a sense in which Pearl has it right, and Eddie has it wrong. The Bible teaches clearly that "alone" is God's way and "crowds" are man's way. Home alone is a theme scattered throughout the Bible. Jesus taught us this by example:

> "When Jesus therefore perceived that they would come and take him by force, to make him a king, he departed again into a mountain himself ALONE." (John 6:15)

Let us never forget that Jesus went to the cross alone, was buried alone, and rose alone!

Remember, God called Abraham alone (Isaiah 51:2). It is when we are home alone that God seemingly has the best chance to call us, talk to us, and direct us. The world is filling our lives with so much noise we hardly hear God any longer. Ours is a world filled with wolverines charging us and frightening us and causing us to flee. Home alone with nothing but God's voice will bring us into a calmness of heart and soul that has no substitute. Gerhard Tersteegen writes:

> Let Him lead thee blindfold onwards,
> Love needs not to know;
> Children whom the father leadeth
> Ask not where they go,
> Though the path be all unknown
> Over moors and mountains alone.

So, the next time the Good Lord leaves you "home alone," turn off the television and listen carefully for that "still small voice." It might just be the greatest alone moment you ever had. I don't know if Eddie will ever learn this precept, but I am trying to follow the example of Pearl on this one.

Chapter Forty-Seven

Behold the Fowls of the Air

"Behold the fowls of the air: for they sow not, neither do they reap, nor gather into barns; yet your heavenly Father feedeth them. Are ye not much better then they?"

MATTHEW 6:26

I HAVE BEEN ENCOURAGED by a flock of ravens my wife calls "the boys" that have settled into our neighborhood. At times they take me back to the days I watched the raven on the family farm in Perham, Maine. A lone winter chickadee can brighten a dreary winter, and a flock of ravens can add great pleasure to the bird-less season in the city. Just ask my cat Eddie?

I write this devotional about Eddie on a bitter cold day in February. To add to the cold was a phone call from my son in North Carolina. Scott is at Fort Bragg "living the dream" in the United States Army. He called to tell me that he had put his shorts on for the first time this year and was heading out for a round of golf. Talk about rubbing it in! Many simple pleasures depart each and every time winter arrives in Maine: warm mildest winters on record with little snow and few sub-zero days, but, when the songbirds of summer leave, I miss the harmony of the bluebird and blackbird. For some the noise of a flock of ravens is an irritation, but for me it is a sound of the homestead. What they lack in harmony they make up in volume, and volume is what is needed to shout out the sounds of the city. When one looks for delight in a dreary day, a flight of ravens, a swarm of seagulls (my mother-in-law, Opal, throws her old bread out to first come first serve) or flock of ducks (my neighbor, Mr. Jordan, feeds the local mallard family) is all you get. Take yesterday for an example. I was having one of those down-days. Was it cabin-fever? Was it a lack of Vitamin D? Was it the onset of the flu? Was it just one of those days you always get in the middle of winter? I don't know, maybe all the above. Whatever it was, I was lifted from my pit by a conversation I had with my cat Eddie who was responding to the ravens in the backyard of the church.

It was a cloudy morning with a threatening sky. Eddie had taken up a favorite position looking out the ceiling to floor windows in the back corner of the sanctuary. From that perch Eddie can survey the entire back lot and lower parking area of the church property. The acre field, once a building and supply business until it burnt, is now a combination dirt parking lot and a lawn. There are a few trees around half the lot and a small forest area to the back. The ravens often show up to glean what they can find in the open field (at least for this year). When my mother-in-law brings over her trash to put into the church dumpster, she usually throws her scraps into that field. If the ravens are quick, they can get a feed before the seagulls arrive, but if not, they only get scrapes. Eddie enjoys watching them through the double pain windows. Every once in a while I will walk the short distance between my study and the windows to see what Eddie is doing. On this day I saw that his eyes had focused on the monarch of the group, an extra-large raven with a proud and arrogant personality. I had tried to talk to him often on my trips between the church and the parsonage, but with a loudly disapproving "caw" he often interrupted my "good morning." Eddie would hear him as well as he walked beside me to the front of the church.

I was never bothered by the comments of the ravens because I too am plagued with that old-fashion disease of grumpiness in the morning. I, too, woke that morning with a bad case. I got in late last night after an extra, long church meeting which normally winds me up anyway. After such meetings it usually takes me a couple extra hours to unwind no matter how tired I am. With less than my normal nine hours sleep (as I near the end of forty years in the ministry, I have discovered eight hours is no longer enough for me so I try to get in nine and if possible ten) I woke grumpy, something that Eddie never does. Having an early morning appointment at eight o'clock, I was running late when I couldn't even seem to get my clothes on. Because we are in the midst of our coldest time of the year, I had to put on extra everything which only slowed me down. And, needless to say as I left my home with Eddie that morning, I wasn't in a very good frame of mind, and a murmuring and complaining raven only mirrored my mood.

Because my dear wife knows of my morning disposition, she tries to stay clear of me until at least noon, and on this morning nothing seem to help my grumpiness. If anything, everything made it worse. "That's just my nature" has been my excuse for years. I have always been like that even in my boyhood. I just didn't like morning, but, when you are raised on a working dairy farm, mornings are a big part of your day. I remember having to get up early to help with the barn chores. My dog Rover even seemed to cut me a wide birth early in the day, but Eddie never has. I often took my grumpiness out on the cows, the cats, and the chickens. I can just imagine them thinking when I would arrive at the barn, "Watch out, here comes that grump again!" You talk about miserable. If things didn't go just right, I was like a thunder cloud ready to sound off. temperatures, wonderful smells, and inspiring melodies from the local birds. Don't get me wrong because we are enjoying one of the Let a calf stepping on my toe, a cow hitting me in the head with its tail, or a chicken peck me and watch out. The problem is this same grumpy spirit came out on this morning from a raven in a tree. I had a lesson to learn this morning from Eddie, but would I be watchful enough to see it?

I don't know what it is about ravens that draw me to them, but like Eddie I like to watch them. My wife loves to feed the ravens (as she loves to feed me), but the local seagull gang usually ends up with most of the meal she prepares for "the boys." You talk about grumpiness. Choice pieces of bread and biscuits devoured by the coastline bandits and all the while the screaming, the murmuring and complaining from "the boys" would make a grump like me proud. Is that it? The ravens on my boyhood homestead didn't have seagulls to contend with. They were the bullies on the block, and all other birds fled before them. Perhaps, that is why I enjoy watching the ravens now. They are reaping what they sowed, and I must admit I get a bit of pleasure watching them lose. On the farm the ravens were not my favorite bird, but in a bird-less backyard at least they have wings, and I have always been drawn to the underdog. So what was it about Eddie's attitude that morning as he watched the competing flocks of birds in the back lot of the church? To those who have had to face my grumpiness I am sorry, but sometimes I can't keep him in bed. It is sad when the pastor's cat has a better attitude in the morning than the pastor! I have improved over the years, and my wife would say it has a lot to do with Eddie, Eddie, Eddie, my morning companion.

Eddie has taught me more than any other of God's creatures how to have a sweet spirit in the morning even when you're confronting a murmuring seagull, a complaining raven, or a grumpy duck. The fowls of Park Street never seem to get on Eddie's nerves so why should I let the folks of Ellsworth get on mine?

Chapter Forty-Eight

Chicken Concepts from a Cat

> *"O Jerusalem, Jerusalem, thou that killest the prophets, and stoneth them which are sent unto thee, how often would I have gathered the children together, even as a hen gathereth her chickens under her wings, and ye would not!"*
>
> MATTHEW 23:37

ONE OF THE NEW fads of our land is urban farming. I never realized until just recently the desire of some folks to return to a time in our national past where you grew your own food and kept your own livestock. A case in point in Ellsworth has recently highlighted this new trend, and right in the middle of it all is my cat Eddie.

I can't tell you when the chickens arrived in our city neighborhood, but now they are a constant reminder of my days in the Blackstone barnyard of my youth. Our neighbors have decided to try their hand at raising chickens, and my cat Eddie sees them as an invasion of his territory. The very yard we believe he was born in is now housing a chicken coop with a collection of the most beautiful (if chickens can be considered beautiful) chickens I have ever seen. As of yet, I haven't seen them cross the road to the church yard or the parsonage yard, but the other day they got close, too close for Eddie to handle.

We were on our way home for supper after a long day at the church office. As is Eddie's custom, he had spent the day inside the church napping and watching out the floor to ceiling windows in the back of the sanctuary. Spring has come early to the coast of Maine, and periodically during the day Eddie had gone outside to make his rounds. It has become his custom of late to remind me that the sun was setting and, therefore, time to cross the street for first supper (half a can of a favorite soft food before an evening walk around the parsonage yard; then around dark he would have a second supper, the rest of that can of cat food). On this particular late afternoon we had exited the church by the side door that faced the street across from the priest's house (Scotty Mower). There, near the road were four chickens pecking away at the ground. As we reached the curb by Park Street, Eddie must have felt the chickens had overstepped their bounds. Straight across the street Eddie went at about half speed. I believe Eddie is a bit intimidated by the size of these chickens, but his passion for keeping the church yard free from intruders overcame his fears.

Instantly, the grey and black foursome sensed danger and turned tail and headed back to the safety of their yard. I had to smile just a bit as Eddie herded the four across the backyard of Scotty's manse. Back and forth, he went as any good sheep dog would make sure our neighbor's chickens got home. Dashing to and fro, crouching like I use to see my childhood dog Rover do as he brought the cows to the milking shed, I couldn't help but remember a time when chickens were a daily part of my life. On my family's farm in northern Maine in the 1950s and 1960s were many animals. Being primarily a potato and dairy farm, we had plenty of Holstein cows, young and old and just about every age in between. Along with the cattle were a few pigs and what would a farm be without a collection of dogs and cats? By the time I came along in 1951 the horses were gone, but the chickens remained.

I already knew Old MacDonald's Farm sounds before I learned his song in school. One of the first I learned on the Blackstone homestead was "with a cluck, cluck here and a cluck, cluck there, here a cluck, there a cluck, everywhere a cluck, cluck!" I was raised next door to a chicken coop. My closest neighbors were a brood of laying hens. One of my first chores in my boyhood barnyard was caring for those chickens. I still remember tagging along with my father to the small coop next to the potato house. Each spring Dad would buy 100 chicks to be raised through the summer and autumn to be laying eggs by winter. They were placed in the small chicken coop to separate them from the mature laying hens in the main chicken coop located in the cow barn. Either place was filled constantly with "cluck, cluck, cluck" multiplied by a hundred plus.

At first, I was only an observer to the ways of a clucking chicken. I can still see my mother with a wire egg basket over her arm walking into the main chicken coop for her daily gathering of eggs. Mother sold the extra eggs to Holt's Store in the village of Perham. Carefully, she would reach into the individual nests that were located in a series of cubbyholes along the side wall of the coop. Each nest was filled with straw and usually a clucking hen. My nose still tickles as I write this memory with the heavy odor of chicken feathers and chicken manure. If I didn't know it, I think I am about to sneeze with the strong smell of ammonia. Next to a chicken's sound, I remember well that chicken smell.

Reaching her hand into the nest of straw, Mother would bring out a freshly laid egg. If there was a chicken in the nest, Mother would reach her hand under the hen and retrieve the prize egg. Usually, a couple of clucks would seal the deal with Mrs. Hen and Mother. I remember thinking at that time that my mother was the bravest woman in the world for doing that. To a small lad a fully mature laying hen was an intimidating creature. I was bigger, but she was louder. I was taller, but sitting on that high perch you could have fooled me. And then there was that beak and those beady eyes! I still recall the first time my mother taught me how to get an egg out from under a setting chicken. I placed my skinny arm gingerly in front of the nest; suddenly, the soft "cluck, cluck, cluck" was changed to a loud "brraack, brraack, brraack." I remember jumping back as a chill ran up my spine and goose bumps covered the back of my neck. Quickly, my mother reassured me that there was nothing to be afraid of so I slipped my hand under the hen again, and this time I came out with my first picked egg. "Cluck, cluck, cluck, to you," I said.

As I watched Eddie return from his expedition across the street to confront his new neighbors, I recalled Jesus' statement recorded at the head of this "meow from the manse." Jesus must have had experiences with chickens as he makes an analogy of a mother hen that tucks a whole brood of chicks under her wings for safety. How he wished he could do the same thing with the inhabitance of Jerusalem, but they refused. Luke also records this declaration of Jesus (Luke 13:34) with the same sad "ye would not!" As Eddie reached the curb with a proud "meow, meow, meow" that I interpreted to mean "I showed those chickens who was boss," I thought of what I hadn't heard as yet from my neighbor's chickens; no "cock-a-doodle-do." Eddie and I had both heard plenty of cluck, cackle, and chuckle, but no "cock-a-doodle-do." Plenty of chickens, but no rooster! That day overlooking Jerusalem Jesus was a rooster calling His chicks to safety, something I believe Jesus wants us to be and do.

Having been a preacher now for well over half of my life, I have a hard time not using illustrations in my sermons or in my writings about what happened during my farmyard days, and, as you know now, my days with Eddie. As you can see, every event, even encounters with chickens have a spiritual overtone with me. Easter has just passed, and once again I recall Peter's lesson from a male chicken (the cock). (Matthew 26:34) Interestingly, all four Gospels record this story in Mark 14:30, Luke 22:34, and John 13:38. Many wonderful concepts and wise precepts can be gleaned from a "cock-a-doodle do."

1. The rooster rises early to use his God-given talent for crowing. How important it is for us to also exercise our Spirit-given gifts every day; the earlier the better! (I Corinthians 12)

2. The rooster doesn't stop crowing because he can't sing like a canary. How very important it is for us to tell and sing the message of God's love whether we have a good voice or not. A warning is more often heard by a sharp shout than a sweet song! (Psalms 100:1-2)

3. The rooster enthusiastically and energetically cries out whether he is praised or not. God is looking for those of us that will earnestly tell and fervently talk of the coming dawn, a dawn that could be for the listener their "day of salvation." (II Corinthians 6:2).

4. The rooster awakens sleepers, a very unpopular thing to do, but also very necessary. We would prefer to stay asleep and so it is with a world asleep in their sins. They need our warning that "the day of the Lord" is at hand and judgment isn't far behind!(I Thessalonians 5:1-8)

5. The rooster is the proclaimer of good news, the arrival of a new day with great opportunities for good. The rooster's motto must be *"This is the day which the Lord has made; we will rejoice and be glad in it."* (Psalms 118:24) Day brings with it a privilege to work for the Lord. We need to work for the night is coming when no man will work, or "crow!" (John 9:4)

6. The rooster is dependable and persistent in his task. Spreading the good news is not a once a week job or once a lifetime occupation, but a daily duty that must be faithfully seen to and through. (I Corinthians 15:1-3)

7. The rooster never murmurs or complains about having to do the same common call every morning. Telling "the old, old story" has become trying to some. There are even others that would change the "crow" of the Christian. Only when the Good Lord changes the crow of the cock will the call of the Christian be changed. (Hebrews 13:8)

It is still amazing the things you think about on a walk home with your cat and a chance encounter with a few chickens!

Chapter Forty-Nine

The Life of an Animal

"A righteous man regardeth the life of his beast . . ."
—Proverbs 12:10

Last week was a sad week in the life of the Emmanuel Baptist Church. We had two deaths in the family. Now, I know at first you might think that two of our parishioners had passed, but they were not members of the church! You might even think I am writing of two family members of individuals connected to our fellowship, but once again you would not be correct. I know this might seem strange, but I am recording this "meow from the manse" to pay tribute to two dogs that had to be put down last week by their owners, Amanda and Austin.

Twenty years ago, even eight years ago (before I got Eddie), if you would have told me that I would be recording the death of an animal as a spiritual lesson I would have told you how crazy you were. However, over the last few years I have come to a different understanding to the proverb I have printed above. That change in theology is because of my cat Eddie and the memory of an old friend as was demonstrated by two couples this week. Solomon was right; righteous people do regard the life and death of their pet. Perhaps, for you to understand why Amanda and Austin were so special I need you to know who these dogs were and the affect they had on their owners.

Amanda you know or at least you have seen her name in these series of challenges before. Amanda was the seeing-eye dog of Michael Griffin, a man blind since early adulthood. Amanda is the only dog I have had attend my church services in nearly 40 years of pastoring. That alone made her unique and special to me. She was a perfect lady at all times as she came into our sanctuary over the last few years directing Michael to his pew. As we sang, worshiped, prayed, and I preached, Amanda remained quiet and reverent under the pew. She was kind and gentle with the church children who loved her. How many get to pat and play with a dog in church? Only once do I remember a bark coming from Amanda, and that was on an occasion when she feared that somebody would step on her. I took it as did the others in the congregation as an "amen" rather than a bark!

About six months ago Amanda stopped coming to church. Her health was in decline (nearing 14), and Michael now had Valerie to help him around, an old love from high school that had come back into his life. We missed Amanda, but we understood why she was no longer attending services. It was a sad day when we learned a few weeks ago that there was the possibility that Amanda would have to be put down. The shock to Michael was great. This was only his second seeing-eye dog. I will never forget what Michael told me after I heard of his decision to put Amanda out of her misery. He told me that he had vowed that he would never get attached to another dog after he had put his first seeing-eye dog down. He told me he broke that vow two weeks after he got Amanda. Now you know how difficult it was for Michael and Valerie to take Amanda to the vet last Thursday. Little did I know until last Sunday that at the same time Amanda was breathing her last, another familiar dog connected to the church was also being put to sleep.

Austin was the family dog of Mike and Debra Hangge. To my knowledge Austin never came to church or was ever in the church building like Amanda. Austin was still a figure in our lives with Mike and Debra. We have been close over the nearly 21 years I have been their pastor. Our connection didn't start with Austin, but rather fishing for Mike and me and making cards for Coleen and Debra. They have been to our house numerous times for meals, and we to their house. For over 15 years a constant figure around their table has been their dog Austin, a friendly dog and a wonderful companion. Austin has been everywhere with Mike and Debra including many trips into the North Maine Woods. I can still see the lad begging for food at the table. Despite the fact Austin had gone deaf and blind over the last few years he was still living a relatively good life with plenty of care and love. Only recently had his general health declined resulting in that difficult decision. Late Sunday night Coleen and I took Mike and Deb out to our favorite pizza place to remember Austin. As we talked around the table, it was as if they had lost one of their kids (they have three and three grandchildren). It was then I remembered my words to Michael. I understand what you're going through because I once had a pet like Amanda and Austin, and his name was Rover.

As a country preacher (Mike is my only parishioner that calls me "preacher"), I have had to deal with death since I first took on the responsibility of pastor. For some this reality of life is difficult and painful, but I learned at a very early age that death was a daily part of life, no matter how sorrowful. Being raised on a working dairy farm, I was exposed to death through the animals on the homestead. Part of my childhood was spent in long hours of feeding, cleaning out, and milking Holstein cows. Besides the cows there were pigs, chickens, dogs, and cats, and then there were the wild animals that we saw on a daily bases. I was surrounded by creatures that lived among us and with us and periodically died. I learned well, at a very early age, not to get attached. I have only broken that rule twice, but how do you not get attached to a dog like Rover or a cat like Eddie?

Rover's body was clothed in black fur with the occasional spot of white. He was a mixture of collie, German shepherd, and maybe a few other breeds mixed in. He had the strength and speed of the shepherd, but the kindness and gentleness of the collie. He had a long pointed nose and a soft appealing face, but mischief danced in his eyes. Though there were always a few dogs on the homestead, Rover became my dog. Whether roaming in the openness and vastness of the pasture land or walking in the blossoms and beauty of the potato land, Rover was by my side (he was my first Eddie). He loved doing anything and everything with me, though most of the time he was more of a hindrance than a help. Rover liked gathering eggs, or so he said, but I knew he loved chasing chickens. Besides chickens he loved chasing cats and cows and anything else that moved fast, including cars. I remember the first time that pain of loss came when Rover got hit by a passing car. I thought I lost him that day, but God was gracious, and Rover survived to walk with me a few more years.

I don't know about others, but since Eddie came into my life I have thought long and hard about my only "best friend" as a boy. Amanda and Austin passing have provoked me to write this eulogy for Rover:

> Rover was a farm dog with a midnight black coat. He was everybody's dog, but he was my boyhood friend. He was such a best friend I never replaced him for nearly forty years (until Eddie, Eddie, Eddie came along). Rover was an once-in-a-lifetime dog. There was no freshly-made pine box for my friend when he died. There were no graveside spectators except my Dad; I didn't even attend. Those were the days when children were not allowed at funerals, grandfathers or family pets (I still haven't forgiven my parents for not allowing me to go to the funeral of my grandfather Barton or my dog Rover). Death was dealt with by not dealing with it. It was just another day on the homestead, and animals die all the time on a dairy farm. It was not the first animal to be put down, but Rover was different, at least to me.

Rover was "just a dog," a crossbreed, a mutt, a mongrel, but he was the best of the best to me. Being a dog Rover knew of no hatred, or envy, or jealously, or evil, but I'm convinced he knew of unselfish companionship and complete loyalty and undying love. Rover was a friendly dog, except towards passing cars. Rover liked people and other dogs and found neither breed offensive. A social dog, Rover was always about proper greeting no matter who came into the barnyard. A vigorous wagging of his long black tail was his handshake, his wave, his welcome to neighbor or stranger. Rover lived a good long life for a dog. His only mistake was getting hit by a passing car which didn't take his life, but, as we learned later, would shorten his time with me. The sum of Rover's life can be the value I place on the time he still walks with me in the meadows of my mind. If life itself can be measured by the contribution one gives to the life of another, then Rover contributed much to my life. Here I am, nearly a half century later, and the memory of that farm dog is still fresh and the separation still painful. I still mourn his departure and desire to hear him bark again.

To this day I still hear the mourning in the voice of Michael and Mike over the loss of their Rover. I am man enough to tell you that a tear still comes to my soul every time a righteous man regards the life of his beast in death.

Chapter Fifty

Sun on Your Face

"The Lord make his face shine upon thee, and be gracious unto thee."
—Numbers 6:25

Ask my wife, ask my kids, ask my closest friend, and they all will tell you that I am not a "morning person." I don't know what it is, but morning is the tough part of the day for me. I have come to believe that you are born that way. But there is one joy in the morning that I do enjoy and, sure enough, so does my cat Eddie.

I might have never found this pleasure if I hadn't been raised on a working dairy and potato farm in northern Maine. If I had been raised in a city, I probably would have slept through all the sunrises of my life; that is, until Eddie came into my life. Rarely does a farm boy get to sleep in as there were cows to milk and chickens to feed and wood to be brought in from the woodshed. The day always began early on the farm, more often than not, before the sun got up. Like Job, ". . .I beheld the sun when it shined. . ." (Job 31:26)

The sunrises I remember most were the ones I saw from the old milking shed located less than a mile from my parent's house. This is where we milked the Holstein herd in the summer and fall. It was more in the autumn when the sun wasn't rising as early that I watched the first light of the dawn making its way over the hill to the east. The bright hue of gold and orange would blend with the changing colors of the trees reflected on the ridge we called the "Sugar Woods." Sometimes the light show was so heavenly that I couldn't blink lest I missed the flash of an unknown color. Since Eddie came into my life, I, too, have noticed his love of the early morning sun and the late afternoon setting sun.

Unlike me, Eddie is an early riser, especially if the sun is out. Normally, just at daybreak, Eddie will climb the stairs from the living room and get into the window over my bed. If it is an overcast day, like it was this morning, Eddie will curl up on the window sill and go back to sleep for a bit longer. But on those clear mornings, when the early morning light invades the backyard, Eddie will become an alarm clock with a multitude of meows. If I don't get up immediately and let him out, I will be bugged every few minutes with a renewed cry to "let me out!" Sometimes, the need is a bathroom break (despite three litter boxes in the basement, Eddie still prefers the "out-house"), but more often than not it is to be outside when the sun comes up over the city skyline.

When I finally get up and get going in the morning, I usually find Eddie sitting in the sun under the porch furniture. We walk over to the church together where I settle into my office while Eddie heads directly to the floor-to-ceiling picture windows in the back of the church. On those cold winter days he enjoys the heat coming through those windows. On other days he seems to just enjoy the sun on his face as he watches over the backyard of the church. I catch him moving from spot to spot as the sun makes its run over Ellsworth creating a different sunny place on the sanctuary carpet. I can't say that Eddie is a sun worshiper; I think he just loves the pleasant heat it gives. As the day lengthens and the sun switches to the back side of the church, Eddie moves into the hallway and enjoys the sun coming through the glass in the side door. This is where I usually pick him up when I exit the church for the parsonage across the road in the late afternoon. You would think Eddie's times with the sun would be over, but they are not. If Eddie loves a good sunrise, he loves a good sunset even better.

Rare is the day Eddie doesn't spend his last moments outside in the backyard of the parsonage. He loves nothing better than to roam the small yard with a constant eye towards the setting sun. Eddie's worst season is when the sun fights to stay up past four in the afternoon. For Eddie his winter sunsets are often viewed from the dining room window in the parsonage. Remember, Eddie loves warmth. There is little heat in a mid-January afternoon on the coast of Maine. That is why the arrival of spring has ushered in Eddie's favorite seasons. Eddie has a curfew (dusk), and he is very faithful to coming in when the sun sets. There have been those odd times he has gotten caught up in some mission (which usually involves the local squirrel family), but when the sun goes down Eddie comes in!

The point for this "meow from the manse" hit me the day before yesterday as I caught Eddie again with his face toward the sun as I met him on the parsonage porch. With the sun on his face, Eddie was enjoying an early morning nap as he patiently waited for me to make an appearance. It was then I remembered the benediction the Lord gave to Moses to give to Aaron whereby he would bless the people of God:

> "*On this wise ye shall bless the children of Israel, saying unto them, The Lord bless thee, and keep thee: The Lord MAKE HIS FACE SHINE UPON THEE, and be gracious unto thee: The Lord lift up his countenance upon thee, and give thee peace. And they shall put my name upon the children of Israel; and I will bless them.*" (Numbers 6:23-27)

As Eddie turns his face to the sun throughout his day, from the beginning to the ending of his day, so, too, should we turn our faces toward God, the Son? I have always loved the words in the old church chorus that says "Turn your eyes upon Jesus, look full into His wonderful face, and the things of earth will grow strangely dim, in the light of his glory and grace."

The more I have pondered my cat's affection for the sun, and the more I have searched the scriptures to understand the spiritual significance of "the Son on my face," I found this verse of exhortation from Isaiah:

> "*Arise, shine; for Thy light is come, and the glory of the Lord is raised upon thee.*" (Isaiah 60:1)

As the sun is to Eddie so the Son should be to us. There was a time as Matthew described it that "*...His face did shine as the sun...*" (Matthew 17:2) John who was there to witness that amazing transfiguration of Christ would write this in his first epistle:

> "*Again, a new commandment I write unto you, which thing is true in Him and in you: because the darkness is past, and the true Light now shineth.*" (I John 2:8)

There is no doubt in my mind what John was referring to in his Gospel when he wrote this about Christ:

> "*In Him was life; and the life was the light of men. And the light shineth in darkness; and the darkness comprehended it not.*" (John 1:4-5)

Today, we have so many who do not know what it means to bask in the warmth of the light of Christ; every day, every minute of every day, feeling that light shining on our face as we look upward into the face of God. I am mindful again of the wonderful truth I saw in the actions of my cat, but I am more blessed by this message of John:

> "*This then is the message which we have heard of Him, and declare unto you, that God is Light, and in Him is no darkness at all. If we say that we have fellowship with Him, and walk in darkness, we lie, and do not the truth: but if we walk in the light, as He is*

in the light, we have fellowship one with another and the blood of Jesus Christ His Son cleanseth us from all sin." (I John 1:5-7)

Will you today "turn your eyes upon Jesus?" Take again this admonition from Eddie and experience the supernatural sunrises and sunsets in your relationship with the Son!

Chapter Fifty-One

Max: The Disabled Dog

"And the Lord said unto him, who hath made man's mouth?
Or who maketh the dumb, or deaf, or the seeing, or the blind?
Have not I the Lord?

—Exodus 4:11

EVER SINCE WE MOVED Eddie's sister (Pearl) into our home thirteen years ago, I have had a renewed interest in the animals that have come into the neighborhood. That perspective has only been heightened with the arrival of Eddie into our house. Because Precious Patience Pearl rarely interacts with other animals their encounters were few and far between, but with Eddie being an outdoor cat some entertaining events have happened as you have already read. I have spoken of some of these creatures in other "meows from the manse," like "the boys," a flock of crows, "the brothers," a pair of gray squirrels (they seem to have gotten a sister or two over the years), "Woody," our neighborhood woodchuck, "Big Grey," the resident tomcat bully, "Willy," the Florida transplant cat; then there are the dogs, most notably "Tucker" and "Max". (At the writing of this Eddie story a new dog has come to the neighborhood, Marius, a white poodle named after a Roman general, and he barks orders like a Roman general. Who knows what adventures Eddie and Marius will have?) Tucker was only with us a short time, an aging brown Lab who came with his owners about a year ago. Eddie liked Tucker because he was mild and mellow, but Tucker died a few months ago so they had few chances to really get to know each other, but this is not true of Max.

A few years back as my wife and daughter were enjoying another wonderful summer evening on the parsonage porch, a new neighbor took her dog for a walk. Since our arrival in Ellsworth in 1991, the yellow house across

MAX: THE DISABLED DOG

the street had seen four residents. The former parsonage for the Congregation Church in town had been sold after the pastors of the church wanted to own their own home, a common practice today. My wife and I have lived in parsonages for 35 of the 41 years we have been in the ministry. Once the last congregational minister to live in the house left, the home has been owned by three other couples, all good neighbors, but the current neighbors have brought a change to the neighborhood. I shared recently about their chickens, but the biggest change they have brought is Max, currently the only resident dog left on School Street, and a very special dog is Max.

Over the years I have wondered why they didn't name School Street Parsonage or Manse Street. Rare do you find three parsonages in a cluster like we had at one time. Beside the congregational parsonage is the Roman Catholic manse (Scotty Mowers home), and our home for the last 23 years is directly across the street, the Baptist manse. Now there are only two, but for those of us who remember, the yellow house just across and up the street will always be a manse. So, now I must introduce you to "the Max of the Manse" and the lesson he has taught me through my cat Eddie who once lived in that manse, but was abandoned by the former owner. Their loss was my gain, as with Max!

As our new neighbor turned the corner from her driveway to the sidewalk, I left the porch with Eddie for the Emmanuel Baptist Church building, also across the street. I didn't take notice at first of the new couple until we met at the corner of Park and School. I noticed immediately the greyhound-type dog only had three legs. Eddie was a bit shy and maybe a bit scared because of the size of the huge black creature hopping down the sidewalk. His master had Max on one of those new extending ropes so he was totally under control. Besides, he didn't seem to be an aggressive dog, just happy to be out for a walk. He was pulling hard seemingly desiring to move more quickly than he was allowed. Despite the dog's handicap, he was moving quite well as we rendezvoused at the corner. Because I had yet to meet this new neighbor, I stopped to introduce myself and Eddie.

Eddie by this time had returned to the porch steps under the shadow of my wife and daughter thinking this would be perfect protection if this new monster should attack. I noticed immediately that I was facing a friendly dog as his nose smelled me, and his carefree wagging of his tail gave no air of danger. Eddie, however, wasn't convinced yet. The lady spoke quickly to reassure me that Max was harmless, and I reached down to pat his head as I made small conversation with his owner. Mrs. Marcozion told me that Max liked cats and that my cat had nothing to fear. Eddie seemed to sense that Max was not an enemy, and he came down the walkway to the street. We exchanged the names of our animals and made small talk for a few minutes before she moved on down the street with Max, and I headed for the church with Eddie. In that short time I was able to understand the reason Max only had three legs.

Max had developed a medical problem that eventually required the removal of his leg to save his life. It had been a recent development just before the Marcozions had moved into the neighborhood. Max was still adjusting to walking on three legs, but exercise was important and we would be seeing them often out walking. Mrs. Marcozion had even asked if she might walk him in the church lot below the church building to which I said anytime. With no danger to Eddie, I was confident that in time the two would be friends and, sure enough, that has been the case. Often, Eddie goes over to his old lot to explore and no doubt encounters with Max have happened. We, too, have met crossing the street as we did on that first evening, and now Eddie will stand his ground, and Max will sniff Eddie. I don't know how Eddie sees Max with his disability, but there seems to be no reaction between how he treats Tucker or Max. They seem to be one in the same with him, and therein lies our lesson for this devotional.

I have believed for most of my life the doctrine explained in the verse that lies at the head of this article. The context is in Moses' encounter with the Lord at the burning bush. Moses is trying to get out from under the assignment the Lord has given him concerning the deliverance of the children of Israel from Egypt. Moses makes the excuses that he can't speak well enough to do the job when in reality Moses was a great speaker. According to Stephen's sermon, before Moses fled Egypt *"Moses was learned in all the wisdom of the Egyptians, and was MIGHTY IN WORDS and in deeds."* (Acts 7:22) It was then the Lord revealed an insightful insight into the source of disabilities and handicaps: they all come from God, but why? We would have to wait for the coming of Jesus, the Son of God, for that answer. In the story of the blind man of Jerusalem this concept was added to the doctrine of the disabled man or animal:

> *"And His disciples asked him, saying, Master, who did sin, this man, or his parents, that he was born blind? Jesus answered, neither hath this man sinned, nor his parents: but that the works of God should be made manifest in him."* (John 9:2-3)

So there you have it! Why the cripple, the blind, the lame, the deaf, the dumb, and any other handicap or disability you can think of? God's glory!

I have for nearly 45 years now visited the disabled wherever I can find them. I am just finishing nearly twenty years at Birchwood Living Center, a home in Ellsworth for extremely disabled persons. If I can be honest, it is one of the greatest ministries I have had over the years.

All the current residents of the home have been disabled since birth. Only a few can even speak, most have mental and physical disabilities beyond description, but like Max they live on (one lady has been there for as long as I have been going). We know from the Bible they were born this way because of the will of God (Exodus 4), and they remain this way to the glory of God (John 9), but to some what good are they? They are a burden, a bother, and blight on society. I still remember when the Lord showed me the blessing of these people. Jesus was talking about the great judgments when the sheep (believers-bema seat judgment; II Corinthians 5:10) and the goats (unbelievers-great white throne judgment; Revelation 20:11) are brought before the throne of God. Jesus spoke of it this way:

> *"For I was hungred, and ye gave me meat: I was thirsty, and ye gave me drink: I was a stranger, and ye took me in: naked, and ye clothed me: I was sick, and ye visited me: I was in prison, and ye came to unto me.* [There are many kinds of prisons and many kinds of nakednesses and many kinds of hungers and thirst and many kinds of sicknesses and who is a stranger more than a disabled, handicap person?] *Then shall the righteous answer him, Lord, when saw we thee a hungered, and fed thee? Or thirsty, and gave thee drink? When saw we thee a stranger, and took thee in? Or naked, and clothed thee? Or when saw we thee sick, or in prison, and came unto thee? And the King shall answer and say unto them, Verily I say unto you, INASMUCH AS YE HAVE DONE IT UNTO ONE OF THE LEAST OF THESE MY BRETHREN, YE HAVE DONE IT UNTO ME!"* (Matthew 25:35-40)

As Eddie goes and visits Max every once in a while, I go and visit Grace and Roland and Brenda and Merle and Dennis and Nicky and Dawn and Terry and Mark, and numerous others over the years. If a cat doesn't let a disabled dog keep him away, should we pull back from a disabled individual? They are the very ones we should be helping and visiting. Is there a Max in your neighborhood you should get to know?

Chapter Fifty-Two

An Angel Unawares

"Be not forgetful to entertain strangers: for thereby some have entertained angels unawares."

—Hebrews 13:2

It wasn't until I was reading a book by a favorite author, W. Phillip Keller that I was provoked to reexamine an old familiar verse, the scripture I have printed for you at the head of this chapter. Was the small, stray cat that wandered into my life over seven years ago a heavenly visitor? Was the poor, paranoid tomcat that entered my wife's and my lives one late autumn day an angel in disguise? Was the terrified, timid tabby really a messenger from on high?

Eddie, Eddie, Eddie is certainly a cat in every sense of the word, but just how he came into my life is still a mystery after all these years; perhaps, the reason I can share these thoughts. Was he accidentally left by someone traveling through Ellsworth? Was he dropped off deliberately by one of those cruel caretakers of cats that just didn't want to care for him any longer? Was he left behind when our neighbors changed homes? Maybe I will never know or maybe there is a higher power involved in this cat story, a greater force than I first imagined. Wherever the source, it was a special day, the day Eddie came into Coleen's and my life. We didn't know at first the full impact Eddie would have in the manse and even in the church we pastor. (I have a home-schooling family in my congregation that is using these chapters about Eddie for their devotional times.) As the years have passed so has our insight into the purpose of Eddie, and the appreciation we have for him has only grown since he came into our care and concern.

The first revelation came when we realized just how loving Eddie can be; almost an unusual, unnatural affection, far beyond the average cat. Of course, we are comparing him to Precious Pearl and the other cats we have had in our marriage. From almost the first day we captured his trust for us, this bundle of fur has displayed a genuine gratitude and an amazing appreciation for what we do for him; most cats show no thanks at all. He has been the only cat that has ever crawled up into my lap and desired just to be near me. When Eddie curls up in my lap, he revels, desires, and asks to be stroked. He will lift his chin and beg me to rub him from top to bottom. He will close his eyes as if he is in heaven. Tickle his ears or caress his back and he will respond with loud purrs that can be heard all over the manse. A case in point took place just last night. My dear wife had been overcome by the flu virus of 2013. Many in the Church have had it, and it finally arrived at the manse on Monday, our day for AWANA, the youth program of our fellowship. Coleen is the kindergarten to second grade teacher, but she was so sick she couldn't go to the meeting. I filled in for her, and, when I got home, I still found her in bed trying to sleep the illness off. I decided it was best to sleep in our spare bedroom and hopefully miss getting the flu. Eddie has often slept with me, but rarely when Coleen is in bed. It has been awhile, but about five this morning Eddie discovered me in our guest room, and then it happened.

Eddie's love of being with me has only intensified over the years (as I write this chapter he is sitting on a pillow on my desk). Wherever I am he wants to be, whether church, yard, my chair watching television, car, wherever and whenever, including the spare bedroom early in the morning. This morning it was a cold nose and a soft meow as if to say, "Hey, what are you doing here, want to play?" that woke me up. He immediately began to paw at the blankets until I let him into my warm bed. All the while his little motor was purring on all cylinders. In and out, purring up a storm, as I tried to get back to sleep. I had had a long day on Monday with a funeral of my boyhood neighbor, Emma McDougal. She was one hundred years old when she died, and her middle son was my childhood best friend. We hadn't seen each other since 1969 (44 years; and what a reunion we had!), but Eddie wasn't about to let me go back to sleep until we had some play time, despite the fact I was still exhausted from a morning of study, an afternoon of a funeral, a hospital visitation, and an evening of AWANA. Hide and seek, touching noses, and plenty of rubbing and patting (my wife calls loving) was necessary to get Eddie to finally settle down. When he did, he curled beside me and went fast asleep for the next three hours. When I finally woke up, there was Eddie by my side.

Eddie came into my life at a time of great sorrow. In January of the year of his arrival my wife was afflicted with breast cancer. As I write, the eighth anniversary of one of the worst days of my life has come. On Sunday Coleen and I visited the new and improved Mary Dow Clinic where we spent many a day during the eight-month battle with one of life's most dreaded diseases.

Seeing the ladies that helped us both so much brought back terrible as well as blessed memories. (As I told one of the ladies Sunday, "The best/worst experience of my life!"). It is inevitable that when family is tried by cancer that here are great gaps of grief that come. What helps most is the support of others, and we had plenty of support from the wonderful professionals at the Mary Dow Clinic. Many wounds are the result of cancer, but there are those the Good Lord brings into your life that heal the hurt and bind the bruises and wrap the wounds with ointment of tears and bandages of trust. My own belief is that we need something as strong as the comforting presence of the Spirit of God Himself to finally get us through. So with the combination of God's grace and the gracious help of others we finally endured the eight months of checkups, tests, examinations, three major operations, and seven painful and sickly chemo treatments. Despite the fact that the medical aspect of the battle was over, there was still years of reexaminations, checkups, follow-ups, and false scares ahead. Annual monograms and monthly self-examinations, fearing and wondering if they got it all, would it return? It was into that period that God in His wise providence injected a feline named Eddie. Coleen's chemo doctor had moved away and there were no more trips to the Mary Dow Clinic; and if Coleen's friends and family had moved on to other things, so had I. I was still concerned, but who would continue to comfort, vitalize, and carry me through the years ahead; a heavenly angel in the form of a tiger cat with a brown chin?

I began to see the animals in the Bible in a totally different light as from time to time God seemed to bring into an empty space the life form of an animal to help a saint through a terrible time. It was not by chance or circumstance that ravens became Elijah's only friends at the Brook Cherith (I Kings 17:5-6). How he must have greeted them with each meal, and how he must have seen them as divine chefs sent directly from God; something to talk to, to be around. Why didn't Balaam understand that his donkey was his friend, not his enemy as he charged (Numbers 22:22-35) foolishly? Interestingly, there is an angel in that story (Numbers 22:25), and what of the angel that fed Elijah after Mount Carmel (I Kings 19:5-7)? Was it not a dove that came on Jesus at his baptism (Matthew 3:16)? Granted, it was the Spirit of the Lord, and I will not establish any doctrine on such illustrations, but for me it isn't beyond the Lord's wonderful graciousness to bring into our lives one of his beloved creatures to bring back joy after a joyless period in our lives!

Take it from me, from my own personal perspective of the Creator God that it was His divine will to send Eddie to me and my wife at a time when we needed an object to distract us from the months and months, years and years that is the post-cancer experience. I learned that the unknown, uncertain, unseen is much more difficult than the known and certain and seen.

From the fear of death by cancer of my wife, God surprised me with the daily delight of Eddie. When I see him, I smile; when I hear him, I laugh; when I am with him, I feel joy; and when I touch him, I know God is near! Such emotion and therapy is a blessing beyond purchase or price. Eddie has been a bonus in my life. Before Eddie I had a great life, and, if he had never come into my life, I still would have been blessed. Eddie has been for me the cherry on top of the banana split; a wonderful tonic, a glorious addition, a heavenly visitation from a stranger that has filled my life with such pleasures that I can only explain it through the reality of time. Just maybe, Phillip Keller was right, Eddie "has come to us as an angel in disguise!"

Chapter Fifty-Three

A Christmas Miracle

"... Lord watch between thee and me, when we are absent one from another."

—Genesis 31:49

I AM PONDERING AGAIN the history of my relationship with Eddie this morning. I have mentioned before the timing of Eddie coming into my life and the miracle that happened that turned this stray cat into my "best friend." They say that the dog is man's best friend, but for me it is a cat. Could I share with you first a 1991 Christmas miracle in my life and then apply it to my 2005 Christmas "cat" miracle?

One of the marvelous advantages of intercession is the long distant effect of such supplications. We don't need to be living in the same community to see answers to prayer. Praying for loved ones that live elsewhere is as easy as praying for loved ones you live with. A case in point is an event that took place unexpectedly just before Christmas 1991 and the answer to prayer that was the result. I wrote about this happening in a short story I called "A Christmas Miracle."

> A quick glance at my daily diary this morning brought to mind this Blackstone homestead memory. It was five years ago today a Christmas miracle took place on the farmstead of my birth that I will never forget or forget to thank the Good Lord for.
>
> My family and I were just beginning our first winter in Ellsworth, Maine, at the Emmanuel Baptist Church when a phone call came from my hometown of Perham, Maine. Despite the two hundred miles between phone receivers, I felt I was there as my mother began to explain how my father had nearly been killed by a falling tree. A man in his late 60s at the time, Dad and my brother Jay were cutting fire wood in the forest near my boyhood home. Just before they broke for lunch, Dad had

logged a large spruce into a stand of trees. Leaving the situation until after lunch, Dad and Jay were hoping that the wind or gravity might bring the tree down before they returned. While Dad was eating, Jay called from his home telling Dad that he had to go to town and pick up a piece for some farm equipment he was repairing. He also asked dad to stay put until he returned and that under no circumstance was he to try to dislodge the tree himself. Dad had taught Jay well! However, after Dad's traditional midday nap was over and Jay hadn't returned, Dad headed back into the woods alone. Arriving back at the spot of their morning labors, Dad discovered that the stubborn tree was still lodged. Despite having preached to us for years about never working in the woods alone, Dad preceded to get his hammer and wedge to knock the spruce loose. Carefully examining the situation, Dad thought he had plenty of room to fell the hooked tree without any apparent danger to himself. Placing the wedge into the partly sawed-through tree trunk, he began to strike the wedge with his big hammer. The blows fell hard and true, and it wasn't long before the tall tree began to groan and crack. Suddenly, everything that could go wrong went wrong. In a split second Dad realized he was in trouble and began to flee the base of the tree, down through a small dip in the terrain to a safe spot, or so he thought. Despite not taking time to turn around, his years of experience in the woods told him the tree had given way, but was falling the very way he had chosen for his escape route. He moved as swiftly as possible over the uneven ground, but deep in his heart he knew he could never outrun a falling timber. The next thing Dad said he remembered was being on the ground with the upper section of the tree across his leg. Fearing the worst, he began to examine himself. Miraculously, the tree had come down over a small hole in the ground just at the spot Dad had gotten to before he was struck. Dad was able to pull his leg out of the hole and hobble to his pickup. Returning to the farm house, he told mother his tale of escape and immediately she rushed him to the hospital to be examined. When Dad's winter clothes were removed, the doctor discovered that Dad's back was one big black and blue mark. The tree had given Dad's back a glancing blow. My father had escaped death by a matter of inches. When the rest of my family heard Dad's story, we decided that we had all received our Christmas present for that year, and that our years of praying for one another had been answered on that day! Dad was bruised and sore for a few days, but suffered no ill effects from his close encounter with a stubborn spruce. At the time of the writing of this "meows from the manse," my father is still alive (he would die in 2017). The Good Lord in His grace has given him twenty-one more Christmases with his family. James 5:16 exhorts us to "pray one for another." I have known of this command most of my life. I was taught as a child to pray for my family members, and I continue this practice to this day. What I learned with my father's miraculous deliverance was that we never know when our loved ones need us to pray for them. Little did any of us know on that December day that Dad would be alone and in a very dangerous situation before the day was over? He would even tell you that he did everything wrong, and that there was no way he should have walked out of those woods under his own power, yet he did. Why? Some would say that it was "luck" that saved him. Neither I, nor my father believes in "luck." Some would say that it was just "chance" that Dad had gotten to a piece of land that would allow the tree to hit the ground, but miss coming down straight on my Dad's leg. Chance and circumstance are only members of the "lucky" family. Had I prayed that morning for the Good Lord to save my Dad from a falling tree? No. Who could have known? Yet every member of my family and the friends who have heard the story believe it was intercessory prayer that prevailed that December day. For years my family and I have claimed the concept I printed at the beginning of this "meows from the manse." We also believe in this precept in Matthew 6:8: *"For your Father knoweth what things ye have need of, before ye ask Him."* That wintry afternoon in 1991, my family needed our Father to protect our father, and He did. Praise the Lord.

I can't say that I have prayed as much for Eddie as I have for Dad, but I do know that it took a "miracle" for Eddie to survive on his own. Eddie had to fight every instinct to run away, but instead he trusted me. It was the Christmas of 2005 that I saw Eddie finally trusted me enough to come into our home to stay, and seven Christmases later he is still with us. Eddie at times leaves to roam and sometimes I can't find him, but the same promise I have claimed for my family I have claimed for my friend. Like Dad, Eddie is in the Lord's hands every time he ventures into the woods alone, and up until now he has always come home safe in answer to my prayers. (As he would for the rest of his ten years, and I for one thank the Good Lord for answered prayer!)

Chapter Fifty-Four

Scarface

"From henceforth let no man trouble me: for I bear in my body the marks of the Lord Jesus."

—GALATIANS 6:17

ON THIS BEAUTIFUL SPRING day in April of 2013, I need to update the legacy that is Eddie, Eddie, Eddie, Emmanuel Baptist Church's resident cat and my companion of nearly eight years. Over those years I have called my cat by various names: the lad, Edwardo, and simply Ed. This morning I have to give him another name: Scarface!

With the weather getting nicer, Ed has wanted to go out earlier and earlier. This morning it was before six. I think the reason has been because of the increased activity of the squirrel brothers and their cousins in the backyard. Eddie spent most of yesterday chasing the squirrel family around. Eddie sees them as invaders so he tries his hardest to keep them at bay. After a few days of cold, periodical showers, the rising warm sun got the best of Eddie, and he was at my bedside begging to be let out, so I did. Big mistake! As my wife got ready for work at McCullough Engineering and Consultants, she noticed Eddie sunning himself on the railing of the front porch. Thinking nothing about it, she opened the door expecting Eddie to come in for breakfast, but he stayed put. It was then my wife noticed a different expression on Eddie's face. Sure enough, a one inch gash running from the tip of his nose to his cheek, a clean slash, a bloody cut. Eddie had been in a fight: Big Grey? It had been a long time since Eddie came home blooded, but his face revealed some kind of altercation, a laceration resulting in a change in his complexion and appearance.

Jesus warned that persecution would hound and haunt His followers, and Paul, too, knew about scars: *"From henceforth let no man trouble me: for **I bear in my body the marks** of the Lord Jesus."* (Galatians 6:17) A simple reading of II Corinthians 11:23-28 will illustrate the kind of scars Paul carried around in his body. Anybody that will get involved in the service of the Saviour will eventually carry with them scars, either visible or invisible. One of my favorite heroes in John Bunyan's classic allegory, <u>Pilgrim's Progress</u>, is Mr. Valiant-for-Truth. Just before he crossed "the bridgeless river" he is reported to have said this: "I am going to the Father, and though with great difficulty I am got hither, yet now I do not repent of all the trouble I have been at to arrive where I am. My sword, I give to him that shall succeed me in my pilgrimage, and my courage and skill to him that can get it. My **marks and scars** I carry with me, to be a witness for me that I have fought His battles, who now will be my rewarder."

To fight is to run the risk of scars for only he who never gets involved has "no scars." I have come to the belief that part of the "hardness" (II Timothy 2:3) that is required of a soldier for Christ is the ability to be wounded in the cause. One has to be tough to endure the pain and shame that will come when one stands up for Christ on the battlefield. I still remember reading the famous book <u>The Red Badge of Courage</u>. I have always been a military buff even though I have no personal experience in military service. Yet I have seen over the years in my reading a similarity between the secular soldier and the spiritual soldier. Paul also makes that connection in a number of his epistles. Often when one speaks to a soldier and they have a visible scar, you ask, "Where did you get that wound?" More often than not the soldier is not ashamed to tell you the war, the battle, and the circumstances surrounding the wound that produced the permanent scar. Why then are we ashamed to tell of the difficulty that has resulted in the mark that is on our lives or the scar that is on our soul?

A few years ago my wife and I made the long trip to southern California, not for the sun and the warmth of that region of America, nor for the joy of escaping a cold Maine winter for a few days, but to visit some missionary friends of ours. The De la Hayes have been special to us because of their willingness many years ago to take our daughter Marnie back to the mission field with them so she could experience being a missionary for a summer. Nigeria was their mission, and Kent Academy was their mission field. They had already experienced once the heartache of living in a chosen field, but having to leave because of persecution in Liberia. The peaceful compound they lived on in Nigeria seemed well protected and ideal for their service for the King among the kids of central Nigeria. Their tranquility and solace was scattered one night when a gang of robbers broke into the compound and tried to steal the money that was in the school office safe. Unable to get the safe opened, the men raided the De la Hayes' home knowing that Marcia, the school treasurer, had a key. In the process, they harmed Marcia, kidnapped Ray (took him for a few hours but eventually let him go), and so traumatized their youngest son Mark (the other three De la Hayes' boys were away at the time) that the scars are still visible today. No physical marks remain, but the emotional scars are still clearly visible after nearly eight years. (At the writing of this chapter, Marcia has just been home in Maine visiting her aging and failing mother, and the scars in her life and especially her son's life are still spoken of as a raw open wound.)

To fight for the cause of Christ in dangerous places like Nigeria is to run the risk of scars; to be scarred in the spiritual conflict is to run the risk of wounds, physical, emotional, mental, or spiritual. To be wounded for Christ is to run the risk of some kind of death, maybe a death of emotion like my friend Mark, a daily dying like my son Scott who returned from the battlefield of Afghanistan with the death of four of his "battle-buddies" on his mind and three permanent concussions caused from being too close to an IED (wounds that earned him The Purple Heart). To gain a scar on the field of battle is by far the best a soldier of Christ can ask, but I ask in closing the question suggested by Isaac Watts in his classic Church hymn <u>Am I a Soldier of the Cross?</u>: "**Must I be carried to the skies on flowery beds of ease, while others fought to win the prize and sail thru bloody seas?**"

You might question the reason why Eddie would fight, but you can't question his willingness to stand his ground against any that would cross his yard because the proof of his resolve is the scar on his face! Where are our scars, marks, wounds for the cause of Christ? Will we stand before Him one day with "no scars?" Surely, if a cat can stand and fight, and, yes, be wounded in the fray, we need to stand as well even if it results in a scar.

Chapter Fifty-five

An American Shorthair Companion

"...and every man his companion..."

—Exodus 32:27

In this book (*Meows from the Manse*) I have been telling you a simple story of a very unique and special cat that started sharing his life with me in 2005. At the writing of this chapter, it is the spring of 2014, and this exceptional feline is still my companion. Though he bears a simple name, Eddie, he has been no ordinary tomcat. The colorful recollections of our companionship together, his loyalty to me and the unbreakable affection we have for each other has only grown through nearly a decade. What has been most amazing and extraordinary to me has been the spiritual lessons God has enabled me to learn through the companionship I have had with this American shorthair. Despite the fact that I have been a student of God's Word for most of my life (I turned 71 a few weeks back!), some of the basic truths of God's divine design have become crystal clear through Eddie's exploits. I never asked for a cat like Eddie, and I didn't put in the local paper an advertisement for the want of a cat like Eddie, but the Good Lord in His wise providence sent me a cat like Eddie and, after all this time, I think I know why.

My first memories of Eddie are nothing to write about, yet I will write about them for the contrast they give to my current opinion of "the lad." I still recall the day I came around the corner of the Emmanuel Baptist Church building and spotted the young cat running across the road. The terror and horror was clearly seen in the countenance of the cat. Eddie was thin, too thin, starving I figured. My very presence invoked panic and flight, but for the first time in my life I was filled with compassion for the little stray. Deep down I was drawn to try and help, and over the next few weeks I saw beyond a scared cat. I saw a keen capacity to survive, an exceptional intelligence to learn, and a real desire to have a friend. I saw a strong constitution and a powerful body that only needed three square meals a day to bring him back into shape. Instead of trying to force the issue, I settled on a daring plan to show the wandering ally cat that I could be trusted. I didn't try to capture Eddie, catch Eddie, or control Eddie. I let Eddie come and go as he wished. In other words I totally set him free, demanding nothing of him, yet all the time I fed his hungry and watered his thirst and gave him everything he needed to survive. We call this "free-will" in theological terms, much like God did with our first parents, Adam and Eve. God wasn't looking for a robot or a zombie when he created man, but a creature free to choose his own companion. (Remember, Adam found no companion until he met Eve. Genesis 2:19-22) I tested this theology on Eddie and found the concept workable, divine!!

After Eddie's would feed by the church, he would flee back to the abandoned barn across Park Street. After each of these short encounters, I wondered whether or not I would ever see Eddie again. Each time Eddie disappeared back into his private, shadowy world I wouldn't see him again for days. Then one day I saw him creeping across the street to see if I had left more food in the cellar-well. I watched through the glass in the front doors so I would not jump him. Each day I put his water and food in its place I would find it all gone the next morning. I fed Eddie day after day, but each time I became visible to him he would run away. I would call after him, but every overture was met with a firm rejection. What I didn't realize, that even these casual encounters were building blocks in an eventual relationship. Like God coming in the cool of the evening, every evening (Genesis 3:8), a companionship, and a kinship relationship was developing.

Unexpectedly, one day after I had just refilled Eddie's bowls, I saw Eddie heading across the street. This time he didn't run from me, though he made a wide birth around me. As he ate, I sat on the front steps of the porch attached to the back of the church building. Over the next few days this was the pattern of our relationship. Then one day to my total surprise I watched as Eddie came over to meet the man who had been feeding him daily for nearly three months. I felt a cold, soft nose touch my outstretched hand. Contact had been made! My heart skipped a beat, and, though it was a momentary connection, it was the turning point in our companionship. We were still weeks away from Eddie coming inside the church to eat, visiting me at the parsonage, and eventually living with Coleen and Pearl in the house across the street, but Eddie had learned that he could trust me. Eddie came to understand that this man had his best interest at heart, would love him unconditionally, and would accept every care for him for the rest of his life. Is this not the way it is when we discover that God will do this for us? It took us awhile to trust Him completely, but once we did have we not found Him to be true and faithful (Revelation 19:11)? Has He not met all our needs (Philippians 4:19)? Have we not found Him to care about every aspect of our lives? Caring to the point that we have learned that we can cast all our cares on Him because He cares for us (I Peter 5:7)?

One of the truly touching results of our growing companionship would be Eddie's utter devotion to me and only me. Where he had been a shy, distant, and fearful stranger, Eddie would become my virtual shadow. Where I go, he goes! Eddie has become essentially a "one-man cat." My wife has tried unsuccessfully to break into this relationship, but Eddie "only has eyes for me." He will tolerate others, unlike the Pearl, but I am his only true friend; he prefers our companionship only. For Eddie, the most difficult command I give him is "stay!" Often when I leave him at the parsonage while I walk over to the church to do something, he sits on the steps leading upstairs and watches through the window until I return. How do I know this? My wife has shared on numerous occasions Eddie's reaction when I leave him home. Coleen tells me sometimes Eddie cries as if to say, "Why has he made me stay?" Once Eddie committed himself to our relationship, companionship has been the result. Is not this what God wants out of our relationship with Him; eternal companionship? How it must grieve the heart of God when those whom He has developed a relationship with Him have chosen after a fashion to break that relationship and no longer walk with Him in a close companionship. We are living in a day when "falling away" (II Thessalonians 2:3) and "departing from the faith" (I Timothy 4:1) is happening on a regular basis in the Church of God. Believers are not only breaking fellowship with fellow believers, but are breaking fellowship with God (I John 1:3). Eddie has taught me what it means to have true devotion to God; to have an undeniable companionship that brings grief if "we asunder part, it gives us inward pain" as the old Church hymn says. Like Eddie, I am a "one-God" man. Are you?

So this is how Eddie and I created a "friendship-companionship." This is how the Almighty God created the possibility of a similar companionship with us. Did not our Lord and Saviour Jesus Christ define this new relationship with God the same way when He said to His disciples just before Calvary?

> *"Greater love hath no man than this that a man lay down his life for his FRIENDS. Ye are my FRIENDS, if ye do whatsoever I command you. Henceforth I call you not servants; for the servant knoweth not what his lord doeth; but I have called you FRIENDS;*

for all things that I have heard of my Father I have made known unto you." (John 15:13-15)

So one of the greatest lessons I learned from Eddie that I have been able to see in my relationship with my Saviour Jesus is that His desire for me from the beginning is that I, like Eddie, would eventually decide to come to Him, trust in Him, place all my care with Him. Discussions and debates on the absolute sovereignty of God as held by the extreme Calvinists and the grave responsibility of man as taught by the Arminians has hounded and haunted me most of my theological life. In my relationship and companionship with Eddie I have come to the conclusion that both views are correct, complementary, and compatible with the teachings of Scripture. The Bible teaches balance, and, though we can't always find a balance, God's sovereignty and man's responsibility can and do work together. The lesson is clear. The call is God's and the choice is His, but He except us to respond, as Eddie did. I called Eddie from the beginning of our relationship and I choice to make him my pet, but it was not until he responded to me did our companionship begin!

Chapter Fifty-Six

Trusting by Senses

"...even those who by reason of use have their senses exercised to discern both good and evil."

—Hebrews 5:14

For the first few weeks and months of Eddie's and my relationship, our intimate acquaintance was still far off; Eddie was like a tightly strung musical instrument. To this day, nearly ten years later, Eddie is still at times on edge, quick to react to an unexpected movement. He will still eye me very carefully when I surprise him. In the early days even the lightest touch would cause a trembling in his being, a fearful reminder of the abuse or misuse he experienced as a kitten? I don't believe Eddie had any harmony in his first family, if he had any family at all. In his sub-consciousness, if cats have such a thing, frightful events still lingered that he had suffered in the wrong house, by the wrong hands, with the wrong person. My conclusion: Eddie was out of tune with his senses. A problem Christians can have as well.

Time after time in those early days I would try to pick Eddie up and hold him close in my arms. At first he would have nothing to do with such intimacy, and even when he did he could only endure the confinement for a few moments. Eddie would leap from my grasp and turn and look at me as if he was questioning my embrace, the hug, the gentle affection I had lavished on him. Trust was the biggest factor in the early development of our relationship, but to become companions trust had to be won. The Hebrew prophet Amos said it best in this ancient question: *"Can two walk together, except they are agreed?"* (Amos 3:3) It was my desire that we become friends, that our lives would interact, and that we would walk together in harmony. Over time, as I stroked his light, lustrous coat, it seemed with each encounter Eddie appreciated the touch and got more comfortable with the sense of touching. Had Eddie never been affectionately touched before? When I carefully examined him for cuts or burs that had gotten on his fur, Eddie became to realize I really cared for him. To this day I still give Eddie an once-over when he returns from a jaunt into the wilderness that is his old haunt around the barn across the street. I am constantly pulling thorns, removing burs, and cleaning his coat. Eddie is all-boy, and he loves nothing better than rolling around in the dirt. He loves to smell like the woods, the ground, and the trees; a natural odor. Now, after I do this grooming, Eddie will lick my hand or touch my face with his nose. Eddie's way of showing gratitude: a touch for a touch!

Have you ever noticed in the Gospels how often Jesus touched? He touched the leper (Matthew 8:3). Remember, lepers were the "untouchables" of that day. How that leper must have felt after months and years without a human touch to receive the touch of Jesus. He touched Peter's mother-in-law (Matthew 8:15), healing her fever. He touched the blind eyes of the blind men (Matthew 9:29) giving them sight. Jesus touched his disciples (Matthew 17:7) in more ways than one. The Gaithers perhaps defined this sense best in their classic spiritual song "He Touched Me." So, too, does the Spirit of God show us compassion and charity by His touch! Like Eddie, we all must respond to the loving touch of God that comes from His divine love for us. *"We love Him, because He first loved us."* (I John 4:19) Eddie learned to love me because I first loved him and showed that love by my touch, and I still can't withhold myself from touching him when he comes near. Eddie would learn, as I have learned in my relationship with the Christ, that a tender touch is the sign of love. Lesson learned, we can trust in the touch of our Lord.

The second sense I used to get Eddie to trust me was the sound of my voice. I used his exceptional sense of hearing to gain his trust for me. In those early months I was constantly talking to Eddie, calling Eddie by name. I even utilized a family whistle to tell Eddie I wanted him to come in, come with me, come here. In time Eddie learned to listen to my voice or the whistle. He came to understand the timbre and tone and tune in my voice, and he came to know his name. No matter how far he roamed in the neighborhood, the sound of my voice and the reach of the whistle would draw him to me. He learned that when he heard my voice, heard the whistle, or heard his name, there would a treat waiting for him when he returned. I have never known a cat that would come when you called, let alone come to you when you whistled. Dogs maybe can be trained, but a cat? Rarely does Eddie linger when I call. Few have been the times I have had to look for him after I whistled for him or called his name. In other words, Eddie has learned to trust the whistle, my voice. I just love to whistle when he is close because I get great pleasure in seeing his ears cock, his head turn, and his tail go upward at the sound of my voice or the tone of the whistle or the mention of his name. More often than not as he comes towards me, he is using his voice to acknowledge his delight in coming to me. There is something amazingly stimulating in the obedient trust of a singular sound. Such is the precept of John 10:3, 4, and 16:

> "To him the porter openeth; and the sheep hear HIS VOICE: and he calleth His own sheep by name, and leadeth them out. And when he putteth for his own sheep, he goeth before them, and the sheep follow him: for they know HIS VOICE . . . and other sheep I have, which are not of this fold: them also I must bring, and they shall hear MY VOICE; and there shall be one fold, and one shepherd."

God has a voice, *"a still small voice,"* (I Kings 19:12) and that voice, the sound of God's voice, has gone out throughout the whole world. He speaks through His Word (II Peter 1:21), He speaks through His creation (Psalms 19:1-2), and He speaks through His Son (Hebrews 1:2). Eddie is always alert to my voice, but am I, are we, always alert to God's Voice? Lesson learned, we can trust in the voice of our Lord.

Besides Eddie's sensitive touch and keen hearing, he also has an amazing nose. The smelling ability of most animals is hundreds of times more acute and accurate than any human. It was this final sense I decided to use in teaching Eddie that he could trust me. To this day Eddie likes to smell me. He is always taking a sniff; I think to verify I am who I am. Often I will reach out my hand so Eddie can smell me, his keen nostrils alert to the right smell or a strange smell. Like with my touch, my voice, the whistle, I tried very hard to create an environment that would make Eddie comfortable around me. That is why he sleeps in my office on the same pillow. In the evening when I watch television, I always put the same quilt over my lap so Eddie will feel comfortable sitting with me. He has always felt uncomfortable in new surroundings, around new sights, and a new smell. You ought to hear Eddie howl when I take him with me to Coleen's mother's house just three miles away. The minute we go beyond an unfamiliar landscape he voices his dislike with a caterwaul of noise that he only uses when we go beyond his neighborhood! Eddie despises the smell of other male cats and, of course, dogs. Some people he likes, but still others he can't stand the smell of. The strong stimuli of new smells usually send Eddie running in the opposite direction. But in time, Eddie came to accept my smell. He came to trust in the creature (how does a cat view a human) that smells like Barry. And such is our relationship with God and others.

It wasn't until I came across this theology found in Paul's first book to the Corinthians that I realized the truth that Eddie was teaching me. Paul writes about "our smell" this way:

> "For we are unto God a sweet savour [**smell**] of Christ, in them that are saved, and in them that perish: to the one we are the savour [**smell**] of death unto death; and to the other the savour [**smell**] of life unto life. And who is sufficient for these things?" (II Corinthians 2:15-16)

How come Eddie accepts my smell and rejects somebody else's smell? One is pleasant to him and the other is repulsive to him. It is the same as our smell as a Christian. To the fellow-believer we are an odor of life, but to the unbeliever we have the smell of death. As Jesus was a sweet savour to God when he died for us (Ephesians 5:2), so we who believe in Jesus are a sweet savour to God as well. We learned to trust in the "sweet-smelling savour" of Christ, just like Eddie learned to trust in my scent. Lesson learned, we can trust in the scent of our Lord.

A sober truth has emerged through my observation of just how much Eddie has come to trust me through the years; that my devotion and trust of God falls far short of the devotion and trust Eddie has for me. My prayer is that one day I will approach the same level of trust Eddie has for me to the level of trust I should have for my Master. Like Eddie, I want a single-minded fixation because, like him, I have learned to trust the touch of my Master on my life, the voice of my Master in my heart, and the smell of my Master to my soul.

Chapter Fifty-Seven

Following the Master's Commands

"Ye are my friends, if ye do whatsoever I command you."
—John 15:14

To say Eddie and I are friends would be an understatement, at least from my perspective. Granted, I don't know. I doubt Eddie knows about friendship because with him it is all about instinct, that inborn tendency to behave as most creatures of his species reacts to certain situations. With the right stimuli, a touch on the belly, a rub of his head, and Eddie will start purring. It wasn't long after Eddie came into our lives that I found a very interesting instinct of Eddie's. If you scratch a place near the top of his back just where his tailbone meets his backbone, Eddie will start licking himself vigorously. I don't know why; the same scratch won't get the Pearl licking. My wife Coleen rebukes me often when I tap into this unique reaction to a certain stimulus on Eddie because it amuses me to see his reaction to a simple touch on a certain place on his body. But, unlike most cats, if not all cats I have encountered throughout my life, Eddie has learned to respond to certain commands, like a dog does. Is that instinct or instruction? Jesus taught in the verse printed above that friendship is directly linked to obedience to commands. It was my observation of Eddie that best helped me understand what Jesus was teaching in this verse and the other verses He shares about "keeping His commandments." (John 15:10)

I never started out to teach Eddie certain commands, but when I began to realize that Eddie would react, unlike other cats like Precious Patience Pearl, I decided I would try certain commands on him. Having had a few dogs in my life, I fell back to the basic dog commands: stay, sit, come, fetch, go, and paw or ask. These commands were short and to the point, simple and not difficult, but would Eddie respond to these clear and explicit commands? Slowly but surely, Eddie began to respond to some of the basic commands as in any good relationship between an owner and his pet. I found that, if combined with a favorite treat, the process would develop rapidly. I learned very early that I could win Eddie over through his stomach. Food for Eddie is life because he had very little of it during his first year, those important development months. Eddie seems to be always hungry even to the point of making sure there is food in his dish, whether church or parsonage, even if he isn't going to eat it now. He wants to make sure there is food for later. So with the powerful stimulus of food Eddie began to respond to certain commands and then repetition took over. Nevertheless, I noticed while I was instructing Eddie, Eddie began to instruct me.

It wasn't long before I began to recognize that Eddie also had a few commands he wanted to teach me. Because we could not always verbally communicate (that's another story), we began to realize that certain actions or sounds would bring a required respond from each of us. I shared with you in the last chapter Eddie's learning the "family whistle" and the sound of his name. While Eddie was learning, I was realizing, for example, that, when Eddie wanted to go outdoors he would scratch on a certain spot just outside my study at the church. He has done this so often now that the scratch marks are visible on the pine boards. In the morning, as happened this morning, when he wants to go outside for his morning constitutional (Eddie still prefers an out-door toilet), he simple comes upstairs and touches the blanket on my side of the bed. He never goes to my wife's side of the bed, and he has trained me to feel that light touch. Only if I am sleeping real soundly will he follow the touch with a simple meow (truly a meow from the manse). My wife is never awakened by him, only me. Haven't I been trained well? Certainly, his sitting beside his bowl in the kitchen is a clear command to "Feed Me!" It was these interactions that taught me that commands happen in two directions, and that as Christ was training me to follow His commands, He was also yielding Himself to follow some commands from me.

Have you ever considered that our relationship with Jesus is not one sided, like with all good friends? What friendship is only one sided or should I say any good friendship? As we give our lives to Him, He gives His life for us (John 15:13). As we follow His commandments, He will answer our prayers (John 15:16). As we abide in Him, He will abide in us (John 15:4-5). Jesus didn't come to simply be a Master over us (that was certainly part of it—*"Ye call me Master and Lord: and ye say well; for I am"* [John 13:13]), but He also came to make friends (John 15:15). This is why Christianity has worked for nearly two thousand years. It is not a relationship based on fear, but respect. Even the Old Testament *"the fear of the Lord"* (Proverbs 1:7) means reverence and respect, not afraid or frightful. The Eternal God certainly doesn't and didn't have to humble Himself to such a relationship, but He chose to do so because of love (John 15:9, 10, 12). I hear it all the time from neighbors and friends when they see Eddie and me together; when they observe how Eddie listens to me and follow's my commands: "Eddie enjoys carrying out your wishes." "Eddie gets pleasure in obeying you." "You really love that cat!" Let us never forget that our relationship with Jesus is a two-way street, and that is exactly what Jesus intended to develop with His disciples and the disciples that would follow His disciples. What the world says, or the liberal theologian says, Jesus has left us with clear commands, unmistakable instructions. His Word is precise and to the point, just like my words to Eddie. Like with Eddie, it is our responsibility to learn to humbly respond and obey those commands. If a cat can do it, shouldn't a Christian do it?

So you don't think my cat is perfect, there are some commands Eddie has trouble with. He certainly has mastered "asking." You ought to see him in the evening using his paw, either right or left (ambidextrous), to ask for his treats, and I rarely refuse his command, just ask my wife. I have also taught him to use his paws to shake hands! He certainly has mastered "coming." Either by calling his name or whistling will bring him running from wherever he has roamed. I have even taught him to fetch a certain toy of his attached to a string. I can throw it into the dining room, and he will chase it down as I pull it back. He has learned to sit pretty well; still working on that; not perfect yet. For Eddie and for us, the hardest has been "stay" and "go," perhaps the hardest commands of all.

To "stay" is sometimes the hardest command when you want to "go," and sometimes to "go" when you want to "stay" is equally as hard. If my cat Eddie finds these two commands difficult to learn, it is not surprising so do humans. Eddie has a hard time being away from me, just like the demoniac after he found Jesus. "Go" suggests the unknown, uncertain, the unfamiliar, and we resist its simple tone, yet powerful instruction, and yet it was one of Jesus' greatest commands (Matthew 28:19). "Stay" suggests the some-old-some-old routine, relations, and relationships, and this is exactly what Jesus told the demoniac to do! How are you doing with these two simple commands? Like Eddie and me, are you still working on them?

Chapter Fifty-Eight
Faithful to a Fault

"Moreover it is required in stewards that a man is found faithful."
—I CORINTHIANS 4:2

DURING OUR NEARLY TEN years together, one overriding quality has emerged in the character of Eddie, Eddie, and Eddie: faithfulness. But in a very strange way, one of Eddie's greatest strengths has become his greatest weakness.

Once Eddie learned to trust me, his presence with me has been a passion with him. As I write this chapter in "Meows from the Manse," my buddy is licking himself on a pillow that sets on a bookshelf in front of my church desk. It is late afternoon, and Eddie is in for a nap before we head home for first supper (Eddie has two: one at five and one at seven). About two hours ago Eddie came in from his daily (except in poor weather like rain or snow) walk around his neighborhood. I still don't know at times where he actually goes, but I have learned that Eddie is very territorial and faithful. Daily he makes sure everything is in order in his world. Eddie gets quite irritated if we keep him in too much. Shirking his duty perhaps? He seems to have an inborn instinct to walk the perimeter of School Street and Park Street which creates an X in our northwest corner of Ellsworth. My wife and I think it goes back to his homeless, wayfaring days when this was where he roamed looking for food and shelter. Now it is simply a task Eddie feels he still must perform, as if he were the guardian of the neighborhood. Over the years I have seen in Eddie's faithfulness the wonderful precept that we, too, must be steadfast and faithful in the place the Good Lord has placed us. Eddie's world is the two blocks bordered by State Street, Oak Street, and Church Street. This is where Eddie was born? And this is where Eddie lives and works and roams! God places us in a particular corner of His world for a purpose, but are we as faithful and loyal to that place as Eddie? Or are we always looking beyond to the "greener-side" of our fence? Are we faithful and content where the Lord has placed us to serve Him?

One of the great temptations in life is the test of "breaking faith" with God's place for us, to move too soon or move too slowly in relationship with God's will and God's way. We are so narrow-minded at times, forgetting that our broad-minded God knows best in place and space. Sometimes it takes a great persistence and patience to be faithful to our post when that post is an unpopular, unimpressive, unrecognized unknown. Eddie never seems to complain that he has spent the entire bulk of his life in a small space doing a simple task. How often I have complained about where I was, what I was doing, and with whom I was living. The Word of God seems to be very clear that the measure of success as seen through the eyes of God is simple faithfulness in whatsoever and wheresoever the Lord has given us to do and go. The Parable of the Pounds and the Parable of the Talents are a wonderful illustration of this concept in the teaching of Jesus: *"His lord said unto him, Well done, good and faithful servant; thou hast been faithful over A FEW THINGS, I will make thee ruler over many things; enter thou into the joy of thy lord."* (Matthew 25:23)

Faithfulness in the annals of God's Word doesn't mean spectacular success, exceptional events, or prestigious places; it lies in a consistent and continual faithfulness to steadfastness in the place that He has placed us.

With such a glowing testimonial, how can I say that Eddie's greatest virtue has become his greatest vice? The case is a simple one. Eddie's faithfulness has made him yield more than once to the temptation that a cat or a flock of crows out of place in his territory is worth fighting over. I have written before of Big Grey, and of the "boys," a flock of crows that have multiplied over the years from seven to well over a score now. The noisy, black rascals, however, are not as menacing to Eddie as male cats (a number over the years with his present adversary Big Black, a huge male tom that has just come into Eddie's neighborhood). I know the other cats in the neighborhood and the local bird population regarded Eddie as an intruder into their realm and they seemingly get great pleasure in taunting him and tormenting him into an altercation. Because of Eddie's size, Eddie is always at a disadvantage; with the crows Eddie is always outnumbered, but numbers and size have never seemed to both Eddie when he thinks his world has been invaded or some gauntlet has been thrown down. Eddie's faithfulness to his sentinel job clouds his judgment and distracts him from a more important faithfulness, that of the faithfulness to himself and his health. Over the years Eddie has received numerous wounds in defense of his world, but faithful without fighting is what is important. How often in the faithful execution of our duties to our Master have we been found fighting the neighbors, other church members, even our own family?

What a temptation it is when we are misdirected from Christ's highest intentions by a fight that turns into some turf war such as the color of the church carpet or how a certain ministry ought to be run, when circumstances which have nothing to do with God's divine purpose overlap, and we start swinging. Some things seemingly so harmless, innocent at first, turn out to be a major cat fight! How our adversary, the Devil, loves to redirect our attention and energy from what is eternal to what is temporary. Like Eddie, sometimes we fail to see the big picture that one squabble is not worth the price it will cost in the long run. What we see as essential only turns out to be a sideshow. I have watched Eddie confront the cats and the crows for years and all it has been is entertainment; so, too, when God's people get into an altercation. People will hear about it, maybe even witness it, then walk away wondering what all the fuss was about. I, too, have watched Eddie defend, for example, our garage from a curious cat, and for Eddie it is worth the wrestling match that happens, but I know the cat was just passing through, that it hadn't come to stay or replace Eddie, but Eddie sees it differently. Temptations can come in many sizes, and one of the most devilish and diabolical is the one that uses our strengths against us. Do you really know how close a humble spirit is to a prideful act (Peter at the last Supper; Matthew 26:33-35)? Do you really know how close love is to hatred (Amnon and Tamar; II Samuel 13:1-15)? Do you really know how close something sacred is to sacrilege (Nadab and Abihu; Leviticus 10:1-2)? Do you really know how close faithfulness is to unfaithfulness (the prophet from Judah; I Kings 13:1-19)? Sometimes the difference between virtue and vice is only a word, only an angry action, only a moment of impaired judgment, only a hiss, only a meow away.

There is within us all, including cats, a tendency to focus on the momentary encounter thinking in ourselves that we are doing something noble, decent, honorable, when in reality we are doing something terribly wrong. Take the story of Saul and his sacrifice in I Samuel 13. Confronted with a vastly superior foe and the delay of the prophet/priest Samuel, King Saul made the decision to perform the sacrifice himself. That one simple event lost Saul the kingdom (I Samuel 13:14). What of the story of Uzziah in I Chronicles 26? Uzziah decides to honor God by burning incense on the golden altar in the Temple of God. His rash act cost him his health for the rest of his life (I Chronicles 26:20-21). Then there is the story of Achan in Joshua 7. In an instant this Hebrew soldier at the Battle of Jericho takes the accursed thing which costs him his life and the life of his family (Joshua 7:24). Eddie has forfeited numerous days of good health and confinement inside after getting bruised or cut in a moment of defending his honor or his homeland. Our usefulness for a time is sometimes destroyed by our misplaced faithfulness. Disaster is often the result of disillusionment of a false understanding of what is courage and resistance and what is foolishness and stupidity. A simple lesson I have learned from Eddie, but also verified in the Holy Writ, is this: it is neither the spectacular stand, nor the sensational struggle, for which the Master asks of us. He is looking instead for us to simply be faithful in the place He placed us, and as He says time and time again in the Bible, *"Stand still and I will fight for you."* (Exodus 14:13-14 and II Chronicles 20:15-17)

Chapter Fifty-Nine

Available for Anything

"... declaration of your ready mind."
—II Corinthians 8:19

I WOULD LIKE TO give some credit to the source of my title for this chapter in my ongoing saga of Eddie, my faithful feline. I got a wonderful gift last Christmas from my wife, a copy of Phillip Keller's classic devotional book <u>Lessons from a Sheep Dog</u>. Even though Phillip was writing about a favorite dog, I saw plenty of parallels between his border collie and my American shorthair. The last chapter in Keller's book bears the same title as this chapter because, like his sheep dog, my special cat also exhibits the same quality of readiness and availability.

It became obvious early on in our relationship that a mutual affection had developed over our courting months. I thought that bond would be broken when after three months I left for India on a six-week teaching and preaching mission. Surely that connection would have to be repaired when I returned, but to my surprise it was if I hadn't even gone. I knew then that something special was happening between me and Eddie. I have a hard time calling it love, but I haven't found another adjective that best describes what there is about our companionship. Even my wife, who lavishes plenty of attention and affection on Eddie, recognized that Ed only has eyes for me. Despite the fact that Eddie has now lived nearly a decade in a pastor's world, he is still "available for anything." He will go where I go, stay with me as along as it takes, and never seems to be bothered with the sudden changes in my life. I have left him alone at the church for hours while I do hospital visitation or get called out on an emergency visit. When I return, Eddie is at the door to greet me back. Even this morning Eddie watched as I shoveled a surprise snowstorm that left a few inches of the heavy white-stuff on our walkway. It is April first, but old-man winter wants to stay around into spring on the coast of Maine this year. Eddie has exhibited this remarkable trait for as long as I have known him, a quality that ought to be found in every Christian believer.

"Readiness" is not often preached, and this Biblical doctrine is not often taught. I chose the verse printed above for the last five words of the verse. I am on a "five-word" mission at the moment. I am in the process of writing a devotional book on some of the great five-word phrases of the Bible. I was inspired by Paul's great challenge of I Corinthians 14: 19: *"Yet in the church I had rather speak FIVE WORDS with my understanding, that by my voice I might teach others also, than ten thousand words in an unknown tongue."* So, as I looked up verses to back the lesson of this chapter about Eddie, I stopped when I found *"declaration of your ready mind"* because Eddie certainly has a readiness, a ready mind, and is ready for anything when it comes to me. Eddie has become totally abandoned to my life, my schedule, my ways. He has adapted to my life, my living, and my lifestyle. He is totally available to go with me, to stay with me, to do with me whatsoever I happened to be doing at any time, even when things change unexpectedly, like last night.

Monday is AWANA night. This is our church's youth ministry for 3- to 12-year-olds. The day started as most Mondays with the knowledge that before the day was through I would spend three hours with over 70 kids. Despite my advance years (71 at my last birthday), I still enjoy ministering to kids, especially 8- to 12-year-olds, my specialty. I never sought a ministry to this age, but the Good Lord in His wise providence seemed to think I could and would, and I have. Between AWANA (over thirty-five years now) and over fifty years of summer camps with that age group I have spent more time with that age than any other age group of kids. Eddie and I were preparing (Eddie on the other hand doesn't like little people) to end our day, he to head home for supper and a nap while I headed to AWANA. The phone rang and my evening was changed. The snow I shoveled this morning started falling late in the afternoon yesterday. It came so fast, beginning as freezing rain that AWANA had to be cancelled. By the time we made all the phone calls needed, a full-blown blizzard had engulfed Ellsworth. Eddie and I fought the wind and the snow home where a warm pelt-stove fire was waiting us. Instead of waiting my return from AWANA, Eddie quickly adapted to an evening home with his buddy. After supper we settled into our recliner and, as he slept on my lap, I watched the end of the first season of Downton Abby again. Are we as ready and adaptable when God changes our routine? Are we as quick to adjust when life throws a curve ball at us?

The Bible teaches that readiness is an important characteristic of the follower of God (Exodus 19:11). Jesus tells a great parable about a king that makes a wedding feast for his son, and, after he said "all things are ready" (Matthew 22:4), he sent his servants out to get the guests, but they were not "ready" (Matthew 22:5-8) to come. In another parable Jesus tells of ten virgins awaiting the arrival of the bridegroom and how five were ready and five were not (Matthew 25:1-10). Those lessons clearly teach "readiness" which is certainly a part for "available for anything," but that isn't the whole lesson. "Available for anything" is not just a readiness, but a willingness to accept the unknown, the "anything." For me a classic illustration for this is Paul's statement of Acts 21:13:

> "Then Paul answered, what mean ye to weep and to break mine heart? For I AM READY not to be bound only, but also to die at Jerusalem for the name of the Lord Jesus!"

Paul was a man ready, available for anything. In Paul's epistle to the Philippians he told them he was ready to live or die (Philippians 1:21-24). This to me is the ultimate "available for anything." I believe this attitude comes from "a ready mind." As Eddie has a ready mind to go with me, stay with me, do with me, so we need a ready mind to be available for anything the Lord sends our way.

I was taught this lesson of readiness long before I met Eddie. When I was in training for the pastorate, one of the first verses I was shown to define my ministry was I Peter 5:2:

> "Feed the flock of God which is among you, taking the oversight thereof, not by constraint, but willingly; not for filthy lucre, BUT OF A READY MIND."

I was taught to be ready at a moment's notice to preach (II Timothy 4:2 ". . .instant in season and out of season"), to share my faith, to go to someone in need. Unlike the instruction today to would-be pastors, I was taught the pastorate was a 24-7 profession. There is no such thing as off-time, down-time, unavailable time. Numerous times in my 49-years of pastoring I have come home early from my annual vacation to bury somebody. It has gotten to the point I do not even have a designated day off. I have tried all six (Sunday has never been a day off for me) and all have ended up days of ministry. Eddie has only reminded me that "available for anything," "ready for anything, at any time" is part of the Christian life. Recently, I was preaching on Jesus trying to get a few minutes off with His disciples because the crowds were unrelenting (Mark 6:31), yet, when the multitude came, Jesus not only taught them, He provided them supper (Mark 6:32-44). Jesus was always ready to heal or to help. He was "available for anything," and His followers should be as well.

In Phillip Keller's book I mentioned at the start of this chapter, he spoke of Lass as always ready to do whatever he asked of her. She was a working sheep dog on a sheep station so her responsibilities and the demands on her were much more extensive than the demands and responsibilities I place on my dear Eddie. Yet, whether in many things or a few things, the attribute of readiness, availability, is admirable in a dog or a cat, but even more so in a Christian. For me the last and best Biblical connection to this quality is found in I Peter 3:15: *"But sanctify the Lord God in your hearts: and be READY ALWAYS [**available for anything**] to give an answer to every man that asketh you a reason of the hope that is in you with meekness and fear."* We ought to live in the expectation and the anticipation of our Master's call for duty. As I woke this morning, Eddie was downstairs, but when I whistled to him he came. He didn't have to (the Pearl certainly would not come at my call), yet Eddie does because he is devoted to the precept that he is ready and available when I call. Oh, that we as believers would be on standby, ready, waiting, available for anything our Saviour would want of us.

Chapter Sixty

Eddie and the Mailman

*"Ask, and it shall be given you; seek, and ye shall find;
knock, and it shall be opened unto you."*

—Matthew 7:7

As they say, this Eddie story is "hot off the presses!" Sometimes it is months between chapters, but at times like this I must write down this tale before I lose the inspiration of the event. This lesson from Eddie's life happened just two days ago on a quiet, seemingly uneventful, Saturday morning in early spring, 2014.

Spring has always meant for Eddie the freedom from being penned in, shut-up, and confined within the parsonage of the Emmanuel Baptist Church. After an exceptionally long winter (snow had been on the ground since December 9th; very unusual for the coast of Maine), Eddie, like the rest of us, couldn't wait for the warming temperatures and the longer hours of a Maine spring. With the early rising of the sun, Eddie was up at daybreak asking (meowing), seeking, and pawing (knocking) to be let out. I remember telling Eddie the evening before that Saturday would be a rainy, windy dawning, and that maybe he would prefer to stay in a bit longer. "Sleep in," I said because I was planning to. It had been another long week, and Saturday was the only day in the week that my wife and I get to really sleep in. I woke early that Saturday morning surprised that Eddie hadn't already been up to our bedroom seeking my help in letting him out. I heard the rain pounding heavily on the parsonage roof and figured that Eddie had taken my advice and had slept in that April morning. Turning over I went back to sleep for another hour when that all too familiar meow could be heard from the hallway. I ignored it at first, but, when the begging meow didn't work, Eddie came to my side of the bed and gently rubbed his paws over the sheets. When that didn't work, Eddie jumped on the bed and into the window located over my head, another sign to "let me out!" I knew the process would be repeated over and over again until I got up and let Eddie out.

Yielding to Eddie's persistent plea, I got up and down the stairs I went. Eddie was already sitting at the porch door waiting my arrival. A raw rain was falling and a gusty wind was still blowing as Eddie ventured onto the front porch. I could tell he was reluctant once he realized just how nasty it was outside, but he no doubt needed to use the bathroom so he proceeded onto the wet deck while I closed the door. Eddie had made his choice and would have to live with the consequences until I got up, or did he? I returned to my warm bed; Coleen did not stir as I got back under the covers. Awake but determined to catch a few more winks, I picked up a book I had started reading the night before and read for a few minutes as sleepiness returned to my eyes. Just before I put the book down and rolled over, I thought I would go to the bathroom lest my bladder woke me a few minutes later. As I left the bathroom to return to my Saturday morning nap, I heard the front door open and close. At first I thought it might be my mother-in-law, Opal, coming over to do her laundry. Opal is an early riser and has caught Coleen and me in bed before. However, the door opened and shut so quickly with no sound of anybody roaming downstairs, so I returned to the bedroom. I did peak out the bedroom window that opens up to the back driveway, but our car was the only car in the yard. I then went into Coleen's craft room across the hall and looked out onto the street in front of the parsonage. The only person I saw was our friendly neighborhood mailman faithfully completing his rounds in the pouring rain. My mind was satisfied when I realized that our mailman must have had a package to deliver and, as he had done numerous times before, he simply opened the door and put the package inside out of the rain. Pulling the covers over my head, I closed my eyes and sought more sleep content that the mystery of the opening door had been explained. However, before I found la-la land again I felt an all too familiar weight on top of me.

I threw the cover off my head and there, looking me squarely in the eye, was Eddie. I had let him out, but who had let him in? Surely, my amazing cat hadn't learned how to open the front door! And then I began to laugh uncontrollably! My wife also woke up and asked why I was laughing. I told her my story, and she, too, began to laugh. As we pondered the event, we came to the conclusion that our postman had in reality let Eddie in. Eddie and the mailman have become good friends over the years, and we suspect that Eddie, after finishing his business, returned to the porch to the only dry spot he could find. It was then our caring, cat-loving mailman was making his Saturday rounds and saw Eddie wanting to come in. No doubt wet and pitiful looking, the sight was too much for the kindhearted postman to ignore. Eddie asked in his feline way and was given access back into a dry parsonage. Eddie sought help from the mailman and found entrance back inside. Eddie knocked (Eddie has learned if he puts his paw up he will get something in return), and the porch door was opened for him. Had Eddie learned Matthew 7:7? Have I? Have you?

While Matthew 7:7 is the precept, Matthew 7:8 is the promise: *"For everyone that asketh receiveth; and he that seeketh findeth; and to him that knocketh it shall be opened!"* This is what happened to Eddie on April 5, 2014, when a mailman in the middle of doing his duty saw a wet cat seeking entrance, and he took an extra second to answer Eddie's plea. Rare is a specific prayer request mentioned by Jesus; maybe Matthew 9:38 (*"Pray ye therefore the Lord of the harvest, that he will send forth labourers into His harvest."*) is the only exception to this rule. Jesus just tells us to ask, seek, knock, and it will be answered, found, and opened. So the teaching is clear. He doesn't tell us what to ask, just to ask; He doesn't tell us how to seek, just to seek; He doesn't tell us when to knock, just to knock. Yet how often do we not use this powerful precept when we are in need?

A few years back I wrote a devotional book I called *In the Pursuit of Prayer*. In one of the devotionals in the series I wrote this:

1. ASKING. Luke 11:9 and James 4:2. There was once a sign in front of a store that read: "If you don't see it, ask!" This same philosophy is taught throughout the Word of God. We serve the God that loves for His children to ask. This is a hard lesson for me because I'm the kind of person that just hates to ask; ask for help, ask for a hand, or ask for a "how do I get there?" All you need to do is ask my wife, and she will tell you that I would rather stay lost than to ask for directions! I would rather break my back than ask someone to give me a lift! This is a sin of pride, and how many prayers have gone unanswered because they were unsaid? (James 4:2) The quickest way to learn anything is to ask (Ephesians 3:11-12), and the quickest answer to a prayer is to ask, even though God knows (Matthew 6:8) before we ask; He still loves for us to ask. (Eddie has learned this; why haven't I?)

2. SEEKING. Isaiah 55:6. Sometimes, however, asking is not enough, and we have to add seeking to our prayer. Many times I have to seek God's will about how to pray because I don't know quite how to pray about certain matters (I John 5:14-15). Writing in Psalms 81:10 ("... *open thy mouth wide* ..."), Asaph tells of a strange custom that existed in his day. At that time, if a king wished to show favor on a visitor or

give an ambassador from another country a special honor, he would request him to open his mouth wide. The king would then fill his mouth with sweetmeats. On very special occasions he might even put precious jewels in the mouth of the one he wanted to honor. This unusual practice accounts for the expression in Psalms 81. Like that king, our King stands ready to grant us answers to our prayers if we would only persistently seek Him. That is why Paul said we could come (seek) boldly before His throne (Hebrews 4:16).

3. KNOCKING. Luke 18:1-8. Not only are we to ask and seek, but we are to keep at it, like knocking. Don't you keep knocking at your friend's door when you know he or she is at home? We know that God never slumbers nor sleeps, that He is always home, so sometimes we need to keep asking, petitioning, pleading, knocking again and again and again at the door of his grace. We must pray without ceasing with all the asking, seeking and knocking we can muster because God loves the child that asks largely, that seeks continually, that knocks expectantly.

In my mind's eye I see Eddie at the porch door waiting the mailman to arrive. I see him look up as if asking to be let in. I hear his purring as the postman rubs his back and understands that Eddie wants to be let in, and I watch as Eddie's paw touches the door, his way of knocking, meaning "let me in!" If a cat gets his request answered by a stranger, surely, we can believe we will get the same and more from our Father. Eddie knows all about asking, seeking, and knocking, but I am still learning. How about you?

Chapter Sixty-One

The Nature of Eddie

"Neither is there any creature [Eddie] that is not manifest in His sight: but all things are naked and opened unto the eyes of Him with whom we have to do."

—HEBREWS 4:13

I DON'T KNOW IF God is a cat lover, but I do know He is an animal lover so I will conclude that He likes cats. It is an interesting study to note that when God made a covenant with man after the flood He included in that covenant the animals:

> "And it shall come to pass, when I bring a cloud over the earth, that the bow shall be seen in the cloud: and I will remember my covenant, which is between me and you and **every living creature of all flesh**; and the waters shall no more become a flood to destroy all flesh. And the bow shall be in the cloud; and I will look upon it, that I may remember the everlasting covenant between God and **every living creature of all flesh** that is upon the earth." (Genesis 9:14-16)

I have often pondered why God would have even saved the animals from the flood. He could have recreated, but He chose to use the animals that already inhabited this world; He saved some, just like He saves some of us (I Corinthians 9:22). When I start thinking down this line of thought I am always reminded what Paul wrote:

> "For the earnest expectation of **the creature** waiteth for the manifestation of the sons of God. For **the creature** was made subject to vanity, not willingly, but by reason of him who hath subjected the same in hope, because **the creature** itself also shall be delivered from the bondage of corruption into the glorious liberty of the

children of God. For we know that the whole creation groaneth and travaileth in pain together until now." (Romans 8:19-22)

I have come to believe the word "creation" refers to all of God's creatures even those below the human level. When man sinned, all of creation was affected (note in the last quote "**not willingly**." Adam and Eve sinned willingly, not the animals). I believe the animal kingdom and the nature world were made subject to terrible things including tornadoes, hurricanes, earthquakes, forest fires, volcanic eruptions, blizzards, famine, drought and floods. (Remember, the ground [the earth] was cursed, [Genesis 3:17-18], and the snake was cursed, and the animals [Genesis 3:14] were affected.) These are just a few example of the imbalance that now governs and guides this world. The animal kingdom, which was at peace with itself, was thrown out of balance. Despite the fact God did this made the choice, He did it in the hope that another day is coming when the deterioration and corruption that plagues this planet will be no more. Surely, this is referring to the Millennial Kingdom of Christ when He gives this world "**the glorious liberty?**" Read carefully these verses:

> "The wolf also shall dwell with the lamb, and the leopard shall lie down with the kid; and the calf and the young lion and the fatling together; and the little child shall lead them. And the cow and the bear shall feed; their young ones shall lie down together: and the lion shall eat straw like the ox. And the sucking child shall play on the hole of the asp, and the weaned child shall put his hand on the cockatrice's den. They shall not hurt nor destroy in my entire holy mountain: for the earth shall be full of the knowledge of the Lord, as the waters cover the sea." (Isaiah 11:6-9)

What a day that will be when peace returns to the earth and the animals!

When my mind travels down this path, I began looking at my cat Eddie differently. Eddie lives in a constant state of fear in the world he lives in. Despite nearly ten years of trying to relieve him of the fear of hunger (constant access to food) and the fear of attack, Eddie still has the nature of the cursed world. He lives on the edge of starvation and slaughter. To this day, on occasion, we find Eddie eating even when he isn't hungry. My wife says he is "stress-eating." Even in the safety of the parsonage Eddie will jump at the slightest noise thinking some other creature is after him, to devour him. Eddie isn't ready, nor does he have the ability to lie down with his newest enemy, Pierre. Pierre is Eddie's latest nemesis. A midnight-black cat with a red collar sporting a bell, Pierre has been in the neighborhood for about a year. Pierre is aggressive and nosy. Just a couple of weeks ago I found Pierre in the church. I had left the front door open so Eddie could come in and out at his leisure. Needless to say, Eddie wasn't impressed and neither was I because I knew a confrontation was inevitable. Sure enough, just a few days afterward I found Eddie and Pierre staring each other down on the front porch of the church. I split them up and chased Pierre off, but within the hour a cat fight of Biblical proportions was happening on church property; no laying down together, no eating together, no dwelling together between these two. Not yet!

When I arrived on the scene there was cat hair covering the landing of the porch. Both cats should have been bald, but there they were in mortal combat as if it was the Battle of Armageddon. Once the two combatants realized there was an observer, they split up, and Pierre ran off. Eddie was left the victor of the field. He even had a trophy. Pierre's signature red collar with the tiny bell was lying on the porch; Eddie had ripped it from Pierre's throat in the struggle. Someday, according to Isaiah 11, Pierre and Eddie could be best friends and even have lunch together, but not now. I returned Pierre's collar the next day and talked to the neighbor about the dilemma, but no solutions could be found, and they won't be found until that Day when the Lord returns and reinstates the creation and the creatures of His creation back to their Eden days. I blame the nature of Eddie on the fall of man. Nature is different, but it can't help itself; it was not its choice to be like this. The animal kingdom is different, but it, too, is but a product of the fall; "not willingly." Adam didn't just send mankind into depravity; he caused the whole of creation to slip into fear and dread and conflict. That is why sometimes when I see Eddie sitting in front of the big picture window in the back of the church looking out upon his domain, I ponder if he isn't thinking, hoping for the emancipation that will come at the Advent of Christ and the manifestations of the saints; a day when he will walk the perimeter of his territory and have no need to watch his back. Without a doubt my cat is in travail, and he groans often. And now I know why!

I don't know about you, but I have a terrible time watching the commercials on television about neglected and abused animals. The cruelty of mankind against animals is legendary, only trumped by his cruelty against his fellowman. Even the wisest man in the world recognized under the inspiration of the Holy Spirit that: "*A righteous man regardeth the life of his beast: but the tender mercies of the wicked are cruel.*" (Proverbs 12:10) Granted, God did give the animals of the world for food *"for every creature of God is good, and nothing to be refused, if it be received with thanksgiving. For it is sanctified by the word of God and prayer."* (I Timothy 4:4, 5) If this was the governing statute in this world today, most of us would be vegetarians! Because few give thanks for the food we eat, let alone the animals that sacrifice their lives so we might eat. Don't get me wrong, I am a meat-eater (I Timothy 4:3). Just last night I received from a parishioner three steaks (and the neck to be used to make the best pie filling there is—mincemeat) taken from a deer killed by her grandson. I will enjoy them without a thought of the white-tail deer, but I couldn't kill one! When man sinned, all creatures became subject to the curse and each fell into "the bondage of corruption." The enmity God put between Satan and the woman, Adam and the ground became the enmity of one creature for another, like Eddie and Pierre. That is why Isaiah's verses are so amazing to read. The wolf eats the lamb rather than them living together. The leopard eats the kid; they don't sleep together. When was the last time you saw a baby playing with a lion? The bear eats the cow. Ever since my trip to Alaska I have had a new interest in a reality show called Alaska's Last Frontier. The story is about a four- generation family who has lived off the land in southwest Alaska. One of the annual events in their lives is herding their beef cows to a meadow for summer grazing. One of the members of the family spends the entire summer watching over the herd because of bears.

I am still looking for my first cobra in the wild, but I would never let my grandchild play with one, let alone put their hand into the asp's den. The animal kingdom is dangerous, and the beauty that once was the relationship between Adam and the animals in Eden is gone. I believe that Adam was a vegetarian as were all the animals (Genesis 1:30). Despite my desire to think so, I still don't believe in the eternal soul of animals. As much as I would love to find Eddie in my mansion when I get to my heavenly home, I don't think he will be there. I do believe when the Good Lord creates *"the new heaven and the new earth,"* (Revelation 21:1) there will be animals, but no sea. I feel that we will have come full-circle, and the relationship we have with nature and the animals will be the same as Adam and Eve had in Eden. I do believe it will be too late for Eddie, but in the nature of this small feline I have discovered a wonderful understanding of why we hear all this groaning and travailing today. I read once of two travellers who were camping on the edge of a great desert. At midnight one was aroused by his companion asking, "What is that moaning sound I hear?" His traveling comrade replied, "That is the desert sighing!" I am hearing that same sigh from my cat Eddie. Can land lament? Can soil sigh? Can ground groan? Can cats travail? I have studied too long (50 years now as a serious student of the Word) the Holy Bible not to know these words from the pen of Paul, "The whole creation *groaneth and travaileth in pain together until now.*" (Romans 8:22) I have walked too long in the natural world not to detect the sighs and groans of this planet in relationship to what man is doing to the land and the ocean and the atmosphere and the animal life (every day a species goes extinct somewhere on this planet). I feel like Goethe who wrote, "Often have I had the sensation as if nature in wailing sadness entreated something to me, so that not to understand what was longed for cutteth to my heart." I fret and fuss at times when Eddie is out wandering, roaming because I know a family of foxes live just over the hill in a woody area of east Ellsworth. They have been seen in the past in our neighborhood. A fox and a cat don't dwell together in harmony; that is, until the great Creator, the Lord Jesus Christ, returns and once again restores the harmony of sod and soil, animals and mammals, creation and Creator. It is amazing to me that after all these years Eddie is still preaching to me, still teaching me another Biblical lesson, still instructing me in the things of God even if he won't enjoy "the glorious liberty" to come.

Chapter Sixty-Two

Paw Prints in the Snow

*"Lest Satan should get an advantage of us:
for we are not ignorant of his devices."*

—II Corinthians 2:11

We have just finished the snowiest November (2014) on record for the Ellsworth area. So much for global warming in Maine! In three heavy snows we got 27 inches of the white stuff. We are not complaining because in the same month Buffalo, New York, got nearly eight feet. But even for us, this has been an early winter blast in late autumn compounded by the water content of the snows. If they had been dry snows, we would have gotten feet instead of inches. One victim of the early snow has been my cat Eddie. Eddie loves to roam and romp around the neighborhood on a daily basis, but Eddie also dislikes snow or rain because he hates to get his feet wet. Despite the discomfort, Eddie will venture out only because he hates a litter box worse. He loves the smell of leaves and dirt when he needs to do his business. The ground has yet to freeze, and there are plenty of leaves still around under the bushes around the church and under the front porch that leads into the sanctuary. So over these three storms (it has warmed between snows and now nearly all that snow is gone, and they are saying a warmer than usual December) I have noticed a series of paw prints around the parsonage, but not just Eddie's paw prints.

In our last article I wrote of Pierre, the black cat from across the road with the red collar and tiny bell. I have yet to introduce to you Lucy, the black cat from behind the parsonage with no collar. Over the summer I had been getting confused because sometimes I would see the black cat with a red collar, and then sometimes I would see the black cat without the red collar. It took my wife and me awhile to figure out that Eddie now had two enemies, not one, in his neighborhood. The plot is similar to one of my favorite movies, *The Ghost and the Darkness*. It is the true tale of a British engineer that was sent to Africa in the nineteenth century to build an iron bridge over a small river for an English rail line that was extending its tracks into the heart of Africa. What he finds when he arrives is a terrorized camp of workers because of lion attacks, man eaters! At first he thinks he is only dealing with one smart lion, but in the end he discovers that it is a pair of lions working in tandem against the camp. This is exactly what Eddie now faces, invasions into his territory from two sides. The deception and danger for Eddie is the fact that both cats are the same size and same shade of black, and I think he gets confused at times. They could be twins except for the fact one is female and the other male, and they came to the neighborhood at different times from totally different families. So now there are more paw prints in the snow to investigate.

The other day as I was taking my daily trip across School Street to my office in the church on Park Street, I noticed a set of paw prints left over from the latest snow. It got me thinking of our archenemy the devil who like a cat (lion) sneaks around looking for someone to attack (I Peter 5:8); much like it appears Pierre and Lucy do, and their prey is Eddie. So how does one know the devil is around and how can one protect himself from the devil's assaults and attacks? Unlike Eddie, we have a great advantage in that God's Word has shown us the devil's paw prints in the snow. We can see him coming, and we can prepare because we have been given his manual of ambush. One of the tragic results of being Biblically ignorant or illiterate is the surprise attacks of Satan when we should not be surprised (amazed, but never surprised) because his techniques and tactics are clearly outlined and highlighted in the Bible. Over the years I have made a study of these "demonic devices," and I share the ones I have found with you now:

A. **DROWSINESS** (I Thessalonians 5:6): This device keeps us sleepy by means of the passions, pleasures, and procrastinations (I John 2:16).

B. **DEATH** (Hebrews 2:14-15): This device convinces us that Satan has the power over death, which he doesn't, another lie (Revelation 1:18).

C. **DEVOURING** (I Peter 5:8): This device so consumes us through sufferings or sicknesses or storms that we feel forsaken (Job 1:15-17).

D. **DECEPTION** (Revelation 12:9): This device uses others to get what Satan wants, like words (Psalms 35:20), ways (Psalms 52:4), works (Proverbs 11:18), witnesses (Proverbs 14:25), and workers (II Cor. 11:13).

E. **DISCOURAGEMENT** (Numbers 21:4): This device tries to keep our eyes off God, like with Jeremiah (Jeremiah 38:6), Elijah (I Kings 19:10), and Jonah (Jonah 4).

F. **DUPLICATION** (II Corinthians 11:14): This device allows Satan to pretend to be something he is not, like an angel of light or a beautiful serpent (Genesis 3:1) or an authority on the Scripture (Matthew 4:6).

G. **DISOBEDIENCE** (Ephesians 2:2): This device was Satan's first (Isaiah 14:13-14) and he has one aim with it (I Corinthians 9:27).

H. **DREAMING** (Isaiah 29:7-8): This device tricks people into thinking that this world can fulfill all their dreams and desires (Luke 18:18-20).

I. **DEFILEMENT** (Judges 14:9): This device tempts us into making us useless for God's service, like with Samson (Judges 16:20).

J. **DESTRUCTION** (Mark 3:5): This device just loves to destroy a person's integrity, reputation, or morals by any means possible (Luke 14:1).

K. **DISTRACTION** (I Corinthians 7:35): This device uses our senses (smell, taste, seeing, hearing, and touch) against us (Isaiah 30:1-3).

L. **DELUSION** (Jeremiah 9:23): This device appears to be real, but it is but a mirage, like prestige (Proverbs 14:12), power (Matthew 16:26), popularity (II Samuel 15:6), and possessions (Luke 12:15) (I Timothy 6:5-9).

M. **DOCTRINES** (I Timothy 4:1): This device uses teaching to deceive, like fashion (I Corinthians 7:31), food (I Timothy 4:3), and fables (I Timothy 4:7).

Time will not allow me to speak of **DECEIT** (Acts 5:3), **DISSENSION** (Acts 6:1), **DIVISIONS** (Acts 11:2), and **DISSATISFACTION** (Acts 8:19).

These are the devil's paw prints in the Scriptures, and we would be wise to pay attention to them because Satan is always on the prowl. We also have been given ample means to defeat the devil, and in another study I came up with these helpful instructions!

THE DETERRENTS FOR DEFEATING THE DEVIL'S DEVICES:

*"Put on the whole armour of God that ye may be able to stand against **the wiles of the devil**."* (Ephesians 6:11)

1. **THE BELT OF TRUTH**—*"having your loins girt about with truth"* (Ephesians 6:14). Most of what Satan throws (Ephesians 6:16) at you will be a lie (John 8:44) or a lie wrapped up in truth so you must know the truth (II Timothy 2:15) and try every spirit (I John 4:1).

2. **THE BREASTPLATE OF RIGHTEOUSNESS**—*"and having on the breastplate of righteousness"* (Ephesians 6:14). You must be covered with that which is right and righteous because Satan's goal is to make you unrighteous, and it can only be one kind of righteousness (II Corinthians 5:21), the righteousness of Christ (I Corinthians 1:30).

3. **THE BOOTS OF PEACE**—*"and your feet shod with the preparation of the gospel of peace"* (Ephesians 6:15). You must be at peace in order to withstand the onslaught of Satan, and that peace comes from one source (John 14:27). It is what we stand on (Philippians 4:7).

4. **THE BARRIER OF FAITH**—*"above all, taking the shield of faith, wherewith ye shall be able to quench all the fiery darts of the wicked"* (Ephesians 6:16). I believe the "darts" are the devil's "devices," and faith (Hebrews 11:1) is our best defensive weapon against them (I John 5:4). We are exhorted to keep the faith (II Timothy 4:7) and defend the faith (Jude 3) to the end!

5. **THE BIRETTA OF SALVATION**—*"and take the helmet of salvation"* (Ephesians 6:17). There is only one defense for the mind (Romans 12:1-2) and that is the knowledge that salvation has secured us no matter the attacks, whether we fail or win (Philippians 1:6). Our confidence in battle relies on the truth that once saved always saved (II Timothy 1:12), no matter whether or not the devil gets the best of us or not.

6. **THE BIBLE OF SCRIPTURE**—*"and the sword of the Spirit, which is the word of God"* (Ephesians 6:17). You must be able to quote it (Matthew 4:1-9) and ponder on it (Joshua 1:8) because it will be the words of God that will put Satan to flight (James 4:7). There is only one way to resist the devil and his devices (Psalms 119:9-11).

7. **THE BATTERING RAM OF PRAYER**—*"praying always with all prayer and supplication in the Spirit"* (Ephesians 6:18). An often ignored piece of the spiritual armour, but notice it is not just any prayer, but *"supplication in the Spirit"* (Jude 20) because even with the armour we need help (Romans 8:26), and Jesus left us with help (John 14:26).

God hasn't given Eddie such insight in his dealing with Pierre and Lucy, but he has given us the means and the methods of dealing with the demons and the devil of this world!

Chapter Sixty-Three

Seeing Christ Everywhere

"And he said unto them, These are the words which I spake unto you, while I was yet with you, that all things must be fulfilled, which were written in the law of Moses, and in the prophets, and in the psalms, concerning me."

—Luke 24:44

It is a late afternoon in the beginning of December as I set before my laptop to record another "meows from the manse" or better known now as an Eddie Exhortation. In the nearly ten years of Eddie's life (our vet thinks that Eddie was born somewhere in the early months of 2005) he has experienced the good and bad of life on planet earth. The bad times came early, a homeless wanderer with a fear of loud noises and big trucks. Things turned around for Eddie when within the first year of his life he found me, and ever since he sees me everywhere and stays close. Today was a typical day for Eddie as we walked together to the Emmanuel Baptist Church building across from the manse. So you don't think he just follows the same path, this morning I had to deposit our family trash in the big dumpster behind the church. This is a completely different route then the one we normally take, and, yet, instead of going directly to the side door Eddie followed me all the way around the church, rarely was I out of his sight for a few minutes. If Eddie can see me, find me anywhere, why is it that we, the totally superior creature, can't find and follow Christ on a moment by moment basis? I would like in this Eddie story to share with you how I came to see my Christ everywhere, whenever, and wherever I looked for Him. It all started when I found Him not just in the New Testament pages of my Bible, but in the Old Testament pages as well. Christ has always been (Genesis 1:1), and He has always been around (Matthew 24:20). A number of years ago I finished this outline of finding Christ in every book of the Bible. I share it now as an example of the precept highlighted in this article.

HOW YOU CAN SEE CHRIST IN EVERY BOOK OF THE OLD TESTAMENT

"And *beginning at Moses and all the prophets, He [Jesus] expounded unto them in all the scripture the things concerning Him.*" (Luke 24:27)

In GENESIS He is seen as "**the seed of the woman**"—3:15 (Galatians 4:4).

In EXODUS He is seen as "**the Passover lamb**"—12:3 (I Corinthians 5:7).

In LEVITICUS He is seen as "**the High Priest**"—8:7-9 (Hebrews 3:1).

In NUMBERS He is seen as "**the brazen serpent**"—21:8 (John 3:14).

In DEUTERONOMY He is seen as "**the great prophet**"—18:15 (Luke 4:24).

In JOSHUA He is seen as "**the captain of hosts**"—5:14 (Hebrews 2:10).

In JUDGES He is seen as "**the messenger of God**"—2:1 (Malachi 3:1).

In RUTH He is seen as "**the kinsman-redeemer**"—4:1 (Romans 3:24).

In I SAMUEL He is seen as "**the great judge**"—2:10 (II Timothy 4:1).

In II SAMUEL He is seen as "**the seed of David**"—7:13 (Revelation 22:16).

In I KINGS He is seen as "**the Lord of Israel**"—8:15 (II Timothy 1:2).

In II KINGS He is seen as "**the God of the cherubim**"—19:15 (Matthew 13:41).

In I CHRONICLES He is seen as "**the God of salvation**"—16:35 (Acts 4:13).

In II CHRONICLES He is seen as "**the God of the fathers**"—20:6 (John 8:58).

In EZRA He is seen as "**the Lord of heaven**"—1:2 (Ephesians 6:9).

In NEHEMIAH He is seen as "**the covenant God**"—1:5 (Hebrews 8:6).

In ESTHER He is seen as "**the God of providence**"—Esther (Acts 24:2).

In JOB He is seen as "**the returning redeemer**"—19:25 (I Thessalonians 1:10).

In PSALMS He is seen as "**the Holy One**"—2:1 (Acts 3:14).

In PROVERBS He is seen as "**the wisdom of God**"—8:11 (I Corinthians 1:30).

In ECCLESIASTES He is seen as "**the Creator**"—12:1 (Colossians 1:16).

In SONG OF SOLOMON He is seen as "**the bridegroom**"—1:16 (John 3:29).

In ISAIAH He is seen as "**a virgin born son**"—7:14 (Matthew 1:25).

In JEREMIAH He is seen as "**the Lord of righteousness**"—23:6 (I Corinthians 1:30).

In LAMENTATIONS He is seen as "**the faithful God**"—3:23 (I Corinthians 1:9).

In EZEKIEL He is seen as "**the Lord is there**"—13:9 (Matthew 28:20).

In DANIEL He is seen as "**the smiting stone**"—2:34 (I Peter 2:8).

In HOSEA He is seen as "**the king of resurrection**"—13:9 (John 11:25).

In JOEL He is seen as "**the giver of the Spirit**"—2:28-32 (John 14:16).

In AMOS He is seen as "**the plumb line** [straight line]"—4:13 (John 14:6).

In OBADIAH He is seen as "**the destroyer**"—8:15 (Revelation 19:11-21).

In JONAH He is seen as "**the longsuffering One**"—4:9-11 (II Peter 3:9).

In MICAH He is seen as "**the God of Jacob**"—4:1-5 (Matthew 22:32).

In NAHUM He is seen as "**the avenging God**"—1:2 (Romans 12:19).

In HABAKKUK He is seen as "**everlasting purity**"—1:12 (II Corinthians 5:21).

In ZEPHANIAH He is seen as "**the King of Israel**"—3:15 (John 19:19).

In HAGGAI He is seen as "**the desire of all nations**"—2:7 (John 12:21).

In ZECHARIAH He is seen as "**the branch of Jesse**"—3:8 (John 15:1).

In MALACHI He is seen as "**the Lord of remembrance**"—3:16 (John 14:26)

Although the Old Testament consists of 39 books, it is nevertheless one book with one Author and one theme. The unifying theme of the Old Testament is Jesus Christ. The Old Testament prepares the people of God and the world for Christ's appearance and predicts His coming in both type (as seen in the tabernacle) and prophecy (as seen in Isaiah 53) as *"God, who at sundry times and in divers manners spake in time past unto the fathers by the prophets."* (Hebrews 1:1)

HOW CHRIST IS REVEALED IN EVERY BOOK OF THE NEW TESTAMENT

> *"God, who at sundry times and in divers manners spake **in time past** [OLD TESTAMENT] unto the fathers by the prophets, hath **in these last days** [NEW TESTAMENT] spoken unto us by His Son . . . "* (Hebrews 1:1, 2)

In MATTHEW He reveals Himself as "**the King of the Jews**"—2:2.

In MARK He reveals Himself as "**the servant of man**"—9:35.

In LUKE He reveals Himself as "**the perfect man**"—2:40.

In JOHN He reveals Himself as "**the eternal God**"—1:1.

In ACTS He reveals Himself as "**the ascended Lord**"—1:9.

In ROMANS He reveals Himself as "**the end of the law**"—10:4.

In I CORINTHIANS He reveals Himself as "**the resurrection**"—15:1-58.

In II CORINTHIANS He reveals Himself as "**the Comforter**"—1:3.

In GALATIANS He reveals Himself as "**the Redeemer**"—4:4-5.

In EPHESIANS He reveals Himself as "**the Head of the Church**"—1:22.

In PHILIPPIANS He reveals Himself as "**the supplier of all needs**"—4:19.

In COLOSSIANS He reveals Himself as "**the fullness of the Godhead**"—1:19.

In I THESSALONIANS He reveals Himself as "**the coming Lord**'—4:17.

In II THESSALONIANS He reveals Himself as "**the consuming Lord**"—2:8.

In I TIMOTHY He reveals Himself as "**the Mediator**"—2:5.

In II TIMOTHY He reveals Himself as "**the rewarding Judge**"—4:8.

In TITUS He reveals Himself as "**the Great God and Saviour**"—2:13.

In PHILEMON He reveals Himself as "**the payer of all debts**"—17.

In HEBREWS He reveals Himself as "**the great Shepherd**"—13:20.

In JAMES He reveals Himself as "**the Great Physician**"—5:15.

In I PETER He reveals Himself as "**the good example**"—2:21.

In II PETER He reveals Himself as "**the beloved Son**"—1:17.

In I JOHN He reveals Himself as "**the word of life**"—1:1.

In II JOHN He reveals Himself as "**the Son of the Father**"—3.

In III JOHN He reveals Himself as "**the truth**"—4.

In JUDE He reveals Himself as "**the Preserver**"—1.

In REVELATION He reveals Himself as "**the Lion of Judah**"—5:5.

John wrote of his gospel and this is true of all books of the Bible: "***And there are also many other things which Jesus did, the*** *which, if they should be written every one, I suppose that even the world itself could not contain the books that should be written.*" (John 21:25)

As I finish this "meow," Eddie is napping on a pillow on top of a bookshelf in front of my desk. It seems as long as he can keep me in eyesight, he is content and confident in what is happening in his life. What is true of Eddie and me is true of Christ and me. As long as I keep my eye on the Christ of the Bible, I, too, am content and confident in whatever is happening in my life, including a three-month illness that has sapped my energy, but hasn't diminished my trust in Christ's perfect purpose (Romans 8:28) for my life—in sickness and in health. As Eddie sees me everywhere, so I see Christ everywhere.

Chapter Sixty-Four

Red Spot

*"And there appeared another wonder in heaven;
and behold a great red dragon,*

*having seven heads and ten horns,
and seven crowns upon his heads."*

—Revelation 12:3

For as long as I can remember Eddie's favorite toy is a small laser that admits a tiny red spot. This brilliant red light has been a mystery to Eddie because he never knows when it will show up. One minute it is there on the wall, and the next minute it is gone. It shows up beside him as he rests on my lap in the evening. Sometimes it has appeared at the church where he spends his days. It has disappeared for months at a time only to suddenly appear again out of the blue, randomly reappearing when he least expects it. His greatest fascination with "red-spot" is the uncanny ability of the "spot" to never get caught. How many times has he gotten his teeth around it only to see it dissolve before him? He has pounced on it, swiped at it with his paw, even corralled it between his paws only to see the elusive "red-spot" disappear to reappear across the living room or on the wall in the back learning center at the church. He has chased it mercifully back and forth across the floor only to have it jump up to the ceiling beyond his reach. He has tried to stare it down, but he has always blinked first, and when he opens his eyes, it is gone again. For years this cat and mouse game has been playing out before my eyes as "red-spot," and Eddie has matched wits with it in a contest of wills. Eddie has yet to figure out his foe, and the more I pondered my cat's dilemma with "red-spot" the more I realized the similarities between me and my "red-spot" foe, the devil.

I find it interesting that John in his ancient revelation would describe our greatest foe as a "red dragon" (see above). *"And the great dragon was* cast out that old serpent, called the Devil and Satan, which deceiveth the whole world: he was cast out into the earth, and his angels were cast out with him." (Revelation 12:9) The Bible is very clear in its definition of just who we are up against in our pilgrimage through this world. Have you ever noticed Lucifer's ("shining one" only found in Isaiah 14:12) many aliases mentioned in the Bible:

A. SATAN—accuser. 51 times the Bible uses this name for Lucifer: ". . . and the accuser of our brethren is cast down, which accused them before our God day and night." (Revelation 12:10) Remember the story of Job and the accusations Satan voiced against him (Job 1:6-11 and Job 2:1-5). I have come to believe that this is the number one ministry of the original "Red-Spot!"

B. BEELZEBUB—lord of the flies. 7 times the Scriptures use this title for Lucifer: ". . .this fellow doth not cast out devils, but by Beelzebub the prince of the devils." (Matthew 12:24) Remember when Lucifer fell from heaven (Luke 10:18) he didn't fall alone (Revelation 12:10), and he is lord of a myriad of "flies" we call demons. Why flies? Because flies are attracted to death and so is the devil. (Hebrews 2:14,15)

C. DEVIL—slanderer. 35 times the Word of God uses this title to describe Lucifer: *Then was Jesus led up of the Spirit into the wilderness to be tempted of the Devil."* (Matthew 4:1) This is one of Lucifer's better known aliases and his angelic followers are more often than not know as "devils" (Matthew 7:22). Next to accuser, slander is the devil's most diabolical ministry.

D. SERPENT—snake. 8 times Holy Writ uses this animal to describe Lucifer: *"But I fear, lest by any means, as the serpent beguiled Eve through subtilty, so your minds should be corrupted from the simplicity that is in Christ."* (II Corinthians 11:3) Remember, this is the instrument that Lucifer used to tempt mankind (Genesis 3:1-14). Interestingly, called "old" serpent (Revelation 12:9, 20:2). Was this his first alias?

E. PRINCE—chief. 7 times we see this title for Lucifer in the Bible: *"Wherein in time past ye walked according to the course of this world, according to the prince of the power of the air, the spirit that now worketh in the children of disobedience."* (Ephesians 2:2) He is also prince of devils (Matthew 9:34), prince of the world (John 12:31), and even sometimes called "the god of this world" (II Corinthians 4:4). His pride has no bounds!

F. ADVERSARY—<u>opponent</u>. At least 2 times this analogy is used in relationship to Lucifer in the Scriptures: *"Be sober, be vigilant; because your adversary the Devil, as a roaring lion, walketh about, and seeking whom he may devour."* (I Peter 5:8) and *"I will therefore that the younger women marry, bear children, guide the house, give none occasion to the adversary to speak reproachfully. For some are already turned aside after Satan."* (I Timothy 5:14-15) As "red-spot" is seen by Eddie as his opponent so, too, must we acknowledge our chief opponent. Only then will we be alert enough to resist him when he strikes.

G. TEMPTER—<u>tester</u>. At least 2 times this analogy is used in relationship to Lucifer in the Bible: *"And when the tempter came to Him, he said, if thou be the Son of God, command that these stones be made bread."* (Matthew 4:3) and *"For this cause, when I could no longer forbear, I sent to know your faith, lest by some means the tempter have tempted you, and our labour be in vain."* (I Thessalonians 3:5) It is in this alias of Lucifer we must apply the precept of James 4:7: *"Resist the Devil, and he will flee from you."* Do you?

And then there is the "red dragon."

Without a doubt the "dragon" is the devil (Revelation 12:9) and "red" is the symbol of war in the revelation (Revelation 6:4). Twelve times (Revelation 12:3,4,7,9,13,16,17; 13:2,4,11; 16:13; 20:2) John uses this description for Satan in the Revelation, certainly a "red-spot" on this age yet to come call the Great Tribulation. I would have you note one other application of the use of these words in two verses in the little book of Jude:

> *"These are spots in your feasts of charity, when they feast with you, feeding themselves without fear: clouds they are without water, carried about of winds; trees whose fruit withereth, without fruit, twice dead, plucked up by the roots; raging waves of the sea, foaming out their own shame; wandering stars, to whom is reserved the blackness of darkness for ever."* (Jude 12-13)

I feel Jude is talking about those individuals, children of the Wicked One, that had crept into the church (Jude 4) and were disrupting and distracting the fellowship of believers. What I like best of the analogy here is the emptiness of these "spots:" no water, no fruit, and no shame. Just like the image of "red-spot" appears to Eddie as being something solid, but in reality just an image, a mirage, here a moment and then gone. So shall it be with the "spots in the feast," and so it will be for the "red dragon." He will cast his "red-spot" for a while on the earth, and then he will be gone (Revelation 20:1-3) for a thousand years. I had mentioned in my opening statement and illustration of Eddie and "red-spot" that it had come and gone over the years. Actually, I had used the original "red-spot" so much teasing and trying Eddie that I eventually wore it out. It was not until recently that I found another one. Eddie's "red-spot" has had several reincarnations over the years and so with the original "Red-Spot," the devil. He has reinvented himself over the millenniums since he left his lofty position by the throne of God as the "son of the morning." His appearance (aliases) in Scripture has been like my playing with Eddie, flashy, drawing, but empty. The devil has always been hard to pin down, but his end, like the "spots" at the feasts, is sure: *"Then shall He say also unto them on the left hand, Depart from me, ye cursed, into everlasting fire, prepared for the Devil and his angels."* (Matthew 25:41) This will only happen when "Red-Spot" makes one more appearance (Revelation 20:7-10) on the earth to finally disappear forever in the lake of fire.

I don't get out "red-spot" every day, just like the devil rarely attacks every day. It is that unexpected moment, that unprepared time, that seems to work best for Satan. That is why we are challenged to "be sober," "be vigilant," and "be watchful" because we don't know when "Red-Spot" will show up in our lives. Like with Jesus, he might depart for a season (Luke 4:13), but he will be back. Eddie doesn't know when I will get "red-spot" out for a romp around the living room, a playful evening chasing his favorite "spot," but as Eddie is always ready to take on the challenge "red-spot" offers, so we must be ready to resist the devices (II Corinthians 2:11) the original "Red-Spot" uses to tempt us.

Chapter Sixty-Five
Beatitudes According to Eddie

"And He opened his mouth, and taught them, saying, Blessed..."
—MATTHEW 5:2, 3

IF OUR BEST GUESS is right, I am writing this "meow from the manse" near the tenth birthday of my cat Eddie. Because Eddie came to us as a stray we can't be sure, but our vet thinks Eddie was born early in the year 2005, and, seeing we are now into the year 2015, my decade old companion has established himself firmly in my heart, and, as you have read, my memory as well. There are few things that bring me more joy than Eddie so on this, my designated celebration of his birthday, I would like to give you a few beatitudes according to Eddie.

It was my Lord and Saviour Jesus Christ that first instructed me by way of beatitudes what I like to call the "happiness is..." verses of the Bible. His famous set of eleven that introduced his greatest sermon (The Sermon on the Mount) will be the template to guide us through this series of beatitudes inspired by Eddie.

1. Blessed were [happiness is] the hours you rested on my lap in the evening as we watched television for they were filled with warmth and joy.
2. Blessed were [happiness is] the meals I gave you for they brought a giving delight, whether first supper or second supper.
3. Blessed were [happiness is] your morning meows that woke me so often for it was the cheerful opening of my day.
4. Blessed were [happiness is] our walks to the church for they brought lasting enjoyment to me and to many in our neighborhood.
5. Blessed were [happiness is] the times you slept on the bookshelf while I worked for they brought a gaiety and ecstasy to the room.

6. Blessed were [happiness is] the times I let you out to roam in the church yard for you brought a cheer to my heart and a rejoicing to my soul that you were still a free spirit and an outdoor cat.

7. Blessed were [happiness is] our times at play with "red-spot" for they brought a glee unmatched as you chased the elusive dot around the parsonage.

8. Blessed were [happiness is] your visits when you returned in triumph with a prey for you made me as proud as a parent.

9. Blessed were [happiness is] the times I watched you through the church window roaming and romping through your Shangri-La for it always brought me great happiness despite my fears that you might never return.

10. Blessed were [happiness is] the experiences we shared in the quietness of just you and me for they brought jubilation sweeter than honey.

11. Blessed were [happiness is] the treats I gave from my hand for they were in a way the way I could say thanks for the wonderful smiles you gave me.

12. Blessed were [happiness is) the purrs I heard from you for they always brought cheerfulness and blissfulness to my heart.

13. Blessed were [happiness is] the times I watched you sleep for I, too, was placed in a merriment and pleasantness unmatched by anything of this world.

14. Blessed were [happiness is] the events of satisfaction that we shared for they brought a mutual gladness to our faces.

15. Blessed were [happiness is] the early mornings when you decided to curl up between Coleen and me for they were the most pleasurable.

16. Blessed were [happiness is] the varieties of meows you uttered for they allowed me to understand "felinese" (the language of cats).

17. Blessed were [happiness is] your exploits with the neighborhood animals for they gave me great insights into my relationship with my fellow man.

18. Blessed were [happiness is] the encounters you had with your archenemy for they taught me wonderful lessons in how to deal with my archenemy (the devil).

19. Blessed were [happiness is] your trips out of your comfort zone for they instructed me how to leave my comfort zone and travel to India.

20. Blessed were [happiness is] your conflicts with your besetting sin (Big Gray) for your struggles helped me more than you can know with my besetting sin.
21. Blessed were [happiness is] the intimate moments we had for they helped me understand my intimate moments with the Almighty.
22. Blessed were [happiness is] the times your patience and contentment with Precious Patience Pearl were inspiring for they spoke to me of the importance of being patient and content with others.
23. Blessed were [happiness is] the occasions I watched your vigilance and watchfulness for they were a sermon to me of the importance of alertness and cautiousness in my own life.
24. Blessed were [happiness is] the simple moments you brought a smile to my face for they highlighted and underlined to me the need to keep my life simple as well.
25. Blessed were [happiness is] the periods of companionship when it was just us for they were special interludes into the wonderful fellowship I have with my God.
26. Blessed were [happiness is] the circumstances that brought us together for they reminded me of the circumstances that resulted in my adoption into the family of God so many years ago.
27. Blessed was [happiness is] the friendship and fellowship we shared for it was by far the best I ever experienced in the animal kingdom.

Happiness can come from a variety of venues. Eddie was just one in my life, but as you can see a vital one at least in the last ten years of my life. I get wonderful joy from my dear wife, my precious children, and already from a little one that is growing in my daughter today. I have only seen him on an ultrasound, but it is enough to bring a new happiness I have yet to experience, the happiness of grand-fatherhood.

If I can find such happiness, welfare, and enchantment from a stray cat, what will be awaiting me with the arrival of my first grandchild (Judah Alan-named after my middle name-was born on August 18, 2015)? God in his will for mankind sought to put them into a place and circumstance that would make them content and happy. With their well-being in mind he placed them in a utopia, a paradise, an Eden. Rapturous and rhapsodic should have been the result, but instead they got so focused on the concept of being "god-like" (Genesis 3:5) they were willing to give up their beatitude for the chance of becoming divine. If I have learned anything from my relationship with my cat Eddie, it is to enjoy the happiness of the moment because such earthly happiness is short lived. (We would only have seven years left!)

Chapter Sixty-Six
Wonderful Graces

*"As every man hath received the gift,
even so minister the same one to another,
as good stewards of the manifold grace of God."*

—I Peter 4:10

I HAVE COME TO believe like with "the fruit of the Spirit" (Galatians 5:22-23) (a fruit that is made up of many pieces, like an orange, is one, but inside it can be broken up into many slices), love, joy, peace, longsuffering, gentleness, goodness, faith, meekness, and temperance, the grace of God also has many pieces (manifold, having many and various forms). I got to thinking down this line of thought one day as I thought of my relationship with Eddie. It is one friendship, but our fellowship takes on many forms. Sometimes it is strictly provider and provide. At other times it is companion and comrade. There are times when it is human and animal. Still, there are times when it is pastor and pet. Depending on the time, the situation, or the circumstance our relationship can and will change, has changed. (I remember ten years ago when Eddie was an unnamed, unwanted stray in our neighborhood and now he is a cherished member of my family.) Such is the reality of God's wonderful grace; it adapts as our life changes. The kind of grace we need now might not be the kind of grace we will need a year from now. I decided to do a little digging into God's inspired Word and see what kinds of slices, or pieces the grace of God transforms itself for us. Here are the different forms I found, and I am quite sure I haven't discovered all the variations:

    A. **Saving Grace.** "*For by GRACE are ye saved through faith; and that not of yourselves: it is a gift of God: not of works, lest any man should boast.*" (Ephesians 2:8, 9) <u>The container of salvation is grace</u> (Titus 2:11). The first step in our relationship with God is a form of grace that results in our salvation. And, as Eddie was a gift from God, so was the grace that came to my heart on June 4, 1958, when I found Jesus Christ, and He became my Saviour and eventually my Lord.

B. **Growing Grace.** *"But grow in GRACE, and in the knowledge of our Lord and Saviour Jesus Christ. To Him is glory both now and forever. Amen."* (II Peter 3:18) The course to maturity is grace (I Peter 2:2). There are some who believe that grace stops with salvation, but as we cannot get saved without grace, neither can we grow in Christ without grace. So there is a saving grace and a growing grace, both parts of God's wonderful grace, but distinct enough to be seen as essential in the ongoing ministry of God's grace in our lives.

C. **Teaching Grace.** *"For the GRACE of God . . . appeared to all men, teaching us that, denying ungodliness and worldly lusts, we should live soberly, righteously, and godly in this present world."* (Titus 2:11-12) The champion of righteousness, sobriety, and godliness is grace. We know from reading the Gospels that *"grace and truth"* came with Jesus (John 1:17), but it was only after His death, burial, and resurrection that we began to see how that grace revealed itself in a variety of forms, and one of those forms was the grace to teach us how to live the Christian life after our conversion. Many believers trust in the Lord for their salvation and their spiritual growth, but then they forget to allow grace to mature them in sobriety, a righteousness, and a godliness; note, "in this present world." Grace is a heavenly virtue without question, but it is most necessary in an earthly setting.

D. **Sustaining Grace.** *"And He said unto me, My GRACE is sufficient for thee: for my strength is made perfect in weakness . . . "* (II Corinthians 12:9). The conductor of strength is grace (Philippians 4:13). This is a very helpful and necessary form of grace because we do not know how many variations of needs we might need in our lives. It appears from the context of our key verse it was a physical shortcoming that was causing Paul some trouble (II Corinthians 12:7, 8). We don't know what it was, but we do know the Good Lord gave him the strength to handle it through grace, to the point that Paul realized that he was better off with the "thorn" and grace than to have grace without the thorn. (II Corinthians 12:10)

E. **Witnessing Grace.** *"And with great power gave the apostles witness of the resurrection of the Lord Jesus: and great GRACE was upon them all."* (Acts 4:33). The conduit of our testimony is grace (Acts 1:8). I don't know about you, but one of the toughest ministries in our service for the King is the work of evangelism (II Timothy 4:5), witnessing.

Without the grace of God I have come to believe it is an impossible task. I struggled with witnessing for many years until I realized that I didn't have to do it on my own. If I only trusted in the moving of the Spirit and relied on witnessing grace, even I could be a soul winner. Since 1970, when I discovered "witnessing grace," I have had the privilege of leading at least one soul to Christ every year. Now that is grace.

F. **Working Grace.** "*And thence sailed to Antioch, from whence they had been recommended to the GRACE of God for the work which they fulfilled.*" (Acts 14:26) <u>The culvert of service is grace</u> (Ephesians 4:7-13). There are many other works the Lord has commissioned us to do besides witnessing. Paul speaks about *"all good works"* (II Timothy 3:17) that we can be furnished, prepared to every good work, but how is that possible? It is possible because of the diversities and degrees of grace available to God's workers. I have come to believe this is what Paul was referring to in I Corinthians 12:4-6. Read it carefully.

G. **Disciplining Grace.** "*For sin shall not have dominion over you: for you are not under the law, but under GRACE.*" (Romans 6:14). <u>The controller of any sin is grace</u> (Romans 6:15). I hear it all the time that many among the Christian community don't think it is possible or practical to live godly in this present world, and yet we learned from Titus 2:11, 12 that is exactly what God wants. How? Grace is the discipline that will manage our lives, keep us from making wrong decisions, help us resist temptations, and guide us through a life of perils and pitfalls. Few believers are tapping into the reservoir of disciplining grace.

H. **Helping Grace.** "*Let us therefore come boldly unto the throne of GRACE that we may obtain mercy, and find GRACE to help in time of need.*" (Hebrews 4:16) <u>The channel of prayer is grace</u> (Philippians 4:6). Who of us hasn't needed some kind of help in our lives? More often than not we seek human help, maybe from family or friend, but often the last place we turn to is grace. Be honest with me, when was the last time you prayed specifically for grace? When I was a kid, prayer use to be called "grace" in my family. Dad would say "grace" before every meal. Granted, as a kid I never caught the connection between prayer and grace, but now I see it clearly in the theology of "grace in a time of need." Have you?

I. **Departing Grace.** "*The GRACE of our Lord Jesus Christ is with you all. Amen.*" (Revelation 22:21) <u>The conclusion of life in grace</u> (II Timothy 4:6, 7). The last form of grace not only seen in the Bible, but will be utilized by all believers on their day of departure is "dying grace." This special aspect of grace will only be administered in the moment of transfer from this life to that life. I have as a pastor been at the bedside of a dying saint and, though I have not experienced it myself, I have witnessed it, and one of the side benefits of this grace is the grace that is applied to the one left behind. Amen!

So what is your relationship with grace? Have you yet realized that Grace is a friend that sticks closer than a brother or an Eddie? It might just be the believers "best friend," and unlike a cat this Grace will never leave you or forsake you, no matter the time, the situation, or the circumstance.

Chapter Sixty-Seven

Purring and Praying

"Be careful for nothing; but in everything by prayer and supplication with thanksgiving let your requests be made known to God."

—Philippians 4:6

Sometimes Eddie just likes to sit in my lap. Is it because he wants to be close to me, enjoy the softness of my lap (plenty of padding now) or does he like the heat generated from my body? Rare is the day that passes that Eddie doesn't jump up on my lap and settle in for a period of purring. More often than not it is in the evening when I am watching a favorite television program. Granted, most of the time I also have to have Eddie's quilt on my lap; how he loves that homemade quilt which was created by my wife for me, but many years ago Eddie claimed it as his own. Sometimes he won't even get into my lap unless I have the quilt situated just right. I have seen him on numerous occasions sit in front of me, stare me down until I get the quilt out and put it on my lap, and then immediately he jumps up and starts purring. This can be very hot and uncomfortable for me in the summer or when the pelt stove is running hot, but no matter to Eddie. He loves the feel of the quilt under his belly and then does he purr. But recently, a lap time took place in my office at the Emmanuel Baptist Church that brought an insight into a very important topic I am still learning about—prayer.

Have you ever considered how prayer is like the purring of a cat? It was Tuesday morning at 9:00 AM when this concept hit me. Tuesday morning at 9:00 AM is India prayer meeting for me. Ever since my last return from India in November 2012, I have been having a private prayer meeting for my friends and the ministries of India that I am acquainted with. The reason I chose that time was to coincide with a pastors' prayer meeting that happens every Tuesday night at 7:30 PM (there is a ten and a half hour difference between Edayappara, Kerala and Ellsworth, Maine) in the home of Shaju Simon. Over my four trips to the State of Kerala (six trips now and this practice on both sides continues-last Tuesday was my 385th combined prayer meeting), I have had the privilege of attending that weekly prayer meeting started by Shaju's grandfather in the 1970s. It is my way of staying close to my adopted country, my adopted family, and my many pastor friends in India. Rarely does Eddie join me at this time, but on that particular Tuesday Eddie jumped up into my lap, settled in, licked himself a few times, and began to purr up a storm. At first I didn't pay any attention because it wasn't a rare happening except for the timing. As I prayed and Eddie purred, the two events began to merge in my mind, percolate in my heart and meditate in my spirit. I soon realized that an eureka moment was happening!

Don't get me wrong. I am not saying Eddie was praying, an action beyond even his amazing abilities. What I am saying is that Eddie's actions are a good way to understand what prayer ought to be like. We all know that prayer isn't a necessary function because of our belief in the all-knowing attribute of the Almighty: *". . .for your Father knoweth what things ye have need of, before ye ask Him."* (Matthew 6:8) We don't pray to tell the heavenly Father anything He doesn't already know. We also don't pray to change the ultimate will of God concerning the matters we are praying about because God's divine will is fulfilled in every answered prayer. *"And this is the confidence that we have in Him, that, if we ask any thing according to His will, He heareth us."* (I John 5:14) We pray because we are instructed to pray and prayer is a simple act of obedience. *"Pray without ceasing."* (I Thessalonians 5:17) Prayer is as much as what we pray as how we pray. This is what the disciples of Christ were asking when they said to Jesus, *". . .Lord, teach us to pray . . . "* (Luke 10:1) What I am saying is simply this. On the morning of my India prayer meeting I learned something more about how Jesus would have us pray, but I learned this through Eddie.

For me, one of the best qualities of a cat is its ability to purr. Purring is a pleasant sound that brings with it a peaceful tranquility and a calming solace. When Eddie purrs, he is telling me that all is well in his world; that he trusts me fully and has full confidence in me; that while he is in my lap he feels safe and secure. Eddie doesn't purr when he is confronting Pierre or guarding the garage against intruders. Purring is reserved for those times when Eddie is relaxed and comfortable. Do you see the application? It hit me like a thunderbolt that when I come into the presence of the Almighty (Hebrews 4:16), I, too, should be exhibiting the same confidence and trust. Prayer ought to be for me a time of tranquility and solace; that I, too, can feel safe and secure as I rest in the lap of my Saviour while supplicating. Do you feel relaxed and comfortable when you pray? Jesus taught us that when we pray we can claim His name, and He promised

His presence (Matthew 18:19, 20). I feel the process of prayer is like the event of the children being brought to Jesus, the encounter that saw the disciples rebuking those who had brought their kids to see Jesus (Mark 10:13). The description in Mark says this: *"And He took them in his arms, put His hands upon them, and blessed them."* (Mark 10:16) Could He have also put them in His lap? I think so.

As I write this section of this *Meows from the Manse* chapter, Eddie has just come in from a trip around the church property. It is nearing noon, and Eddie is looking for a place to have a nap. But before he settles down on the pillow on the bookshelf in front of my desk, he has decided to snuggle into my lap for a few minutes of what we call cuddle time, a rubbing of his ears and a stroking of his back. He is also purring heavily as if to reassure me that he is well and thanks for being here. Spiritually speaking, isn't this exactly what we do when we bow our head and open our heart in prayer to *"Our Father which art in heaven. Hallowed be Thy name?"* (Matthew 6:9) That is our opening purr, acknowledging our entrance into the presence of our God. As with Eddie, we come boldly (Hebrews 4:16) because we don't fear Him. If anything, we are coming into the presence of a friend (John 15:13) as Abraham did so very long ago (James 2:23). I still remember the days my two children use to run and jump into my arms and settle into my lap after I came home from work. Their joyous laughter and childish chatter was like Eddie's purring. And I have come to believe that our heavenly Father hears our prayer, supplications, and intercessions as I heard my children's conversation then and Eddie's purring now. It is not the words that are as important as the pleasure and passion that comes when hearing a contented request, a confident petition, or a purring plea.

The next time you go into your closet to pray (Matthew 6:6), imagine yourself a little child again walking into your father's room before you go to bed. Do in your spirit as you use to do in the flesh. Reach out your hands to a loving Dad (Galatians 4:6 *"Abba Father"*) and allow him to pick you up and sit you in his lap. Feel His warm embrace and soft kiss on your forehead as you are wrapped in His massive arms (John 10:28-30). Feel a song (prayer) coming to your heart, a song without words but full of meaning like a purr, a prayer. Its melody is heard and grows in volume as you rejoice in sharing your heart's desires with a benevolent Deity. You know, as Eddie knows with me, that God will take care of you, provide for you, and protect you. Is there any wonder you are purring?

Chapter Sixty-Eight

The Comforting Cat

"Blessed is God, even the Father of our Lord Jesus Christ, the Father of mercies, and the God of all comfort."

—II Corinthians 1:3

I HAVE FOR YEARS been blessed with a string of "comforters" as long as my arm. I have never not known a time when the Good Lord hasn't sent me the exact "comforter" I needed in a time of need. Over the years my study of the Word of God has revealed that though there is only one source of "comfort," comfort doesn't always come from that source. Note, Paul tells us that God is *"the God of all comfort."* (II Corinthians 1:3) I recently finished a handout sheet on this topic and these verses:

"Who **comforteth** us in all our tribulation, that we may be able to **comfort** them which are in any trouble, by the **comfort** wherewith we ourselves are **comforted** of God. For as the sufferings of Christ abound in us, so our **consolation** also aboundeth by Christ. And whether we are afflicted, it is for your **consolation** and salvation, which is effectual in the enduring of the same sufferings which we also suffer: or whether we are **comforted**, it is for your **consolation** and salvation." (II Corinthians 1:4-6)

Note "all" because there is not just one kind of "comfort."

1. **SOVEREIGN COMFORT.** The source of all Comfort is certainly the Almighty God, but the Bible is clear, He administers "comfort" through:

2. **SAVIOUR COMFORT.** "Now our Lord Jesus Christ himself, and God, even our Father, which hath loved us, and hath given us **everlasting consolation** and good hope through grace, **comfort your hearts**, and stablish you in every good word and work." (II Thessalonians 2:16, 17)

3. **SPIRIT COMFORT.** "*And I will pray the Father, and he shall give you* ***another Comforter*** *that he may abide with you for ever; even the Spirit of Truth; whom the world cannot receive, because it seeth him not, neither knoweth him: But ye know him; for he dwelleth with you, and shall be in you.* ***I will not leave you comfortless.***" (John 14:16-18)

4. **SCRIPTURAL COMFORT.** "*Or whatsoever things were written aforetime were written for our learning, that we through patience and* ***comfort of the scriptures*** *might have hope. Now the God of patience and* ***consolation*** *grant you to be likeminded one toward another according to Christ Jesus: that ye may with one mind and one mouth glorify God, even the Father of our Lord Jesus Christ.*" (Romans 15:4-6)

5. **SAINTLY COMFORT.** "*Wherefore comfort yourselves together, and edify one another, even as also ye do. And we beseech you, brethren, to know them which labour among you, and are over you in the Lord, and admonish you; and to esteem them very highly in love for their work's sake. And be at peace among yourselves. Now we exhort you brethren, warn them that are unruly,* ***comfort the feebleminded****, support the weak, be patient toward all men. See that none render evil for evil unto any man; but ever follow that which is good, both among you, and to all men.*" (I Thessalonians 5:11-15)

Let us never forget that we are in the comforting business as well; and then last night I discovered that God can bring comfort through "a comforting cat."

The spring of 2015 brought a new affliction into my life. In all my 64 springs before, I had never had trouble with allergies. Others I have known have fought the pollen and mold of the allergy season, but as for me never a sniffle or a sneeze. Then last Saturday, the first real day of spring despite the fact six weeks had passed since the official start of spring, I decided to rake the old leaves and dead grass off the parsonage lawn. As usual, I seemingly was unaffected by the annual activity, but by the next morning my nose was running and my eyes were watering like I have never experienced before. At first I thought I had a spring cold, a head cold, a sinus infection, something I had experienced, but with each passing day I realized this cold wasn't like any other I had endured through the years. Within a couple of days I was miserable with my nose flowing like Niagara Fall and my eyes crying like I had just lost my best friend. The pressure was increasing and my head was getting ready to explode. I started taking medicine both up my nose and down my throat, and the struggle to breathe and see finally came to a head on the fourth night. It was then I discovered there was another "comforter" living at the manse.

My pregnant daughter (carrying my first grandchild) had gotten home from California for a baby shower. She had settled into the spare bedroom, and Eddie had claimed the second twin bed because of a quilt (how Eddie loves quilts) my wife had placed at the foot of the single bed. Eddie normally spends his nights on a quilt in my recliner in the living room, but with the coming of warmer weather he loves the guest bedroom with the open window. That night as I headed for bed I checked on Marnie and Eddie and found them both sleeping; I on the other hand was far from sleep. I just couldn't get comfortable with my nose running, my eyes watering, and my head aching. I tossed and turned for about two hours until finally I had to sit up on the side of the bed to catch my breath and calm the pressure in my nose. I was quietly hoping not to disturb my wife when an unexpected visitor showed up. Sure enough, Eddie must have heard me or sensed I wasn't feeling well and decided to comfort me in the late night hour.

In the ten years I have had Eddie this was the first time he had done this. As I settled back down, Eddie found a place on my stomach and purred me into a more restful state. Even modern science has documented the therapeutic value of an animal during a time of illness or sickness. That is why nursing homes and boarding homes now have resident cats, and hospitals allow comfort dogs into patient rooms. There is something about touching and caressing a cat or a dog that even calms one's breathing. Eddie stayed with me for about half an hour before he returned to his quilt in the spare bedroom. I think he sensed he had done his job and relaxed me enough to fall off to sleep. As I pondered his comfort, I realized I had discovered another one of my God's great "comforters." I thought how the ravens that came daily to Elijah must have been a great source of comfort to the hunted prophet (I Kings 17:6), and the comfort the dove must have given to Noah (Genesis 8:8-12). If God is the God of all comfort, then He can use His creative creatures to bring to us a measure of comfort, can He not? Eddie has been a lot of things to me over the years, and now he has become a "comforter" in a time of sickness. I would encourage you the next time you need a comforter to look beyond a human to an animal.

Chapter Sixty-Nine

Does a Cat Have a Soul?

"In whose hand is the soul of every living thing, and the breath of all mankind?"

—Job 12:10

HAVE YOU BEEN WONDERING when I would get to this debatable question? You have noticed I have left it to the end of this book, a book, at the time of the writing of this chapter, has been twelve years (the age of Eddie) in the making. My wife believes in the positive answer to the questionable question becoming convinced of its validity by her experience with "the Pearl," her cat of nearly 19 years. But I have struggled with the theology of her belief because of the Biblical interpretation that has been long held that only the human animal got a "soul" at creation (Genesis 2:7). I still don't know if I am as yet convinced, but I would at least like to share with you an insight I got when I was writing a book about my boyhood dog Rover. As I wrote the early chapters of that book I called <u>Rover: A Boy's Best Friend</u>, (also published by Wipf and Stock Publishers) I recalled a series of verses my father pointed out to me when I was just a lad. They are found in the first book of the Bible, not Genesis, but Job. I have come to believe in an extensive study of Job (over a three-year process) that Job is the first book of the Bible chronologically speaking. Living during the days of men like Abraham, I believe Job was a saga, a very wise man, inspired by God I believe (II Peter 1:21). I believe he wrote the account of his amazing trial, and in his speaking to his three friends he makes this inspiring challenge:

> "But ask now the beasts, and they shall teach thee, and the fowls of the air, and they shall tell thee. Or speak to the earth, and it shall teach thee: and the fishes of the sea shall declare unto thee. Who knoweth not in all these that the hand of the Lord hath wrought

this? ***In whose hand is the soul of every living thing, and the breath of all mankind.*** " (Job 12:7-10)

Most of the scholars who look at this old use of the word "soul" feel that a better word would be "life;" that what Job was talking about, was more, the breath of life that God breathed into Adam than "the living soul" part. As Daniel told Belshazzar: "*. . . and the God in whose hand thy breath is . . .* " *(Daniel 5:23)* This is similar to the thoughts of Paul in his great *"to the unknown God"* sermon: *"For in Him we live, and move, and have our being. . ."* (Acts 17:28) I am not here to debate the doctrine of the creative and life-giving power of God because I believe all life comes from Him, including man and mammals. What I am here to consider is if the animal kingdom got something more, such as a soul, an eternal part. Job suggests that there are lessons, instructions, teachings that we can learn from the beasts, the birds, the bluffs, and the barracuda! That God can use the planet, the predators, the puffin, and the pink salmon to proclaim to us a Godly statute. The Psalmist seemed to take us down Job's train of thought when he wrote: *"The heavens declare the glory of God; and the firmament sheweth His handiwork. Day unto day uttereth speech, and night unto night sheweth knowledge."* (Psalm 19:1, 2)

Whether looking at the sun or the stars or the clouds in the sky, they speak of the nearness of God. Every animal, every bird, and every creature that crosses our path on a given day is a sign from God that "God is near." The heavens declare, the earth teaches, the birds tell, and the beasts teach us something about God, but are we listening, looking? As I pondered this profound path, I realized that this entire book, Meows from the Manse, has been an exercise in this concept. Eddie has been a constant source of instruction by the Almighty to my watchful eyes. Granted, I probably have missed more instruction than I took in, but I was at least listening. And as I have written so often, Eddie is different than your normal cat, even different than "the Pearl." Eddie breaks all the theories about cats being solitary creatures, self-centered, and stand-offish. Eddie has sharp eyes, soul penetrating eyes, and his all-embracing benevolence and tolerance is of another world. If a cat ever had a soul, a spiritual side, it is Eddie!

Eddie has always had a calming demeanor; you touch him and his motor starts and that relaxing purr begins. If Eddie is a preacher sent by God to preach to me, he is not your "fire and brimstone" kind of preacher. He always speaks in soft tones and kindly gestures. Where the animals of the saints live "God is near," and I still can't be sure Eddie will be in my mansion (John 14:2) in glory because God's Word isn't clear in my opinion, but I hope James Herriot is right, that my wife is right, because my cat Eddie has shown the characteristics of having a soul more than many people I know that have a soul. Oh, didn't I tell you? The title of James Herriot's chapter was "Do Dogs Have Souls?"

Chapter Seventy

Eddie and Judah

"... therefore she called his name JUDAH ..."
—Genesis 29:35

It is only fitting that if I have written about nearly everything in my life, I would have to write about my first grandson. Over my nearly thirty years of writing, I have written books on my childhood dog Rover, my adulthood cat Eddie, my homestead in Perham, my parents, my wife, my father-in-law, my children (Scott and Marnie), my grandparents, and I could go on and on. I have written a book on every one of my overseas adventures including books on India, Australia, England, Israel, and then there was Paris, my second book I had published about a 40-hour trip to Paris and back to pick up Judah's mother from a mission's trip to Togo, West Africa. Oh, if I only knew then the grandchild Marnie would present to us on August 18, 2015. The reason for this chapter now is the grand 15 days we had with Judah Alan Legaspi celebrating his first birthday. A year ago he was just a baby, cute, with a head-full of reddish hair and beautiful blue eyes, but we were still trying to figure out who he was—his traits, his personality and all that.

To say that we have waited a long time for Judah's arrival would be an understatement. We have friends who have grandchildren ready to have children. Over the years my wife and I have taken solace in the fact that we have had the opportunity to be grandparents to children in our church, and we have; a multitude of children that we have shared in their birth and have watched them grow up before our eyes. We have been able with their parents to see them brought up in the *'nurture and admonition of the Lord.'* (Ephesians 6:4) We have rejoiced in the fact that we have had a small part in their upbringing, but deep in our heart we wanted one of our own. And our hopes sprang eternal when we heard from Marnie that she had found God's man. Finishing her last year at Dallas Theological Seminary, she met

Josue Legaspi. The courtship was short as Marnie prophesied years before. In her thirties by this time, Marnie had already spent half her life either in higher education or missions work. Now it was time for a family. Within six weeks of her graduation she had a June wedding, before Christmas she was pregnant, and just two months after her first year wedding anniversary she delivered a healthy baby boy and *"she called his name Judah."*

Despite the fact I live on the Atlantic Ocean coast of Maine and the Legaspi family lives on the Pacific Ocean coast of California, it has not stopped our getting together. When my wife and I visited Judah on his first birthday, my wife had already been to Salinas, California, four times, and I had been there two times. Grandsons can do that to you. Time and distance mean nothing when it comes to your first grandchild, and your first grandson has to meet your best friend Eddie, and it was in the manse of the Emmanuel Baptist Church that they first met and became great friends.

Judah was born in August of 2015, and by November of 2015 he had made his first cross-country trip (at this writing Judah is only 19-months old, but has already crossed this great land from sea to shining sea six times) to see his grandparents in Maine and the rest of his Blackstone family. Judah and his mother came for a Thanksgiving gathering of the Blackstone clan and what a gathering we had (including a four-generation picture on both his father's side of the family and his mother's side of the family). Because his father, Josue, is allergic to cats, Judah had never met a cat before, nor, should I say, two cats before. Quick to see the addition to the family, both Precious Patience Pearl and Eddie, Eddie, Eddie were quite curious about the little person that had invaded their space. Pearl soon voiced her disapproval with plenty of growls and hisses. She would keep a wide birth of Judah during their nearly month-long stay. Eddie on the other hand kept his distance at first, but as he became more familiar with the little lad, he warmed up. This was not like Eddie because Eddie doesn't normally like little people either, but there was something in Judah he would tolerate as Thanksgiving passed and we headed towards Christmas.

Being the onset of winter, Judah did enjoy his first snow, his first Christmas parade, his first encounter with his great-grandparents, and a cat named Eddie. Barely moving, except for the occasional attempt at rolling over and the kicking and thrashing of his limbs, Judah was just a permanent fixture wherever he was placed. This made it easy for Eddie to check out the lad, but at the same time escape if the legs and the feet of this tiny creature would get too close. My favorite picture of that first encounter was a photograph my daughter took which I had enlarged, and it now sets on a filing cabinet in my office. The picture is of Judah sitting on my lap as he fed Eddie his evening treats. Marnie snapped the camera just right as

Judah placed a tiny treat in Eddie's mouth. If there is anything that brings Eddie near, it is his favorite, fishy treat. The focus of both Judah and Eddie are priceless as the two made a memory for Bubba (Judah's name for me). I wanted them to be friends, but how do you know until sometime passes? It was well over a year before the two would meet again.

The events surrounding Judah's second trip to Maine were not as festive. In October 2016, shortly after Judah's first birthday, we learned of Judah's only uncle's cancer. Diagnosed with Stage 4 lung and liver cancer, within three weeks Judah and his mother and father flew to North Carolina to find out what was going to be done for Scott. My wife and I drove down from Maine the same day that Josue, Marnie, and Judah flew in on a "red-eye" from California. Eddie, of course, wasn't there, but that event would set up Judah's next visit to see Eddie. Over the next six months (we flew Scott home to Maine in November to care for him at the parsonage we live in) Judah's mother would fly to Maine to help with Scott's care. Scott had made Marnie his Power of Attorney so there were plenty of legal papers to prepare and plenty of things to do to get Scott's house in order because the doctors told Scott the same thing Isaiah told King Hezekiah: "... *Set thine house in order; for thou shalt die, and not live.*" (II Kings 20:1) Between November and January Marnie came to Maine twice without Judah. It was after the second trip Marnie realized she would never do that again because when she got back the second time Judah would have nothing to do with her for three days which broke Marnie's heart. So, near the first of March 2017, it was time for another trip and Judah came along, but this time Eddie was in for a totally different experience with the lad from Salinas, California.

Judah was now walking, running, climbing, talking, and touching as any year-and-a-half-year-old will do. Despite Judah's limited vocabulary, he quickly picked up the word "Eddie," more like "Ed-dee." Eddie at first sought only flight as this three foot, ball of energy, came after him. As before, the Pearl took one look at Judah and ran upstairs, and thereafter when in his presence, she would vocalize her displeasure of Judah's presence in her domain by hissing and growling up a storm. (Judah never mastered "Pearl," but simple mimicked her "growl." Judah was learning animal sounds so "growl" became Pearl's name.) Judah soon learned to keep his distance from the Pearl, but Eddie was another story. Because Eddie didn't just stay at the parsonage, as has been our routine for years, Eddie would each morning come to church with me, and who was staying at the church but Marnie and Judah.

With Scott staying with us there was not extra room at the parsonage, but there was a prophet's chamber in the sanctuary of the Emmanuel Baptist Church across the street. Used more often than not for visiting missionaries, the church allowed us to set it up with a crib and a bed for Marnie and Judah's visit. It gave them some space and a place for Judah to rest (Judah was still having afternoon naps and was in bed early in the evening) without bothering his Uncle Scott who by this time had declined in health dramatically compared to when Judah saw him in October. It was here that Judah and Eddie were to become friends. Each morning I would bring Eddie over, and within a few days (Marnie and Judah stayed for eight days) Judah was chasing poor Eddie into the basement. It took us a few days more to teach Judah he needed to be gentle and quiet, and Eddie wouldn't run away. Once Judah understood the ground rules with dealing with Eddie, a friendship emerged. It wasn't long before Judah could go into my office, where Eddie spends his days, and pat Eddie and sit beside Eddie without Eddie racing out the door for the basement. Soon I could hold Eddie, and Judah could touch him and talk to him without Eddie bothering to move. "Eddie" this and "Eddie" that became Judah's favorite new word, and before they left I gave Judah a picture of Eddie to take home with him. One of the first videos I got from California after the pair returned home was Judah taking Eddie (the picture) for a ride on his scooter. His mother is heard asking, "Who is that?" and the quick reply, "Eddie" as Judah pointed to the picture with his finger.

Eventually, even over at the parsonage, Eddie and Judah became close as every time Judah would visit Uncle Scott he would ask were Eddie was. On the morning of the "last" goodbye (this would be the last time Marnie and Judah would see Scott-he passed away on April 1, 2017), Eddie was still sleeping on our bed so I took Judah up to say goodbye. By now Eddie didn't even move when Judah came into the room, but the Pearl was still growling in the hallway. I set Judah on the bed beside his new friend, and they had a few bonding moments as the two new friends said goodbye. When will Judah meet Eddie again I know not; I know not if they will ever meet again, but for the master and the grandfather in this story I was glad they met.

Postscript: Eddie and Judah and later his sister Elena would have plenty of visits over the next four years with a number of visits from California, and eventually the entire family moving to the coast of Maine in the spring of 2020 and buying a home eight miles from the manse!

Chapter Seventy-One

The Sentinel of the Brush Pile

"... set up the watchman ..."

—JEREMIAH 51:12

My dear cat Eddie just turned 13. Three days ago Eddie had his annual checkup with the local vet (Bermeister) and was found to be in good health. Eddie had even gained a few ounces, almost ten pounds now. The vet was pleased with his countenance for a cat of his age, over 90 in cat years. I was glad to think I would have "the lad" for a bit longer. Eddie is slowing down, sleeping more, but one thing hasn't change and that is Eddie's desire to be outdoors more than indoors. Winter keeps him in more, but now that we have arrived to another "spring-summer-autumn" season, Eddie is enjoying again the parsonage porch, exploring the land behind the church, and his number one passion, guarding the brush pile in the backyard.

When my family and I landed in Ellsworth in the summer of 1991 (it is now the summer of 2018), the men of the church had just stabilized and resurrected an old one-door garage in the backyard. Between the garage and the neighbor's cedar fence they created a brush pile for the bushes, shrubs, and tree limbs they cut down to clear the area around the garage. Over the years my neighbors and I have only added to the pile of branches, twigs, and trees we have cut down to trim and clear other parts of the yard and their yards from unwanted brush. Year after year the pile has expanded and shrunk as the snow crushed the pile every winter and the rotting of the wood decreased the pile. Despite the changing of the pile, there has remained for 27 years now a pile of leaves, grass, twigs, and decaying branches covering an area about twenty feet long, six feet deep, and four feet high, given the time of the year. Within this maze of limbs and other stuff, the local squirrel family has made a series of tunnels and no doubt rooms. Almost from the first time I let Eddie out into the parsonage backyard, the brush pile has been a magnate to

Eddie's interests of protecting the area from unwanted visitors. Periodically, I would find Eddie sitting in front of the pile just staring. Over the years my wife and I would wonder where Eddie had roamed on a given day, but in the warmer months we could be assured to find him at the pile, guarding against the squirrels or other creatures using the brush pile for cover, a home, or just a stopping-off place. I can't remember whether it was my wife or myself who gave Eddie the title of "the sentinel of the brush pile!"

The other day I was watching Eddie at sentry duty when I realized there was another spiritual lesson in Eddie's actions around a backyard brush pile. In the Bible "a watchman" was an admired profession, those who watched over a city, or a field, or a house. It was a needed occupation because of the dangers from raiders or warriors seeking plunder or conquest. They might be found on city walls (II Samuel 18:24), in watchtowers (II Kings 9:17), or on a hilltop (Jeremiah 31:6). They were responsible to warn and ward off anyone or anything that might bring harm to those or what they were guarding. These were the sentries and sentinels that guarded and protected people and property in Biblical times. Besides the practical occupation of the watchman, there was the spiritual application given in the Bible to the men and woman we called prophets. They were the spiritual sentinels (Isaiah 21:6 and Jeremiah 6:17) responsible for watching for and warning of impending doom or judgment delivered to them by Jehovah Himself. Listen to these words given to Ezekiel because in them we learn just how serious God saw the duty of the spiritual sentry:

> "Son of man, I have made thee a watchman unto the house of Israel: therefore hear the word at my mouth, and give them warning from me. When I say unto the wicked, Thou shalt surely die; and thou givest him not warning, nor speakest to warn the wicked from his wicked way, to save his life; the same wicked man shall die in his iniquity; but his blood will I require at thine hand. Yet if thou warn the wicked and he turn not from his wickedness, nor from his wicked way, he shall die in his iniquity; but thou hast delivered thy soul." (Ezekiel 3:17-19)

Long before Eddie reminded me of my responsibility as a "watcher," I was sobered by this verse in Hebrews 13:17: *"Obey them that have the rule over you, and submit yourselves:* **for they watch for your souls, as they that must give account**, *that they may do it with joy, and not with grief: for that is unprofitable for you."* Being a spiritual sentinel or being a watchful sentry over the lives of others is serious business.

Surely, if a simple tomcat can spend hours and days watching carefully a pile of brush, we can be sober and vigilant in watching over the souls of others. Time and time again Jesus invoked the word "watch" (Matthew 24:42, 26:41). Paul invoked the same word in Acts 20:31 and I Corinthians 16:13. John in the Revelation says: *"Behold, I come as a thief. Blessed is he that **watcheth**, and keepeth his garments, lest he walks naked, and they see his shame."* (Revelation 16:15) If a cat can do it, certainly we can do it!

Chapter Seventy-Two

The Death of a Pearl

"...gold and precious stones and pearls..."

—Revelation 17:4

I know her name hasn't been mentioned much in this "Meows from the Manse" chronicle, but she has been a part of the history of the manse of the Emmanuel Baptist Church in Ellsworth, Maine, for nearly 22 years of the nearly 29 years my wife Coleen and I have lived at 50 School Street. Precious Patience Pearl was certainly not our first female cat, but she has been and probably will be the longest living cat my wife and I will ever have (May 13, 1998 to November 8, 2019). The Pearl, as we called her, died liked she lived, independently, on her own terms. Originally brought into the manse because our daughter Marnie was heading off to college, the classic "empty-nest" syndrome, the Pearl became my wife's cat, a strictly indoor cat, and a highly temperamental cat. Only in her last days did the Pearl warm up to me, allowing me to feed her treats and even getting onto my lap. I believe this happened not because Pearl's personality had changed, but because her physical health made her thirsty and hungry all the time, and she would do anything to satisfy her cravings. During the last weeks of her life our family from California was visiting (a 29-day stay that was glorious for two grandparents coveting the companionship of their only two grandchildren, Elena Hope and Judah Alan), and even then the normally shy, hands-off cat was friendly, even with a four-year old and a 20-month old. Again, I believe it was because of her declining health versus a change in attitude. Our only desire was that the Pearl would survive the visit, and she did, by three days.

However, shortly after our son-in-law Josue and our daughter Marnie and their children left to return to their home in Salinas, California, my wife and I began to notice a dramatic change in the Pearl's behavior and actions. Within a day of the Legaspi's leaving the Pearl stopped eating, and within two days her breathing became labored. She could hardly walk two steps without stopping to lie down and panting up a storm. On the day of her departure from the manse my wife and I determined that, if she survived the night, we would take her to the vet, something she despised! That Friday night we watched her labor as we watched television. About nine she disappeared, and we thought she had moved behind Coleen's chair. We watched two more programs before heading upstairs for bed. As I got to the second floor landing, I saw her laid out on the door stoop to Coleen's craft room. Somehow, she had managed to climb the stairs one more time, dying alone near her master's room where she had spent a lot of her time over the years. Eddie was on our bed within sight, but Pearl died alone as, I suspect, the way she preferred it.

Pearl's death was a shock to my dear wife, but not a surprise. Few cats live into their teens, let alone into their twenties. I have never known a cat to live as long as the Pearl, both our own and others. Pearl had certainly lived a long, carefree, and on her own terms life. She had been the queen of the manse for her entire lifetime (she had actually been born in the home of a parishioner just a couple of blocks from the parsonage of the Emmanuel Baptist Church in the spring of 1998) and had been pampered and provided with all she could ever want, including "fish and shrimp" for most of her life. Granted, she did escape on those rare occasions, but I believe she never spent more than a few minutes at a time outdoors at any one time for all of her life. She had an easy life which probably contributed to her long life. But, like Eddie, Pearl taught me many lessons, including this final one from the day of her death and the day of her burial.

Like humans it is appointed for cats "once to die." (Hebrews 9:27) Since the fall of man death has been a part of the life of everyone and everything that has ever lived on this planet, including animals. Sometimes, we don't recognize the parallel between the death of a human and the death of an animal, but both are true. Life can only survive so long, a short life or a long life, the end is the same, death, and it is that death that reminds me of the greatest humbling my Lord and Saviour ever did: *"But made himself of no reputation, and took upon him the form of a servant, and was made in the likeness of men: and being found in fashion as a man, he humbled himself, and became obedient unto death, even the death of the cross."* (Philippians 2:7, 8) The Author of life (John 1:1-4, Colossians 1:16) actually yielding to death is the most profound truth about Jesus I know. Think with me for a minute and realize that Jesus was willing to humble Himself to die like the Pearl died, alone, in a struggle for breath, and the yielding up of life itself.

When I think of a pearl in relationship to Jesus, I recall one of Jesus' great parables: *"Again, the kingdom of heaven is like unto a merchant man,* seeking goodly pearls: who, when he had found one pearl of great price, went and sold all that he had, and bought it." (Matthew 13:45, 46) There are those who teach that "the pearl of great price" is the Church, but I have come to believe and teach that the "one Pearl" is the Christ. What is it about the Christ that makes Him so valuable that the person that finds Him is willing to give all to attain Him? I teach and believe it is and was His willingness to die for us: *"Greater love hath no man than this that a man lay down his life for his friends."* (John 15:13) Who wouldn't love and desire someone that is willing to lay down their life for us, to die so that you will not have to die in your sin. *"For the wages of sin is death; but the gift of God is eternal life through Jesus Christ our Lord."* (Romans 6:23) Whether or not Pearl will be found in Coleen's mansion (John 14:2/see Chapter Sixty-Nine) or not is not the point I am making (though my dear wife believes it). The point I am making is the fact that in life there is eventually death, and in death there is an eventual burial.

The morning after Pearl's death I arose early after a frosty night to dig a grave for the Pearl. We had placed her body in a wooden crate she had used for sleeping during the last years of her life. We wrapped her in the bedding, and I made a wooden cover. I found a sunny spot (Pearl loved to be warm, whether the rays of the sun or the flames of our pelt stove, the Pearl could be found most times in a warm place) behind the clothesline beside the garage. I only had to break through a thin layer of frost to get to a soft gravel section of the backyard. I dug deep and wide giving myself enough space for the Pearl's coffin. After getting the burial site prepared, I went into the house to get Coleen. It only took a few seconds to place the box, cover it with sand, return the sod, and cover the whole space with the fallen leaves of autumn. Is not this what Joseph and Nicodemus did with the body of Jesus (John 19:38-40)? Granted, the grave was different, the body preparation different, but, as with the Pearl, the body of Jesus had to be buried. One of the aspects of the Gospel we often overlook is:

> *"For I delivered unto you first of all that which I also received, how that Christ died for our sins according to the scriptures;* **and that he was buried**, *and that he rose again the third day according to the scriptures."* (I Corinthians 15:3, 4)

Is there anything more common than a burial? They might be more elaborate, attended by more people, contain more weeping, but a burial is a burial whether the Son of God or the manse cat. For me Coleen's and my Saturday burial of our beloved Pearl was simply a reminder how far my Saviour was willing to go for me, but the greatest contrast is that after three days (the time of this writing) Pearl is still buried, but Jesus arose!

Chapter Seventy-Three

Sadie Mae, the Frightful Feline

"... but we were troubled on every side; without were fightings, within were fears."

—II Corinthians 7:5

The manse has a new cat, or should I say that a new cat is now living at the manse of the Emmanuel Baptist Church in Ellsworth, Maine. After the death of Coleen's cat, Precious Patience Pearl, my dear cat-loving wife took a few months to grieve the departure of her cat-of-a-lifetime, but decided in the end to try and replace the Pearl. For weeks she looked through the websites of the local ESPA shelters and found a cat or two she liked the looks of, but each and every time she called the number given on the site the cat had already been adopted. Deciding to wait until after our annual Christmas trip to Salinas, California, to be with our daughter and family, Coleen restarted her search the first week into the New Year, and on Thursday, the second, Coleen made up her mind to go to the local animal shelter and find her next cat. She asked if I would go with her, and I did. When we arrived we found the shelter overflowing with adoptees, both young and old, cats and dogs, and a few other species of animals. I advised Coleen to get a kitten, but she was determined to rescue an abandoned cat. As we went from cage to cage, none of the orphans jumped out to her until she came to a cage in the corner with a name tag reading "Emerald." The multi-colored short hair was in her bed sleeping showing no interest in being touched. Deciding to hold Emerald to see if she was a "snuggler," Coleen's number one quality for a cat, the attendant look Emerald out of her cage and took her (a seven year old abandoned female) and us to a seating room so we could get to know each other better. Our bonding period lasted about half an hour, and in the end Coleen felt that Emerald was the cat for her. Because of the protocol of the shelter, we had to fill out adoption papers, and the shelter would check with our vet to see if we had a good reputation with animals. A final checkup would be made overnight on Emerald, and, if everything and everyone checkout, we could pick up Emerald the next day.

Early that next morning I got a phone call from the shelter that we had checked out, Emerald had checked out, and that all we needed to do was to show up and pick her up. That afternoon, that is exactly what we did. Taking Pearl's old cat-carrier with us, Coleen gave the shelter **one hundred dollars** (in our nearly fifty years together we have had a score of cats, but Emerald is the very first cat we have ever bought!) for the privilege of taking her home. Emerald was up-to-date on her shots, she had been fixed, and she had a complete and clean bill of health. Only one thing had not been provided to us from the shelter and that was a mental assessment! Little did we know what was going on in Emerald's mind when we put her in the cat carrier and into my car and brought her into our home? What baggage was she bringing with her? What was her sad story? In her seven years what had she experienced from man? When we got her home, we soon realized that there was something wrong with Emerald and changing her name didn't help.

Coleen had already decided the night before that Emerald wouldn't be the name of her new cat. She suggested Sadie to me, and I liked it. It wasn't long, however, before Coleen was calling her Sadie Mae, and even Eddie didn't seem to mind though at first he was standoffish as he gave Sadie a wide birth (a cat half again as big as him). For the first few hours Sadie simply sat on Coleen's lap and snuggled. Things were starting out in the right direction, and our first evening with Sadie seemed to verify Coleen's choice.

But late that night Sadie decided to play hide and seek with us. Over the next four weeks we might have seen Sadie four times. We discovered her first two hiding places in the basement and tried to convince her to join us upstairs, but to no avail. As I write this, she is still playing hard to get so the verdict is still out on Sadie Mae. Some days Coleen talks of catching her and taking her back to the shelter, while on other days Coleen speaks of being patient and tolerant, waiting for Sadie to lose her fear of us and join our family. The decision seems to be up to Sadie, but whether she goes or stays she has been in the manse long enough now for me to see a wonderful lesson for all of us.

Sadie reminds me of a favorite illustration that I have used numerous times over the years to hopefully make my point. The story is of a passenger on a great ocean liner traveling from the United States to England in the days when boats were the only means of transportation between the two great continents. Having never been on a boat before and learning that the trip might take four or five days, the passenger made preparations for the long journey. Having bought his ticket he also packed enough food and water for the crossing. Though the passage was very smooth, the first-time traveller rationed out his meager supplies. As he neared the end of his trip, his fears were that he would run out of food and water before the ship docked. Great anxiety overcame him when on the fifth day there was no land to be seen, and he ate his last meal and drank his last cup of water. It was then a steward came to his cabin to check on him because he hadn't been seen the entire trip. To the steward's utter amazement a great ignorance had resulted in an overwhelming, great fear. As the steward asked for the man's ticket, he was shocked to discover that the ticket the man had purchased included eating at the captain's table and free access to every part of the ship. Instead the man had locked himself away in a small space eating only that which he had brought along for the journey across the Atlantic!

I have often used this illustration to highlight and underline how many Christians sail through their pilgrimage not taking advantage of the wonderful benefits that are theirs in Christ: *"Blessed are the God and Father of our Lord Jesus Christ, who hath blessed us with all spiritual blessings in heavenly places in Christ."* (Ephesians 1:3) Sadie still confines herself to a damp, dusty basement living on meager fares we place there for her when she has been adopted (like us in Galatians 4:5, 6) with all the privileges of the warm second floor and comfortable third floor. There are always treats and more food than she could eat, but she seems to be like the traveler of our story unaware that her ticket to travel with the Blackstones includes all necessities and more. Will she ever realize that she doesn't need to hide in a duck vent, or behind the wood pile, or between the insulation and the ceiling? Time will tell. We hope the day will come that we can convince her that she has nothing to be frightened about because even our other cat Eddie would welcome her if she would simply realize she has become a part of a caring, loving family that has committed themselves to her health and well-being with all expenses paid.

Are you today struggling, fearful of the journey you are on to heaven's distant shore? Are you isolating yourself against a world that frightens you, barely making it, hungry and thirsty, wondering where your next spiritual meal will come? Have you yet realized that you are on a ship called the "Church" (Matthew 16:18), powered by the Holy Spirit (Acts 1:8) and Captained by Jesus Christ Himself (Ephesians 1:22-23)? Do you realize that you have numerous traveling companions that want to pray for you (Ephesians 6:18), that want to help you (I Thessalonians 5:11), and that want to bear your burdens (Galatians 6:2)? Come out of your basement and join the Captain at His banquet table!

Chapter Seventy-Four

Scaredy Cat

"Terrors shall make him [her] afraid on every side..."
—Job 18:11

Two months have passed since we brought a new cat into the manse of the Emmanuel Baptist Church of Ellsworth, Maine. Sadie Mae has proven to be the most unique cat we have ever had. Granted, we have had some interesting felines over the years, but none as strange as Sadie. In my first article on this frightful female I highlighted her immediate impulse to hide from us, and that quality has continued for over 60 days now, and, when I say hide, I mean hide, most of the time. In our time together I might have seen her a dozen times, my wife a few more, but whenever she is caught out in the open the phrase from Job printed above describes exactly how Sadie responds to our encounters!

Coleen and I have come to the conclusion that something traumatic happened in Sadie's short seven years of life that has resulted in her being afraid of men. Sadie and Eddie seem to get along well, and the adjustment to a strange cat for both Eddie and Sadie hasn't been a big issue. Within days Coleen witnessed them playing together, but unlike with the Pearl who Eddie respected and honored by being the oldest member of the family, Eddie from the very start made sure that Sadie knew who the head-of-household was. The same seems to be true with Coleen, though it did take weeks for Sadie to trust Coleen and that trust hasn't reached sitting on her lap or even touching her, but Sadie will come out when Coleen is around and stays out. Sadie has jumped up on the bed a number of times and settled down while Coleen was still in bed, but for me no such respect. Whenever Sadie sees me, she returns to her comfort zone under the spare room bed. Remember in our last article I mentioned that she had found hiding places we couldn't even find. Now we know where she is when we can't see her, but that doesn't mean we see her any more often. But a pattern has now materialized in these two months, and that being when I go to bed Sadie comes out and heads downstairs for supper. On the odd occasion we have met in the hall, back under the bed she has gone. Once, she jumped up on the bed thinking Coleen was there, but the minute she saw me, back to the shared bedroom she went. I have yet to touch her since that first touch at the animal shelter over two months ago. Sadie is afraid of men, or at least that is our verdict as for now.

I don't know when Sadie will become a real part of our family or if she ever will, but once again Sadie has got me thinking about something and that is the topic of "being afraid." When I dug out my concordance, I was amazed just how many times the Bible speaks of "being afraid" (over 200 times). Because of that high number I realized that "being afraid" or being in "terror" was a topic the Almighty knew would be a thorn in the side of most humans. I remember when God was working on downsizing Gideon's army that one of the things He said was:

> "Now therefore go to, proclaim in the ears of the people, saying, **whosoever is fearful and afraid**, let him return and depart early from mount Gilead. And there returned of the people twenty and two thousand; and there remained ten thousand." (Judges 7:3)

Being afraid was like a pandemic in Gideon's army which also reveals just how widespread "being afraid" can be in any situation or circumstance. Remember, it was "being afraid" of the people of Canaan that kept the Israelites out of the Promised Land for forty years:

> "The great temptations which thine eyes saw, and the signs, and the wonders, and the mighty hand, and the stretched out arm, whereby the LORD thy God brought thee out: so shall the LORD thy God do unto **all the people of whom thou art afraid**." (Deuteronomy 7:19)

Being afraid can grip a cat, an army, or a whole nation. It is a scourge that can cripple a cat, paralyze an army, and stop a nation in its track. It is an emotion that can cause you to stay under a bed indefinitely!

I would ask you to remember other "being afraid" and "being in terror" stories of the Bible like the disciples in the storm (Matthew 14:27), or the disciples on the Mount of Transfiguration (Matthew 17:7), or when Jesus visited His disciples after His resurrection (Matthew 29:10). But in all three occasions, Jesus told His disciples not to be afraid. I have come to believe that all disciples get afraid, but my theology teaches me we are not supposed to be afraid. What was true in the New Testament was true in the

Old Testament. A case in point was Joshua just before he led the children of God into the Promised Land:

> "Have not I commanded thee? Be strong and of a good courage; **be not afraid**, neither be thou dismayed: for the LORD thy God is with thee whithersoever thou goest." (Joshua 1:9)

I do not know what Sadie is afraid of. It appears to be me, but I know she has nothing to fear from me. When Coleen chose her to live at the manse, I committed myself to her protection and provision for the rest of her days or for as long as I could. (And though Coleen passed away two years ago I have keep my promise to care for Sadie) In time will I convince her of that? I don't know, but I feel the same problem is in the heart and minds of many. The Bible is clear, like me with Sadie, God will protect and provide so what have we got to be afraid of? It was David who wrote:

> "The LORD is my light and my salvation; **whom shall I fear?** The LORD is the strength of my life; **of whom shall I be afraid?**" (Psalm 27:1)

David's theology was sound, but is yours?

"Behold, God is my salvation; I will trust, and not be afraid: for the LORD JEHOVAH is my strength and my song; he also is become my salvation." (Isaiah 12:2) I wish I could be as bold to say that I have never been afraid, but you would know that I was a liar. There have been times in my life where I have acted more like Sadie. I, too, have been in a new place, in strange surroundings, with people I didn't know. I still remember the first time I travelled nearly half way around the world to a small village in Kerala State, India. I hadn't been out of the country for 24 years. I had never been to India, and I still recall the terror that swept over me the moment the door closed in the room I would spend the next 42 days. The climate was hot, the sounds coming from the window were strange, and the prospects of the unknown were almost paralyzing. I took a deep breath and questioned what I had done to myself. Not since the first day I left home for college and walked into a room with four other guys at Bob Jones University 1500 miles from home had I felt that fear, that terror, that being so afraid. Yet it was in those events, the first one took a bit longer, but the second event in India only took seconds before I laid claim to my theology, and the fear and terror that had overwhelmed me in a moment was gone in a moment. I have never been afraid in India again, and at the writing of this article I have spent 137 days in India in five different trips (165 days in 6 trips now). I have told all who will listen I fear nothing in India, nothing in India terrorizes me, and I am afraid of nothing—the elephant, the cobra, the Bengal tiger, the Moslem, the Hindus, or the Sikh.

Sadie is a cat so I will probably never convince her in the near future she has nothing to be afraid of with me, but I am not writing this article for a cat, but for the Christian that is having trouble with fear, or terror, or being afraid of something or someone. *"But and if ye suffer for righteousness' sake, happy are ye: and **be not afraid of their terror**, neither be troubled."* (I Peter 3:14) What do we need to be afraid of with the Lord on our side (Romans 8:31)? I don't know what you are afraid of, but with the Lord on your side you should fear nothing. Only cats called Sadie should be Scaredy Cats, not Christians!

Postlude

An Ode to Eddie

"Praise the Lord from the earth, ye . . . beasts . . .
Let them praise the name of the Lord: for His name alone is excellent;
His glory is above the earth and heaven."

—Psalms 148:7, 10, 13

I know there would be those who would say that no creature can praise the Lord, yet over and over again in the psalms the psalmist seems to exhort the animal kingdom to do just that. I would be the first to say I know not the mind of man let alone Eddie, yet I have come to believe, as you have read, that my cat Eddie had indeed been an instrument of God in my life for praise. In his own way I believe he did fulfilled this exhortation written above.

The first time I approached Eddie I found him in a forlorn state. He met me with frightful eyes, a low growl, and raised hair on his back. He did not want me to touch him or even get close to him. He trembled at the sound of my unfamiliar voice, and my very presence was terrifying to him. He resisted my approach. He resented my outstretched hand. He recoiled in my presence. In time, his eyes sparkle when I draw near. He spoke to me in pleasant tones as I approach him. He craved a touch, to be held, to be caressed on his back, behind his ear, and under his belly. My whistle and the sound of my voice draw him, and my presence was sheer delight to him. Once he despised companionship, but eventually our friendship was all in all. Once the mention of his name would result in flight, but eventually "Eddie, Eddie, Eddie" resulted in a cheerful trot to my waiting arms, but the transformation was beyond amazing; I believe it to be divine. I am convinced after all this time (seventeen years) that Eddie had been for me one of those "angels" Paul describes in Hebrews 13:2.

AN ODE TO EDDIE

Interestingly, a year after Eddie came into my life I sat down and composed this bit of verse titled "An Ode to Eddie" that is fitting in this my last chapter in Eddie's book:

A year ago you were not fat,
And when I came, you would scat;
Across the road to your habitat,
And that was just that!
But I played the diplomat,
As day by day we had our chat;
And back and forth, tit for tat,
You played the aristocrat.
I watched you close as you sat,
Upon the steps with your white cravat;
And then it happened, a simple pat,
I was allowed on your black top hat.
Would I call you Ellie, or maybe, Nat?
How about Eddie, or maybe, Pat?
But I could not tell the kind of cat,
For I could never get you on the mat.
With plenty of food I filled a vat,
And soon you gave me a little tat;
And I could see you'd been in combat,
And then I knew you were a tomcat.
So Eddie you became, for you were no Matt,
And soon we discovered that you were no brat;
But a mild mannered kitty cat,
And certainly, no polecat!
A problem developed with the autocrat,
For Pearl had never known another cat;
And soon you two began to spat,
With conflict and acrobat.
You loved her sprat,
Better than rat;
And whereat?
You were no hellcat!
Despite the occasional bat,

From that other cat;
To you it was only a drat,
From that democrat.
You love the warmth of the thermostat,
And that your new world has no gnat;
For you there is plenty of plat,
And now you are a fat cat!

Eddie had been taken from a world of want to a world of wealth by cat standards. Would that not be something to be thankful for? Eddie's life compared to the average cat was way above normal, and I believe he was thankful for that. Eddie lived in a safe environment where people care for and love him, and his very actions tell me he was grateful. As you know by now, I was led to India at the same time Eddie was directed to me. In India I saw sights unimaginable to the point one would think that I was on another planet; sights of poverty, plight, and persecution. Surely these two worlds, America and India, can't exist together and yet they do. I occasionally see the stray cat wandering the neighborhood and wonder what their life is like, and then I think of Eddie. I came back from India full of praise for the blessings bestowed on me. I am not a rich man in America by anyone's standards, yet, compared to India standards, I am rich beyond belief. The last lesson Eddie taught me was that my God has blessed and benefited me beyond value. Compared to my Indian brothers and sisters, I have had an easy life, just like Eddie. I want for nothing, and I fear no hostile faction in my ministry. I am the "fat cat" and so are you. One trip to a third-world country should make every American Christian into an instant voice of continual praise! What should you be thinking and thanking God for?

My prayer was that these "exhortations" from Eddie, these meows from the manse, these purrs from the parsonage, have reminded you of the Great God we serve and the multitude of blessings that are ours in this land because of Him. Next time you need to be challenged by some spiritual precept, maybe, just maybe, you only need to observe the pet in your own home. It worked for me!

(*Postscript*: After seventeen years of life Eddie developed cancer and had to be put to sleep on a Tuesday afternoon at 3:30 PM by his vet. (Because I was away pastoring another summer of kids at Living Waters Bible Camp, not in Canada this time but in Maine, it is only fitting that I started this book at such a camp, and would end this book from a similar place!) Because I wasn't there my daughter Marnie took him wrapped in his favorite quilt made by my wife. According to a text from Marnie "he purred to the end!" Marnie and my good friend Mike buried him in his favorite spot in the backyard of the parsonage of the Emmanuel Baptist Church where he loved watching and chasing the squirrels that lived in the brush pile behind the garage. It's just feet away from where we just a year and a half ago buried his beloved Pearl. Many a day he would spend in that spot. If you have read any of my latest books, you know that it has been a tough few years for me with the death of my beloved father and dear son weeks apart in 2017 and the death of my loving wife and my gentle mother weeks apart in 2020. Could I be honest with you? Eddie's passing feels like the third punch in the stomach for me. I will miss him terribly when I return to Ellsworth in a few days, much like the first time I returned home from a ministry trip and Coleen was not there, but Eddie was, and now he is gone, too.)

Barry Blackstone

July 13, 2021
(The day I had to put Eddie to sleep because of throat cancer.)

www.ingramcontent.com/pod-product-compliance
Lightning Source LLC
Chambersburg PA
CBHW070244230426
43664CB00014B/2407